## Praise for S

"Thought-provoking . . . informative, a
*Stuffed* will certainly get people talking and thinking."

—Forbes.com

"Straightforward and sobering. We all know the food industry is big business, but Cardello shows in clear terms just how big it is—with suppliers all over the world—and why this makes it so slow to improve."

—*Milwaukee Journal Sentinel*

"Hank Cardello, a former food industry executive with Coca-Cola and General Mills, has his own solution . . . serve up a tasty, profitable business scenario and let the industry take the forefront in shrinking America's growing waistlines. Cardello's ideas may not win over food purists, but his ideas derive from practical, real-world experiences."

—*Los Angeles Times*

"Former food industry executive and current anti-obesity advocate Cardello calls on his erstwhile colleagues to become custodians of their customers' well-being. . . . The point zings home: The food industry knows how to sell; now it has to sell the right thing."

—*Kirkus Reviews*

"Hank Cardello paints a clear picture of the economic and market forces that have converged to feed the global epidemic of obesity. *Stuffed* makes a forceful and compelling argument that the right mix of regulation and voluntary restraint by the industry will be a topic of legitimate debate for years to come. There is no question that we must find a way to create a level playing field on which the food industry can promote and sell products that support rather than subvert the health of Americans."

—Walter Willett, MD, PhD; author of *Eat, Drink, and Be Healthy: The Harvard Medical School Guide to Healthy Eating*; chair of the Department of Nutrition, Harvard University

"Anyone who is interested in their health and thinks they're educated about nutrition needs to read this book."

—Bookbrowse.com

"An interesting look into the psychological world of the 'Big Food' business. . . . *Stuffed* is a great book because it is honest, and Cardello does not mince words when it comes to the reality of our nation's misguided obsession with food." —Eats.com

"Hank Cardello offers insights into the obesity epidemic that no author or scholar has had. He illuminates how the food sector confuses and ultimately controls us, explains how pricing in supermarkets works, and details how restaurants and many other elements control our eating patterns."

—Barry Popkin, PhD; director of the Interdisciplinary Obesity Center, UNC-Chapel Hill; author of *The World Is Fat*

"Food companies would be more profitable and keep their customers longer if they adopted the ideas in *Stuffed*."

—Tom Ryan, former chief concept officer of McDonald's Corporation

"We can't underestimate the role that healthy lifestyle choices make in reducing the incidence of any number of life-threatening diseases, breast cancer among them. Cardello's book provides insights into our nutrition choices that, hopefully, will help us to make the right decisions about what we eat and avoid health problems down the road."

—Hala Moddelmog, president and CEO of Susan G. Komen for the Cure

"One would think that enlightened self-interest would cause everyone in the food industry to help their customers live longer, healthier lives. Unfortunately this has not happened. Here Cardello makes the case for how and why the food industry, the government, and the media must change, so we don't all eat ourselves to death."

—Bob Goodale, former president of Harris Teeter Supermarkets

# stuffed

*an insider's look at who's (really) making america fat*



hank cardello

WITH DOUG GARR

ecco

*An Imprint of* HarperCollins*Publishers*

A hardcover edition of this book was published in 2009 by Ecco, an imprint of HarperCollins Publishers.



HarperCollins books may be purchased for educational, business, or sales promotional use. For information, please write: Special Markets Department, HarperCollins Publishers, 10 East 53rd Street, New York, NY 10022.

FIRST ECCO PAPERBACK EDITION PUBLISHED 2010.

*Designed by Ralph Fowler / rlf design*

Library of Congress Cataloging-in-Publication Data has been applied for.

ISBN: 978-0-06-189674-3

10 11 12 13 14 ID/RRD 10 9 8 7 6 5 4 3 2 1

*For Mary, Erin, and David*

# contents

# preface

Ever have a day that you consider to be a life-changing experience? Mine was on May 15, 1995. As I waited outside the Atlanta Cancer Clinic in my car, I read—again—the notes my physician had shared with me leading up to this moment:

*Date: April 20, 1995*

*The patient has a CD-10 elevation and very high levels. This is linked to a type of leukemia.*

*Date: May 8, 1995*

*The patient's CALLA is up. We need to do a bone marrow.*

Leukemia. Bone marrow. Not words you want to appear on your medical chart.

How did things get to this point? It had started about five months earlier, on a sunny January morning. I couldn't get out of bed. I felt weak and ached all over. I was absolutely miserable. I did the usual self-diagnosis. Maybe it's just a bad case of the flu. I babied myself for a week, but the "flu" didn't go away. Maybe it's mono, since I had had it in high school. But this was no mono.

This was Beyond Crud.

I called my doctor and was soon functioning as the proverbial pincushion, going through a battery of tests. Initial findings revealed "nothing unusual." Sessions of antibiotics and traditional medicines proved ineffective.

After weeks of curling up on my living room couch watching, zombie-like, as the O. J. Simpson drama unfolded on CNN, I thought I would try a different approach. I'd find a doctor who practiced complementary medicine, who looked at the complete picture and not just the symptoms. I wanted a physician who could probe deep into my lifestyle and look beyond the typical symptoms.

I found such a doctor, and learned early on I could trust him. Most core test results like heart, lung, and kidney function were normal. Interestingly enough, however, he discovered a wide range of nutritional anomalies. Nutrients like magnesium (necessary for energy and helping to prevent restless sleep) were woefully deficient. Some more vanguard assessments showed a slow liver function, but he felt this could be dealt with by adjusting my diet.

You can imagine how surprised I was when two test results came back with a positive (that means bad) signal on leukemia.

Here I sat in my car, in another Atlanta office parking lot so familiarly fenced in by the perennially green southern pines, mulling over my future or what little was perhaps left of it. I was suddenly faced with the reality of a worst-case scenario. I ran a little how-did-it-happen review. Was I about to pay the price for years of poor eating habits? Or burning the candle at both ends? Or was it just a matter of chance? I was only in my forties, and I accepted that anything can happen to anyone, at any time. Nobody is promised tomorrow's wake-up call.

Thinking about my upcoming appointment, I felt there would likely be one of two possible outcomes: "Everything's okay. You're fine." Or " Bad news, you've got twelve to eighteen months to live." As I reflected on the second one, my anxiety, fear, and tension began to ebb. The more I thought about my possible condition, the more a quiet, serene feeling came over me. One never knows how one will react to bad news. Was there trepidation? Sure. But somehow, that feeling dissipated and was replaced by the knowledge that this situation could result in something positive.

Okay, there's no way you can negate the truly inevitable, so if the clock was ticking dreadfully fast, the least I could do was to try to help others facing similar situations to live longer, healthier lives.

I was no longer thinking as a business executive. Market share, revenues, the bottom line, suddenly had no relevance at this moment. Being a part of the human community (and beyond) took hold, and it felt so natural—so effortless—to commit to the preservation and extension of life.

I didn't realize it at the time, but I had just crossed my personal Rubicon.

It was time for my appointment. I was ushered into a nicely appointed room with pleasant wood furnishings. Much nicer than the stereotypical cold, sterile doctor's office, I thought. Dr. Cooper stepped in and introduced himself. He mentioned that he had reviewed my doctor's notes and wanted to first take a look at me before proceeding to extract a bone marrow sample. After a brief examination, he shook his head and said, "Something's up, but I'm not sure what it is. I want to look at your blood first before we go through the bone marrow procedure." Sounded like a good idea to me. Anything to keep me intact a little bit longer.

After a nurse collected the blood, Dr. Cooper said, "Come with me. Let's go sit down with the lab biologists and see what they find." When we arrived, a young woman in a white lab coat was already busy at work, her eyes glued to a microscope. "Mmmmm. Huh!" She didn't sound very encouraging, I thought. "Ummm . . . ," she purred. "What do you see?" I asked. She continued to manipulate the controls on the instrument, then finally she peered over the side of the microscope and said, "Look here," surrendering her seat to me. "These are your blood cells. They sure look like they've been through a war—beaten up, I would say—can't tell you for sure." Then she said the magic words: "But I see no blast cells or other evidence of leukemia. Not today."

Breathe out. That's what you do. You just exhale.

. . .

It's been over a dozen years since that indelible day in May. The road traveled is not the one I had originally mapped out. But somehow, it's more real and more purposeful.

For nearly twenty years before meeting Dr. Cooper, I had served as an executive and adviser to some of the largest food and beverage corporations in the world. My focus centered on what you might expect of a consumer products marketer—building your brand, improving the bottom line, getting the consumer to buy more of your products. These are the things you think about. That's what you're paid to do. And much as in most businesses, that's how you get promoted, by delivering the goods.

It turned out that what was wrong with me was not cancer, but chronic fatigue syndrome, and this diagnosis meant that I could no longer eat whatever I wanted and burn the candle at both ends.

After my personal health crisis, I came to a realization about my role in the food industry. Not only did my own nutrition need to change, my purpose needed to change. I could no longer advocate products and practices that contributed negatively to consumers' health the way that I once did. My work, like my life, was in need of a new direction, and with that in mind, I set off to do my part to reenvision how the food industry dealt with health.

Most of the folks I have come across in the food industry have been well intentioned. When you look at the passion a brand manager has for his or her product, you realize that the brand becomes their "baby." And what parent wouldn't do everything to ensure the nurturing and growth of their child—even at the expense of others?

But historically, to achieve a company's objectives, the well-being of the customer has not been a deciding factor. This doesn't mean that companies don't care about those who purchase their products and services. If they're smart, they do. It just means that when it comes to delivering the bottom line, they'll do what's best for themselves financially. And sometimes, more than most of us would like to admit, that has been at the expense of the consumer.

In the decades leading up to the turn of the twenty-first century, there was less need to be concerned, because the consumers' increasing weight problems hadn't fully surfaced. It wasn't a big issue among food purveyors. "Let them eat," we said—and that was precisely what they did. But as times changed, the food industry marketing model has not kept pace. In matters of health, it has either remained static, or regressed in some very harmful ways. The conventional methods of marketing are increasingly out of sync with the long-term needs of the consumer. More is no longer better.

Unfortunately, at the moment only a small cadre of companies is truly committed to making a difference in the long-term health of their purchasers. The vast majority of producers and retailers in the food chain are slow to accept that they must take custodianship of their customers' well-being first while they make their money more responsibly.

You will note in the following pages that sometimes I am harsh on the food industry—and myself—for some of the questionable practices that have been the industry standard for far too long. However, I do not intend to join the ranks of those who attack the food industry as if it were the Evil Empire. I want to be very clear that the food industry is by no means alone in contributing to our nation's ever-growing obesity crisis. In fact, a number of great forces are complicit in creating and sustaining this crisis, whether they contribute knowingly or not. Simply put, there are many people responsible for making us stuffed.

Have we witnessed any government programs and regulations that have proven to lower the rates of obesity in this country? Do the activist groups demonstrate that they understand banning or taxing certain foods not only hurts industry, but also hurts the consumer? Can they acknowledge that all of us live in a market-based economy and companies must make a profit to stay in business, pay their employees, and feed the nation?

And where does the consumer weigh in? Is there not some shared responsibility to take care of one's health? Do we really believe that the vast majority of consumers can be counted on to suddenly implement healthier eating and lifestyle programs?

The health crisis as it relates to nutrition is a profoundly complex matter that doesn't offer easy answers and solutions. If solving the obesity crisis were simple, almost all of us would already be svelte and happy, and there would be no need for books like this. But inscrutable as it may first appear, I don't believe in my heart that this problem is intractable. Just because it's hard to find our way to a permanent national transformation doesn't mean we shouldn't explore new ideas. We must take some risks. We must change the way we prepare and sell our food. Our children's future depends on it; of this I'm certain.

*Stuffed* is an outgrowth of my professional experiences and personal commitment to ensure that all of us remain healthy longer. Just as I did in my own health crisis, I will ask you to join me in looking beyond the symptoms. I will offer a view of the issues through a slightly different prism, since I have been on the inside as the issue has festered and unfolded. I will help you see how and why decisions are made that affect the way you eat. You'll understand how the siren song of *perceived value* seduces you to buy more, and subsequently eat more. You'll meet spin doctors on both sides of the obesity debate and learn how they might be attempting to manipulate you to believe many things that are only partly true, or not true at all.

My hope here is to try to explain rather than blame. Pointing the fickle finger of fat responsibility at any one group is ultimately futile and will do little to solve the problem. I'm not here to harangue. I'm here to invite and persuade. My goal is to help people in the food industry and their customers understand why we consume what we consume and how we must change the model so we don't all eat ourselves to death. Ultimately, I firmly believe the only way we can fix the obesity mess is to begin with the food industry itself—not because it is the only one to blame, but because it's the only one that can truly make a difference.

# 1

# a boxcar full of turkeys

It all started with a turkey. Well, actually, not one turkey but many turkeys. The year was 1953. Thanksgiving had passed, the economy was booming, and Christmas shoppers around the country were getting ready to throw down some of their hard-earned cash for a little bit of Christmas cheer.

But the mood wasn't so great at C. A. Swanson & Sons, an Omaha-based frozen food company. Somehow, Swanson had over-estimated America's hunger for turkey that Thanksgiving, and they found themselves with more than half a million pounds of unsold turkeys. This would have been a lot of food in any era, but back then it was astronomical. Not to mention that Swanson didn't have enough refrigerated warehouse space to keep the turkeys from spoiling. Facing the prospect of having to write off all these birds as a huge loss, Swanson piled the turkeys into refrigerated boxcars while they searched for a buyer. As the boxcars traveled back and forth from Nebraska to the East Coast, the company's owners looked for a solution that would save them millions of dollars.

As the legend goes, one of their salesmen, Gerry Thomas, had been in Pittsburgh, checking out the catering kitchens of Pan

American World Airways when he heard about the company's problem. On the flight home, he began doodling, thinking about the hot tray the airline used to keep food warm. Why not use it to keep food cold, he wondered. In his sketches, Thomas ended up designing a three-compartment tray—a sort of takeoff on the old army mess kits, but also something that drew upon the airline's reliance on serving different foods steaming hot. The food in these trays would be kept in the freezer until it was ready to be eaten, at which point it would be heated up and served. In a matter of minutes dinner could be served with little to no preparation.

Initially, nobody at Swanson's headquarters was bowled over by the idea, and they produced only 5,000 of the meals. But eventually they warmed to the concept. They initiated Operation Smash, a national marketing campaign consisting of a blitz of television and print ads. Two headlines read: "Swanson's fixed it for you! Complete turkey dinner on a tray." "My boys are crazy about Swanson TV Dinners."

Soon enough consumers responded with a demand that far outpaced the supply. The company was blindsided by the fact that Americans seemed fascinated by the prospect of eating this new, convenient meal in front of their televisions. And just like that, the TV dinner was born.

Though Swanson did not invent the frozen food concept, its multiple compartments and use of leftover food changed the way the food industry made money and the way America ate its meals. Almost overnight, it seemed that millions of kids were plopped in front of the black-and-white televisions with the aluminum pan in front of them. A few slices of bland turkey in gravy with some cornbread stuffing, sweet potatoes, and perhaps the sorriest-tasting—certainly the sorriest-looking—peas on the planet. It wasn't very appealing, but it was convenient, and the postwar generation quickly and steadily bought into this new concept of convenience foods. Mom and Dad had the evening out, and the babysitter stood in as cook and waitress. In its first full year, more than 25 million tins were served in living rooms and kitchens across the nation. A phenomenon was born, and in one single moment, the face of food in this country began to shift.

There are many people who trace the beginning of our national obesity epidemic to the start of the fast-food chain, to a man named Kroc and the Golden Arches that he started in Des Plaines, Illinois, in 1955. While I'm the first to admit that fast food and all of its offshoots played a big role in our current situation, for my money, the story of the Swanson TV dinner holds the real key to understanding why we're so fat. The TV dinner marked a lot of firsts: the first time that we embraced en masse convenience over cuisine; the first time that it was better to be easy than to taste good; the first time that a preprepared (frozen) meal was served ready to heat and eat at home.

But of all these firsts, perhaps the most important, the one that has affected our waistlines and our taste buds the most, is that the Swanson TV dinner marked the first time that a food industry marketing gimmick seduced what might have been our better judgment. After all, the TV dinner was just a way to boost a company's struggling bottom line and cut its losses. On the surface, from a food perspective, there appeared to be little benefit to the consumer. The taste was awful, the food unappealing, and the choices limited. I mean, seriously, who wants to eat frozen Thanksgiving turkey in February?

And yet it turned out that was exactly what a lot of people wanted, and they wanted to do it because of how it had been sold to them. They had been sold on the idea that the convenience of this product was their ticket to a happier life. It had nothing to do with the actual food, and everything to do with the *image* of the food that had been projected. It had to do with the convenience, the slick packaging, and the easy cleanup. Anytime, anywhere, you could have a meal that you knew. It might not have been a good meal, but at least it was familiar.

The Swanson TV dinner appeared at a moment when our culture was changing how it thought about food. Televisions were making their way into people's homes, and food companies had begun to use this new medium to advertise their products, feeding consumers hungry for new ideas with spoonfuls of new ways to spend money on food. The idea that convenience trumped taste played right into the mind-set of that moment and it was all too infectious—from the boardrooms of the nation's food consortiums to the glass doors of Madison Avenue. Food shopping, which up until then had been more of a local endeavor, started to become a national enterprise, and when people went to the store, there were certain brands they expected to see—the brands from the television commercials.

Swanson TV dinner was a turning point, not so much because of what it was, but because of what it represented: Our expectations for food were lowered. It proved that convenience was king. McDonald's, Burger King, Stouffer's, Wendy's, the prepared food in your supermarket, takeout pizza, cheap Chinese food—none of these ideas could have taken off as they did if Swanson hadn't paved the way with a simple equation that millions of Americans embraced: TV dinners = more free time. Who cared if it tasted bad? Who cared what was in it? It was easy to buy and even easier to make. It wasn't gourmet, but hey, few things were.

The one upside to that first batch of Swanson TV dinners was that they were humble in their portion sizes. Although high in sodium, the classic roasted, carved turkey dinner weighed in at a modest 250 calories. There was no way that a nation gorging itself on TV dinners would become overweight. The servings of turkey and peas were not only foul tasting, they were anemic by any of today's standards.

That was soon to end.

For over thirty years I held various executive posts at some of the country's largest food and beverage corporations, and while I wasn't there for Swanson's revolution, I was certainly there for its wake. During the second half of the twentieth century, America ate like there was no tomorrow, consuming all manner of restaurant fare, prepared food, and packaged goods, and in the process making a handful of well-heeled, well-funded companies like Swanson incredibly profitable.

Every day during those thirty years, the ideas and methods we employed came straight from the example that Swanson had set, even if Swanson itself was not explicitly mentioned. The names of the game in the food business became convenience and marketing. With these two concepts employed in just the right way, you could sell almost anything. Swanson was never used as a case study and never spoken of as the definitive moment in food history that it was. In truth, it was a story that I'd heard passed around for years, but it was rare that people referred to it as a paradigm shift. Nevertheless, the lessons it represented and the implications it offered were clear to the entire industry. Cut losses and maximize profit through creative marketing and attractive packaging. If you can accomplish this, all else is secondary.

Today these ideas of packaging and marketing don't seem revolutionary, but at the time they were precisely that. Before Swanson, most meals were prepared in the home, not purchased in a ready-to-heat-and-eat form. That's the way it was. Swanson set the stage for convenient meals at an acceptable price and passable taste. No longer would poor-tasting products be rejected out of hand.

Swanson inverted that tried-and-true thinking. They dropped product quality—and by extension, health—from the equation and found large-scale results. It paved the way for a whole new means of gauging consumer satisfaction when it came to eating habits. If the consumer demands bigger portions, you don't raise the price; you use lower-grade ingredients and adjust the taste to a manageable level. If the consumer demands a lower price, you don't sacrifice the product's gimmick; you rejigger the recipe to compensate for shifts in palate. If you manage to make it taste good in the process, great. If not, leave it to the marketing department. It's their job to come up with a way to make it sell.

At the time I joined the food industry and for almost twenty years after, no one in the business, myself included, anticipated how detrimental this strategy would be to our nation's well-being. Obesity wasn't even on the radar screen. We simply didn't think about the future health consequences of our actions, and the few who did worry about them certainly didn't worry too much. As a result, from the 1970s to the early 2000s, America's caloric intake increased by 10 percent and American food production per capita went up by 20 percent. But none of that really mattered to most of us who worked in food. Ours became a party that would never end. All we had to do was keep our ingredient expenses down and our marketing innovation up. Invest in tasty new product design, not in healthful, quality ingredients that cost more—unless we could charge more for them.

Ultimately, these tactics worked well, far too well as it turned out. They worked so well that the food industry got addicted to the results, and sadly, America had little choice but to go along for the ride. We are now paying the price for that addiction. Our culture of excess consumption, poor-quality ingredients, unhealthy products, supersize burgers, party packs of potato chips, and 64-ounce Double Gulp soft drinks have catapulted us into the middle of a health and nutrition crisis. Two-thirds of Americans are overweight, and the nation's enormous collective girth is getting larger and younger every day. Dr. Jeffrey M. Friedman, a Rockefeller University researcher, estimates that the nation has 4 billion pounds of excess baggage, a major factor leading to high levels of hypertension, heart disease, stroke, cancer, and other life-threatening illnesses. We've been feeding at the food industry's all-you-can-eat buffet for over fifty years, and there is virtually no disagreement among health officials, doctors, nutritionists, and scientists that it's been killing us slowly ever since we started.

We've all heard the scary statistics about America's weight

problem, but there is more than just shock value in the numbers. Every year there are countless studies commissioned and public health reports released, all of which warn us about the gravity of our current state of affairs. All these are well-intentioned, but oftentimes the white noise they create only obscures the important numbers that prove this obesity problem is shared by everyone in America—regardless of race, gender, location, income, or ethnic background.

People have long been eager to believe that their ethnic group, region, city, or income bracket is immune to serious problems of obesity. There was a point in time when I agreed with this sentiment, thinking that the national obesity crisis was driven strictly by money and class. If you were an immigrant or poor, or both, you were a "leftover" who lacked the means to afford a healthier lifestyle. If you were affluent you could easily pay for a healthy diet. But I was wrong, and this theory was far too provincial in its premise. Like many diseases, those related to bad diets and obesity are starkly ecumenical and apolitical in whom they attack. If you take a look at the long lines in the waiting room in a standard dialysis unit of any hospital, amid the grim faces you'll see the mosaic of the American populace. Old and, yes, young, Caucasian and every other color of skin you can imagine. The people I'm describing defy categorization by demographic or ethnic origin.

What's really alarming is how we're mortgaging our future in the health care crisis. Obesity, especially among children, is one of the prime causes of future health problems and high mortality rates. One in three children born at the turn of the twenty-first century are expected to become diabetics at some point in their life, and half the black and Latino children are expected to be afflicted. David Ludwig, the head of the obesity program at Children's Hospital in Boston, warned, "If the current epidemic of child and adolescent obesity continues unabated, life expectancy could be shortened by two to five years in the coming decades."

In support of this point, the American Heart Association and the Centers for Disease Control released some revealing data in 2005. Even though the overweight percentage among African American adults showed them to be among the highest-risk group according to rate, the raw numbers are greater among non-Hispanic whites. Some 14 million blacks were overweight or obese; 14.5 million Hispanics; and a whopping 77 million non-Hispanic whites. And while obesity rates do tend to be higher for lower income groups, surprisingly, the highest *growth rate* is in the highest income bracket. If you're well off, you're far more likely to become fat faster than any other economic segment out there. In other words, money alone will not buy your way out of risk.

While some of America's obesity problem can be explained by our lineage, some of it can also be explained by where you live. Regionalism is also very apparent in the overweight sector. In the Midwest, we know that meat and potatoes are American staples, and fried chicken and biscuits tend to rule in southern kitchens. Regional cuisine is a wonderful and defining characteristic of American food, but as it has been practiced, it is also woefully heavy. According to the Centers for Disease Control's Behavior Risk Factor Surveillance System, the East South Central states (Alabama, Kentucky, Mississippi, and Tennessee) had the highest obesity rate. Mississippi has been fingered as the fattest state. The West South Central states (Arkansas, Louisiana, Oklahoma, and Texas) were only a percentage point behind. To be fair, several other regions were right up there on the "fatness" scale.

Shifting the focus from the regional level to the city level, the numbers change little. *Men's Fitness* magazine publishes an annual study of the cities in the country with the most people who are overweight. The editors use several criteria including air and water quality, availability of parks and open spaces, drinking alcoholic beverages, length of commute, percentage of overweight and sedentary residents, smoking, and sports participation. And the magazine added number of fast-food restaurants as an additional factor for the first time in 2006. Though the magazine's results are not based on strictly scientific study methods, they are worth noting because they offer a different array of data. While Las Vegas earned the number one ranking in 2007, four of the top ten of the fattest cities were in Texas again: Dallas, Houston, San Antonio, and El Paso.

In New York City, the Department of Health and Mental Hygiene found a lack of healthy foods in the Bedford-Stuyvesant and Bushwick neighborhoods in Brooklyn. Those areas have some of the city's highest obesity rates. In Bedford-Stuyvesant, for example, 30 percent of adults are obese, while the average city rate is 20 percent. The agency reported that only one in three bodegas (small corner Hispanic markets, which are often the main food shopping locations in neighborhoods that lack larger supermarkets) in Bedford-Stuyvesant sold reduced-fat milk, even though 90 percent of the surrounding supermarkets stocked alternatives like Lactaid or 1% or 2% milk. Alarmed at the makeup of the standard bodega's offerings, the city began promoting a milk program in neighborhoods like central Brooklyn, the South Bronx, and Harlem.

The report also revealed that bodegas were much less likely than supermarkets to stock fruits and vegetables. While the majority of bodegas and supermarkets carry some kind of fresh fruit, only 21 percent of the bodegas in Bedford-Stuyvesant offered apples, oranges, and bananas. Leafy green vegetables like spinach and kale were found in only 6 percent of the bodegas surveyed. When asked, bodega owners were honest in their replies: They did not carry healthier foods because they didn't sell well. "Not their fault" was the explanation. And we wonder why our Hispanic neighbors suffer disproportionately from obesity and diabetes.

The obesity problem is endemic in other large cities. When CNN did a special report on nutrition in 2007, its team visited a woman in Chicago who had turned a vacant lot into an organic vegetable patch—pure backyard farming in the middle of an urban zone. It was a courageous experiment in every way because it was impossible to find anything resembling a fresh tomato anywhere in her neighborhood. She said, "You could probably buy right now, if you wanted to, illegal drugs. . . . If you wanted to buy a gun, you could buy a gun in this community. But if you wanted to find an organic tomato in this community, if you didn't want to come to our urban farm site, you wouldn't be able to buy one."

The unsurprising revelation from these studies and findings is that we're fat just about everywhere. Serious obesity and its accompanying health issues have become a panethnic, pancultural, and paneconomic problem. The size of this high-risk group is approaching two-thirds of the nation's population; it doesn't matter whether you're grabbing tonight's dinner from the El Barrio Superette or dining out on *canard à l'orange* at a French bistro. Those most at risk are the least likely to change their dietary behavior because of where they live, what they have available, and what their routine is, or because they are simply unwilling or unable to change their eating habits.

Of course, the food companies insist that the only thing obese Americans have in common is that they choose to be unhealthy. Diet is your personal choice and your responsibility, they remind you with a shake of the finger and parental scolding. All they do is provide and market the food, and most also provide healthier options. If people choose to eat the products that are unhealthy, so be it. That's not the food companies' concern. The only commonality among overweight Americans is that they all make bad decisions—end of story.

While the basic notion of personal responsibility is an important one, not to be ignored, the food companies are far more culpable than they like to let on. To put all the onus on personal responsibility ignores the trends and developments of the last fifty years in the food industry. In practice, personal responsibility accounts for a only a small fraction of the decision making that goes into what you eat, and it fails to address the litany of questions that potentially trump responsibility: What happens when your environment or routine restricts those choices? What happens when food industry marketing practices and advertising dollars make your decisions much more difficult? What if it's easier to get fast food than fresh vegetables? What do you do when a company's focus-grouped, test-marketed $20 million advertising campaign for doughnuts is designed to ensure that people in your precise demographic will struggle to select a healthier alternative over their product?

Whether it's paying school systems to have soda machines on campus, advertising their new, most sugar-filled cereals during Saturday-morning cartoons, or using a heart-stopping cooking oil because it's cheaper, the recent history of the food industry is littered with examples of questionable business practices that are employed to eliminate the role that conscious choice plays in decision making about food. In the process, these businesses boost their own bottom lines at the cost of public health. Simply put, they have risked our health for too long because change did not offer the easiest short-term business model.

After hearing all of this, it's only natural to wonder how it happened and to find yourself curious about what the food industry has done to make us fat. I'm the kind of person who can tell you; I know, I was there. I share in the responsibility. I saw companies sit idly by while they knew Americans were gaining weight, and I saw them resist all manner of health-conscious change because it was not beneficial to their corporate earnings reports. These stories lie at the heart of this book.

The story might begin at Swanson, but it certainly doesn't end there. It looks at the common denominators among all of these disparate parts, examining the forces at work in your food that you don't even know about. It's a complex equation that involves far more than just the consumer and the producers. Along the way there are many complicit parties—lobbyists, nutritionists, activists, producers, restaurants, supermarkets, consumers—each of which has its own agenda and its own reasons for trying to change or for maintaining the status quo.

My goal is to pull back the curtain on the food industry and all of the other players involved to show you the secrets about how they do business and expose the truths that explain how so many different Americans, who eat so many different things, in so many different places, all became unwitting coconspirators to the horrible health situation of today. I will examine the way the various components in this drama have behaved and interacted, to demonstrate why certain solutions will never work. In the end, I hope to deliver real-world solutions that can be implemented once and for all to solve this grave problem.

Ultimately, those who are overweight are up against the motion of all these forces—the system of business, government, nutritionists, and themselves. The problem is too big for one single reform, and this book looks at the developments that need to occur for real change to take place. Offering solutions that work within the system, I'll examine how each of these parts needs to do its share to get our nation's health back on track. Eating habits aren't going to change overnight, and may in fact not change much at all. But the public itself can have an effect on how they consume what they love to eat by gradually influencing what the food industry offers for sale. It's my contention that the real solution must come from the food industry. They hold all the cards. The food business ultimately will change because it will serve them well to change—on their bottom lines.

The gears of the food industry do not have to produce food that leads to obesity, and they do not have to produce food that depletes our pocketbook. There is plenty of room to still make a profit. There is a way to create and market cheap, convenient, healthier food, but before we can effectively accomplish any plan to get our eating back on track, we must first have a sense of our edible history. We need to learn the system and tactics that made us fat in the first place, so that we can turn them around and get on the right track.

# 2

# how food executives think

My first assignment at General Mills was as a marketing assistant for the Betty Crocker line of cake mixes. As a twentysomething guy, practically the only thing I knew about cake was how to order it. Sure, I liked cake, but that was the extent of my knowledge and experience.

When I began at General Mills, Pillsbury was cleaning our clocks because they sold, well, a "moister" cake. So how do you launch a counteroffensive? If you're a marketing guy, you walk into the test kitchen and yell, "More water! We need moist!" The home economists in our kitchen rolled their eyes at me. What did a marketing guy know? It turned out that what we really needed was more of a special starch that released moisture during the cooking process. The decision was made to relaunch the Betty Crocker line as "SuperMoist," better-tasting, and, well, a cake with more moisture. Very creative. Take that, Pillsbury.

This was the predawn of the nutrition age. We still used lard and highly saturated fats as ingredients and nutrition labeling was not even a gleam in the eye of the Food and Drug Administration (FDA). The most important aspect of marketing a product was its taste and texture. I threw myself into my work, and I quickly earned the sobriquet from colleagues—"Cardiac Cardello."

In preparing to introduce "SuperMoist" I spent a lot of time sampling the reformulated eighteen flavors in the Betty Crocker kitchens. If I hadn't been as young as I was, I would have put on more than five pounds during that stint. When the company's senior honchos pronounced the products ready for prime time, there was only one task left: supervising the "beauty shots." Home economists and food stylists in the Betty Crocker kitchens would spend countless hours prepping sliced pieces of cake for package photography. I never dreamed how much intricate detail an expertly manipulated toothpick could create on the surface of a cake. I swear, some days the photos were so appealing that I could have eaten the box.

At the time, we were just following logic: Make the food look as appealing as possible so that people will want to buy it. Nowadays with Photoshop, computer imaging, and graphics, it's easier than ever to make food look good, but the market-tested lessons from the photography of old still hold true. The look of the food and the aesthetic of the packaging are two of the most important factors when it comes to convincing consumers to spend money.

For every product you see on the supermarket shelves, there are hundreds of people whose combined talents went into making that product appealing. When I entered the food industry I became part of that invisible army that coerced you into buying Coca-Cola, Sunkist, Michelob, or Betty Crocker products. We manipulated you because, well, you were so docile and easy to sell. By that, I don't mean you're foolhardy. On the contrary, you're smart. But you're still easy to dupe, and it's not your fault. We're just clever. We have the playbook and you don't.

Basically, you're a consumer; I got you to consume.

And now we're all the worse for it.

In order to talk about the people who are contributing to the

American way of fatness, we have to examine a cross section of an expansive industry and uncover the kinds of people like me who bring you your daily bread. The term "food and beverage industry" is a broad phrase used to describe three very different types of companies—packaged goods, supermarket chains, and restaurants. Packaged goods companies produce the items you find on the shelves at your grocery store, companies like General Mills, Kraft, Coca-Cola, and Frito-Lay. Most of these companies are sprawling enterprises that consist of hundreds of individual brands sold around the world. Supermarket chains are the national and regional companies that sell groceries straight to you, places like Kroger's, Ralphs, Shaw's, and Whole Foods Market. Finally there are the restaurant companies—varying from mom-and-pop operations to national chains like McDonald's, KFC, Wendy's, Burger King, T.G.I. Friday's, Chili's, and Applebee's.

While there are overlapping interests among all three parts of the food industry, each segment acts independently of the others to address its own specific concerns, priorities, strengths, and weaknesses. Nevertheless these three groups combine to control almost everything that the average American eats.

And yet to treat packaged goods, supermarkets, and restaurants as a monolithic bloc is to greatly oversimplify the food industry and the people who comprise it. Each arm of the food and beverage industry possesses a drastically different business model, and with each business model comes a uniquely tailored mind-set designed to meet the priorities and methods of that segment. A big part of understanding what's wrong with our food is understanding the unique psychology of each segment. Getting to the heart of how food executives think and seeing what motivates them speaks volumes about how we got to our current conundrum. Before we can come up with an adequate solution, we need to understand this mind-set driving the players behind America's food. We need to get inside their heads and figure out how they operate, so that we can show how their thoughts have contributed—intentionally or subconsciously—to making us all fat. Only then can we piece together a real-world solution.

When I was a cocky and ambitious young grad student at Wharton, my fellow marketing majors looked to the three most prestigious consumer product companies to land a brand-management job—General Mills, Procter & Gamble, and General Foods (now part of Kraft Foods). These were the plum assignments. Get a summer position with one of the big three, and your career path was already paved in gold. You'd have to be an idiot not to covet one of these jobs.

I'd already had two fairly attractive job offers in New York City, but my friends encouraged me to try for one of the big three. I was scheduled to have an interview with Ted Cushmore, the Mills exec doing the recruiting. Cushmore was the typical executive of his day: tall, chiseled face, an athletic build, but very serious and low key. The kind of guy you wanted to emulate if you aspired to be a successful executive in any field. I went to my meeting with him brimming with confidence—maybe overconfidence—and after the usual round of questions, he asked me about my dreams, my lifelong goal. I knew this was the make-or-break question, so I decided to have a little fun. After all, I had nothing to lose. And who wanted to go to Minneapolis? All I knew was that Minnesota was somewhere west of New York.

"My lifelong ambition is to be the brand manager on Count Chocula." ("I vant to eat your cereal!" was the tagline—I kid you not.)

Cushmore did not reveal the slightest discomfort with my glib reply. The interview was routine from that moment on.

I got the job.

After getting my graduate degree I went to work at the company full-time. From day one, I don't recall discussing anything about the nutritive value of General Mills's cake mixes or other products, new products, or corporate responsibility to provide healthy foods to our customers. It was just not a topic that ever came up in any of our meetings.

In the late 1970s, Ted Cushmore took me to lunch. He was particularly distracted that day because he was fretting over a big decision. He had been spending sleepless nights over the pending introduction of Honey Nut Cheerios, the first line extension to that iconic brand. All he talked about was whether the new cereal would cut into the market share of Cheerios, already a brand legend and cash cow for the giant food concern. Would Honey Nut Cheerios cannibalize the sales of a hit product that had been on breakfast tables for more than forty years?

That's what consumed him, and, by extension, all of us at General Mills. The questions we worried about revolved around what packaging colors would attract kids' attention in supermarkets. Could we persuade them to beg Mom to buy two with a toy (called a "giveback" in industry parlance) gimmick? What new geographies hadn't we penetrated? Can we sell more oats in Alaska? The answers to these questions pointed to our annual bonuses and ultimately bigger jobs. In the end, it was all about how many boxes of cereal and cake mix we could move.

Cushmore exemplified the model food executive before nutrition and health became an issue. On one hand, he served his firm and its shareholders well by playing it safe and returning sustainable growth and profits. On the other, it was not in his—or my—job description to address a nonexistent obesity problem. The senior decision makers had a vested interest in increasing profit margins and their companies' revenues and market share. These were public companies, and there was a responsibility for the managers and directors to return profits to their shareholders. As a result, these companies were incredibly entrenched against change. Or, as a food executive who has had a number of high-level positions told me, "Big brands do not like to make big changes."

Until recently, most everyone in packaged goods thought this way and operated in this manner. Change that could adversely affect the bottom line was to be avoided at all costs. Of course, companies were always inventing new products and trying new things, but large-scale shifts in ingredients and quality were generally avoided. With this mind-set came a fundamental belief in consumer research and market testing. The only problem was that all the consumer feedback frequently seemed to push them in the wrong direction from a health perspective: Bigger is better; it equals more bang for your buck.

The better consumer packaged goods firms are very responsive to consumer needs. They generally employ multiple levels of research techniques to understand existing customers: taste testing, in-market testing, simulated test market analyses, message testing, and so on, and now even brain wave testing to determine the impact parts of commercials are having on viewers. Yet despite this arsenal, market performance is not perfectly predicted. Executives fall short of their sales objectives, and brand strategies miss the mark. More than four out of five new products fail. The result is few hit products, many failures, and a sea of mediocrity. This causes risk aversion. In many cases, it's better not to introduce a truly new product (unlike a simple line extension) for fear of failure and a career setback. It's easier to add new flavors and raise your market share half a point than to swing for the fences.

As such, food executives are geared to listen to consumer feedback and address unmet consumer needs. If in a particular category the consumer demands more value (for example, Hamburger Helper), they offer a better price. Larger portions have come into play with products targeted to the "he-man" customer—Campbell Soups, Manwich, and others.

I suppose the introduction of the two-liter soft drink bottle traded consumers up to a larger size. Consumers felt that while they were paying a little bit more, they received a better value. It's more likely that the 20-ounce bottle that has become so prevalent in convenience stores and vending machines is the real culprit since it is sold as a single-serve container.

This speaks to the bottom line: Consumers want "more for less."

I don't recall ever seeing consumer research where consumers would pay "whatever" for a product. This generally makes it difficult to raise prices. The exceptions are superpremium products like Grey Poupon and Häagen-Dazs, which are viewed as so special that consumers feel they're worth it and are willing to pay almost any price increase for these kinds of items.

Oftentimes the changes that did get made were about size. The executive mantra was bigger packages, bigger servings, and more of everything per container. In the process, portion size got dangerously out of hand. We went from "buy one, get one free," to "buy it by the dozens and save." Unfortunately, this also dictated *how much* we ate. We began to crave oversize entreés and 20-ounce Mountain Dews, and the packaged goods companies were more than willing to oblige, ignoring the inherent risks behind a nation fueled by processed foods and gallons of soda.

This was the mind-set that governed the packaged goods companies. For years they rode this tidal wave of money straight to the bank, based on the idea that you could make Americans eat just about anything, so long as you sold it right. Of course, there were some famous colossal blunders along the way—"New" Coke and "Clear" Pepsi being among the most memorable—but on the whole, the packaged goods industry subscribed to the mantra "If you market it, they will come."

Here's a typical example of the rationale that pits profits and brand extension before the best interests of consumers. When I was a brand manager at Anheuser-Busch for Michelob, my superiors issued me a challenge. Although Michelob was a solidly entrenched and successful premium brand, it was under siege by an army of imported beers. I was put in the hot seat: Could I increase revenues by extending its reach into a broader market? The idea my team came up with was to sell a malt liquor under the Michelob banner. The product would be different, because it would bring Michelob's upscale imagery and "smooth taste" to a downscale market. There is some risk to this move ("devaluing" or "eroding" the brand—a marketer's worst nightmare), but when it works you can make a lot of money. (Think about how in the past decade or so Mercedes-Benz successfully developed lower-priced models to attract a less affluent buyer. At one time you had to be wealthy to own a Mercedes. Now all you need is a steady job with a reasonable paycheck.) From a business perspective the malt liquor launch was an easy one to make. It would expand the brand's reach and deepen our market penetration in urban areas where much of the consumption of malt liquors was well established.

The development group proceeded to gear up for a test run. We chose to try it out in Detroit where there was a heavy concentration of target users in the inner-city neighborhood. We'd wanted to get Michelob Malt in the delis and convenience stores. At the time, it never crossed my mind that marketing 40-ounce bottles (yes, 40 ounces, more than half a six-pack) of a more potent alcoholic beverage (malt liquors typically have alcohol content levels that range from 5.7 to 5.9 percent, whereas regular beer is around 5 percent) to inner-city customers, primarily African Americans with higher than typical unemployment levels, might be—there is no other way to put it—more than a little irresponsible. In retrospect, given the superpremium platform where Michelob competed, there were better opportunities to capitalize on, other than exploit, the inner-city market.

At the end of the day, it didn't work out. We decided to leave that market to Colt 45 and Schlitz Malt Liquor. But though our strategy was not a success, this incident proved a perfect example of how decisions were made with little to no care for the consumers' well-being. We just didn't think about such things. All we thought about was market expansion and our own bottom line.

When you sum it up, the packaged goods marketers are pretty

plugged-in to their consumers and recognize trends as they emerge. In their best moments they can be quite nimble and responsive to their users' needs. Some have moved to reshape their business models and practices to be in alignment with the trend to healthier eating. Most have not. But there is hope, because among all the players in this game of obesity, these marketers have the most capacity to change.

For decades most products sitting on supermarket shelves were born out of market expansion and saturation. Even most of the "healthy" products were more about market share than actual health. Because virtually every supermarket is overflowing with packaged goods, there is quite a lot of interplay between these two branches of the food industry. Packagers and supermarkets work closely with one another to ensure that the aisles remain filled with the old standbys as well as packages and displays that lure customers into new products.

Despite this overlap between packaged goods and supermarkets, there are distinctly different forces that motivate supermarket success. Supermarkets are challenged to make a profit. Their net income is only 1 to 2 percent, compared with consumer packaged goods and restaurants, which generally reach 15 percent or so (but can vary as much as from 5 to 25 percent). The supermarketers are not the innovators; rather, they're master merchandisers. When they agree to take on a new product, they have one goal: to shelve-display-promote it in a way to maximize grocer profits. Everything has an "expiration date" on it; they must move the products out the door. Inventory turnover is paramount. This limited profitability and need to lower their carrying costs makes their business model much different from consumer packaged goods firms and restaurants.

Because there is so much pressure on the bottom line, they look to cut costs and extract the maximum promotional dollars from the producer companies. Basically, they're in the real estate business—you want to rent space in my store, you pay me for it. It wasn't always this way. With the grocery trade consolidating over the last decade or two along with the rise of Wal-Mart, grocers now have more clout with the producers and continually find ways to extract more money. Their biggest challenge is to differentiate themselves from their competitors. On one end, there's low cost (Wal-Mart is now the nation's leading supermarket), and on the other end there's high cost (Whole Foods). This gap leaves a sea of middle-ground companies to battle it out on price alone.

The term "slotting allowance" was coined by the supermarket industry when it charged food companies for shelf space when they introduced a new product. It is kind of a nonrefundable advance payment just in case the product fails. This is not just blatant extortion on the part of the grocers. They understand the high failure rate. They can't afford to leave unsold, expired goods on their shelves without making instant changes.

Do you think those megadisplays of Coke and Pepsi are free? Think again. Location. Location. Location. The highest traffic areas command the most money—and they are effectively exploited. Would Coke rather have end caps (product displays at the end of the supermarket aisle that make products highly visible to the shopper), stand-alone displays near the front entrance, and 20-ounce bottles at the checkout counter, or be buried on an interior shelf? You know the answer. This is the game-within-the-game. Even though producers and supermarkets are partners in bringing you a cornucopia of branded foods and beverages, they also have their various tugs-of-war to generate their respective sales and profits.

Unlike the packaged goods people, supermarket types are not going to lead the parade. Their strength is in execution and implementation. They will not be the ones who come up with solutions to the obesity problem. They don't have the luxury of spending the time or money to do so, given their limited resources and profits. But they can play an important role because they own the real estate and can influence what goes on the shelves.

. . .

One day recently, a colleague and I were ruminating over a bagel and coffee at a restaurant about the obesity crisis. We were in Manhattan, where he lives, the bagel capital of the world, at least from the point of view of New Yorkers. The bagels in question were from H&H, a legendary Upper West Side bakery known by insiders as perhaps the best bagel in the city (others consider Ess-A-Bagel to be the gold standard, but let's not argue). My colleague and I are about the same vintage, and so the first thing he brought up was the ever-increasing size and weight of the bagel. Remember when we were kids? The bagel was roughly three to three and a half inches in diameter. Today's bagel is about five inches in diameter, much bigger, we both agreed. In fact, it's nearly doubled in size. (Consider the bran muffin and the corn muffin, and other breakfast pastries that have also morphed into supersize breakfast fare.) That light breakfast you just had with your two cups of coffee probably exceeded half the suggested caloric intake for the day.

He wondered how the bagel grew so big. Did the bagel eaters suddenly become hungrier over the years, he asked? I laughed, and told him that it was simple college economics. If you make a small bagel and it costs fifteen cents to make, and you sell it for fifty cents, you make thirty-five cents a bagel. Not bad. But if you make a much bigger one, your ingredient investment is only slightly higher—certainly not double. So you invest, say, twenty or twenty-two cents and then you sell it for $1.30 (the price of an H&H bagel at the time of this writing). Your revenue is much higher, of course, but your profit also has more than doubled to over a dollar, and it certainly doesn't take that much longer (or more fuel) to bake the bigger ones. Only a very backward baker would sell the smaller bagel when he knows you'll buy the bigger one. And if you're truly a stoic, you'll eat only half and give the other to the pigeons or share it with the person in the next cubicle.

Marian Burros, a respected food writer for the *New York Times*, did a bagel survey for a story back in the mid-1990s. She analyzed several versions and found that the largest one weighed in at 7 ounces and had 552 calories—with *nothing* on it. She called it calorie "sticker shock." The average bagel has 70 to 80 calories per ounce. How did they get this way? The bagel of old was simply a combination of flour, water, and malt. Today the bagel has sugar or honey, or may even have Crisco, not to mention other flavorful additives. In short, to create a bigger, great-tasting bagel, you put more ingredients in it.

I relate the bagel story not to point the finger at the makers of one our great national foods. I love bagels, and I certainly wouldn't stop eating them just because they're potentially fattening. But they do provide a window into the workings of how restaurants go about making their money. They're a clear example of how the practice of ever-larger portion sizes have contributed to the nation's expanding waistlines.

Why do restaurants push bigger sizes? Simple: more profits. If I make my muffins bigger, my ingredient costs go up, but not as much as the price I can charge. Therefore I make a higher profit with the larger size. Same holds for french fries. Same holds for beverages. It's in the mind-set of a food executive to squeeze more profits out of what he sells. In the case of restaurants, almost one-third of their costs are tied up in ingredients. That's a huge chunk. So if you can find ways to stretch your dollars, that's a big plus, especially since labor costs (another third of expenses) are even harder to control.

When the opportunity arises to supersize a given item, or introduce combo meals, or sell larger bagels and muffins presents itself, these food purveyors are not thinking about your waistline. *They're thinking about survival.* If I can't produce more profits, I may be at risk of losing market share to my competitor down the block, or worse—going under. The executive is worried about losing his job. Take, for instance, a time of flagging national economy. Restaurant traffic and sales are soft (a nice industry euphemism for a no-growth environment). This reverberates back through their suppliers (soft drink manufacturers, french fry producers, bread bakers, and everyone else in the supply chain). The consumer—also stretched financially—is looking for even more value, and as such, more bang for the buck is not only a smart thing to do, but a necessary thing to pursue. It's a classic example of getting more for less.

America eats out more than ever before. This is a recent—meaning approximately the last half century—cultural concept, fomented in part by our endlessly busy lifestyles. Mom and Dad are working and they're exhausted after picking the kids up from after-school activities, so they don't have time to cook. And authorities agree, the more you rely on someone else to cook your food, the less you know what's in it. While fast-food outlets are easily identifiable targets for this trend, the casual family restaurant chains—Applebee's, Red Lobster, and Olive Garden, for example—have become popular destinations as well. Mostly, the time-pressed consumer eats high-calorie, low-nutrition fare. Nobody eats grandma's cooking anymore. (If we're not eating out, then we're bringing prepared foods into the home at a greater pace than ever.)

Are the restaurants trying to make us fatter or less healthy? Not intentionally. They just haven't figured out a better way to improve their bottom lines.

This also ties into the nature of the restaurant industry's personality: They're operators. While the initial restaurant concepts can be creative, once you're in business, it's all about operations. So guess what? The people doing the day-to-day work—cranking out those fries—are focused on making things work, not on coming up with creative solutions or the next big idea. Collectively, the industry is prone to react to change, not create it. It will dig in and defend its traditional stances rather than be open-minded to better ideas. While our packaged goods friends tend to be more strategic, the restaurant crew must focus on perfect execution—otherwise they'll die.

The restaurateurs' historical business model demands a keen eye to managing costs and executing well. Creating breakthrough solutions is not their priority. If you have a good thing, you stick with it. When it comes to managing a restaurant, the health of the clientele is not even a factor in the equation, no matter how simple or complicated it may be.

Somewhere, somehow, someone in the fast-food business invented the "combo" meal. Probably, he noticed long lines at a McDonald's outlet during the dinner rush hour, and people staring at the menu boards while waiting to order. When it's your turn, if you're not absolutely certain of what you want, you perform sort of a brain grope while you piece together your meal (Do I want fries or onion rings today?). Why not just include the burger, fries, and soft drink in one single price? Induce the customer into buying the combo meal and he won't even have to *think* about it. Sure, there's a small price break, as the whole is less than the sum of the parts. But the average check goes up, because the combo meal encourages the customer to buy more. Not to mention that the line moves much faster, resulting in quicker turnover in the kitchen. When you net out the benefit to the franchise operator, you see an increase in sales.

What a brilliant idea. Every burger chain imitated this innovation, and customers loved it. You felt like you were getting a bargain, even though sometimes you were saving as little as 10 cents on a multidollar purchase. Those medium- and large-size soft drinks included in the deal did nothing to make anybody thinner. Coke and Pepsi, which sell huge amounts of beverages through these chains, were happy, too. What are you thinking when you get an empty cup and are asked to help yourself? Free soda, that's what. Buy one, get the next one free. What a deal. The franchisee is thinking: less work for my staff, greater efficiency, more profits.

The combo meal really made a difference in the fast-food dinner experience. People think, "If I don't take advantage of this offer, I'm losing money." Nobody really does the math when they're on the ordering line. Perhaps no restaurant chain has jacked up its portions more than Burger King. Since 2006, it has introduced a Triple Whopper, the BK Stacker with four beef patties, and an Enormous Omelet sandwich, which is a sausage, bacon, and cheese omelet on a bun. But that seems small compared with its Meat 'Normous, a breakfast sandwich that the company flogs with the slogan: "A full pound of sausage, bacon, and ham. Have a meaty morning." So much for having it "your" way (the "custom" Whopper), which was Burger King's move to stand out against the combo-meal trend that became so popular. McDonald's has responded, too, ever mindful of the fierce competition. And at the time of this writing, they introduced the Angus Burger, which at a third of a pound, is 25 percent bigger than their famous Quarter Pounder. When industry critics say they're still heading in the wrong direction, I find it difficult to muster a counterargument. But what if McDonald's didn't match their competitors? They'd claim they'd lose customers to the other fast-food outlets down the street. And they'd be right.

When the burger chains went big, the major pizza chains quickly added larger pizzas to their menus. In the early 1990s, *Time* magazine pictured an example of one of the new megapies superimposed over a shot of a toddler, describing the new effort as "a pizza a boy can hide behind." The combo meal's effect is far-reaching. In the end, the bargain pies sold by Pizza Hut and Dominoes only accelerated the overeating phenomenon. All the actions, reactions, and imitations added an intensity to the eating experience that fed our obesity tsunami.

So where do we stand? A toxic alchemy results when our lack of table discipline collides with food executives' marketing practices that encourage consumption of less healthy foods and beverages. All of the above "failures" point to the fact that much of what we eat—and what we're served—has more to do with perception than reality. Food executives make their decisions on what they understand to be consumer preference and demand. They ignore the evidence of the adverse health impact that their decisions create, and many stick with the status quo as long as they can. I call this "conspiracy by human nature." There's nothing insidious about it on any intrinsic level, but it's pervasive throughout the industry. It can be discouraging when you realize how this kind of thinking affects our overall well-being in the long run.

One thing that binds them together is their goals; they're in business to make money. They do it well, and up until recently, nobody has given any real thought to modifying a model that was not designed to address the health and well-being of the consumer. And that's what has to change. Nobody is thinking on a macro level. Their models are outdated. They're missing a key ingredient: the welfare and longevity of their valued customers.

The risks to Americans' health that this presents are not always immediately apparent, but there is a darker reality here that few people take seriously. You start with those packaged goods with high calories and sugar, and that jumbo order of fries at the fast-food emporia that dot the American landscape today. Cut to the overcrowded hospital rooms of tomorrow and a society burdened with obesity and diabetes. There are several dots to connect the food with an overburdened health care system that will eventually affect the well-being and economic status of every American, obese or not. But anyone can see this line being drawn and its ultimate impact. The powers that be in today's food industry must take a long look at their marketing tactics and the products they're selling and developing, and ask themselves the tough question: How do I reconcile today's profits with the future health of my customers?

# 3

# what grocers don't want you to know

I want to take you on a little private tour. It's a path you've undoubtedly traveled many times on your own, but I want to make a few stops and let you ponder the view from the perspective of a couple of food executives.

It is hard to resist the marketing allure of the supermarket itself. After all, we're all hungry, avid gourmands to some extent. And the supermarket ambience has been periodically changed and upgraded to accommodate us. In recent years, we've seen the advent of more in-store advertising—not just the daily specials—but prodding in ways that are ever more creative, or annoying, depending on your point of view. There are television screens in some stores, and audio messages booming over the loudspeakers. People buy more when they hear music they like. No need to clip the newspapers, either. The discount coupons are often available in dispensers on the shelf right next to the item. There are ads everywhere, of course, including on the backs of shopping carts.

The supermarket is the gateway to the food industry. In many ways it's the closest that most shoppers will ever get to going behind the curtain. Of course, everything is well-disguised and hidden in plain sight, but if you know where and how to look, suddenly the strings of the food industry start to become all too apparent.

To look at a supermarket like a food executive is to see things not as food for your family, but as products ripe for consumption. In this world, the entire space is well thought out and carefully planned. It's like taking a choreographed tour through Disney World. Everything from store layout to the products to the packages that contain the products has been focus-grouped and test-marketed to ensure that a consumer fitting a specific demographic and income level will buy one thing or another. Little is left to chance. No one sets out for the grocery store saying, "I'm going to buy food that makes my family fat," yet somehow people find themselves constantly coming home with the same combination of items that are unhealthy. It's everything they don't see that keeps them returning for more.

None of this occurred over night, of course. The methodology of this type of retailing has evolved over the past seventy-odd years. The idea of the "super" market actually began to evolve at the beginning of the Great Depression, in 1930, and the concept is generally credited to an assistant store manager named Michael Cullen who worked at a Kroger grocery store. Cullen submitted a plan to Kroger president William Albers that envisioned developing very large ("monstrously large," as he put it) no-frills self-service stores with low overhead and a cash-and-carry policy that would make it possible for a food merchant to charge very low prices without sacrificing profits.

Cullen hypothesized that extremely low prices for one thousand staple food products would draw unprecedented hordes of people to the stores and create high-volume turnover. Replacing the ubiquitous retail clerks with self-service would greatly reduce the payroll, and it would also be a catalyst for what would become known as "impulse" buying. Shoppers would be free to browse about, inspect the merchandise, and retrieve the things they wanted from the shelves themselves—something they could not do in the vast majority of grocery stores of that era.

Fate played a pivotal role in the supermarket's history. Kroger's president never saw Cullen's letter. His immediate boss, Kroger's vice president of retailing John B. Bonham, summarily rejected it. Frustrated, Cullen quit and formulated a plan to open his own retail business. On August 4, 1930, he successfully launched King Kullen, the world's first supermarket, in an abandoned garage at 171st Street and Jamaica Avenue, in Queens, New York.

Cullen's business philosophy—low food prices and low operating expenses—is still the core of the supermarket movement, but what is perhaps more important is the concept of the store's architecture. The grid system layout is commonplace, but it was a radical notion in the 1930s. Cullen knew that merchandise displayed within easy reach of shoppers would encourage them to add items they hadn't planned to buy.

For every American family, food shopping would never be the same.

It had been some time since I'd been through a supermarket on a pure reconnaissance trip, so as a reality check, I asked Bob Goodale to accompany me. Goodale spent his career as president of three food-processing, distribution, and retail companies: Finevest Foods, Sunstate Dairy and Foods Company, and Harris Teeter, a major food retailer in the Carolinas and Virginia. During his tenure at Harris Teeter, revenue doubled, the operating income tripled, and the number of stores increased from 75 to 125. He sat on the board of Peapod, Inc., an online grocery shopping and delivery company. In the mid-1990s, Goodale served as North Carolina's deputy secretary of commerce.

Goodale is eminently qualified to comment on how retail supermarkets stock their shelves—and more important, how they get you to buy the products they want you to buy, instead of what you should be buying. He is a master at merchandising and has conducted strategic studies at Purdue University to analyze and assess consumer patterns in the grocery store. He coined the metric known as the "Index of Exposure," which indicates how much of a grocery store a particular customer actually sees while he packs his shopping cart with goods. It is rare for the average consumer to see more than 40 percent of a supermarket; the goal was obviously to increase the buyer's exposure to as many products as possible.

We decided to return to one of Goodale's haunts, Harris Teeter, an upscale southeastern grocery chain in the mold of Wegmans (in the Northeast), Ukrop's (Mid-Atlantic), Marsh (Midwest), Byerly's (Upper Midwest), and Vons/Pavilions (West Coast). The typical Harris Teeter target buyer falls someplace between a Kroger or Safeway shopper and a Whole Foods aficionado. Goodale is a spry, white-haired man in his seventies, with a gleam that reveals the energy he had for this business. He explained how Harris Teeter creates a department store–like shopping experience. Goodale's executive team made an effort to correlate how much time people spent in a supermarket with how much they spend. The more time they spend in the store, the more they're going to buy.

"We want to settle the customer down right away," he said. "Women hate to grocery shop, but they love to department store shop." The opening section sets the stage so that the customer will want to spend more time in the store. So you see lots of colors up front, and that's why they direct you to the produce or the floral section. If it were at the exit, he said, you would be all shopped out. He explained, "This section is a high-contribution area to overhead," meaning it's important to the store's profits.

Every grocer uses "power" items to drag the customer through the store and disperse impulse purchases everywhere. Products such as bread, milk, bananas, ground beef, chicken, and eggs are major examples of power items. The meats and breads are in the back, pulling the consumer through the store. In essence, the shopper is manipulated through the aisles.

By the time we reached the meats, he grinned and said, "We've picked their pocket by now." A customer is fully engaged once they get to this point. As we continue our walk through the store, Goodale notes that beer and wine here are sold together with snacks. The beer pulls the customer in, and then he is exposed to the higher-margin wine and snack products.

As we started to look at shelves, Bob identified the "arc of activity." This represents the critical six inches above and below five foot six (the average female height).

"Eye level equals buy level," he noted, adding that eye level placement is the most coveted spot for any product. This is where a new product can achieve critical mass. Gatorade is aimed at men (the label is at five feet eight inches, right in front of your typical male face) and Propel, an energy drink targeted to women, is shelved slightly lower (five feet even, because most women are shorter). We noticed several Harris Teeter private-label offerings were shelved at eye level. These products have good profit margins, and it was obvious that Harris Teeter was pushing these products by their shelf location.

Higher-priced brands such as Grey Poupon mustard are clearly "in the arc," as well as items that provide the grocer a higher profit margin. The slower-moving items are on the top shelves, harder to find, and thus reserved for the "destination shopper." People are specifically looking for these items. For example, this shopper might typically be looking for a certain item such as Tabasco sauce, so it does not have to be at eye level. Often, smaller sizes fall in the arc due to their higher margins.

He also pointed out that larger sizes normally are placed on the bottom shelves. Typically these are commodity products such as ketchup, or high-demand icons such as Cheerios and Kellogg's Corn Flakes. Other brand staples are on the lower shelves where they know consumers can always find them.

While these rules are fairly constant, there are, of course, occasional exceptions, many of which involve products aimed at kids. Goodale revealed how supermarkets sell products to your children, bypassing your scrutiny and best intentions for good nutrition. When kids were in the shopping cart, he noted, they induced the parent to spend up to 50 percent more. For example, in the cereal aisle, some drinks such as Capri Sun and Hi-C were shelved directly across from the cereal. There were also small toys adjacent to these sections. Once again, presweetened cereals were shelved at the kids' eye level (the two shelves above the bottom). Goodale laughed as he recalled that grocery insiders also refer to the bottom shelf as "the underwear shelf" (because women must bend down to retrieve the items).

Though the cereal aisle is a frequently cited illustration of food marketers and supermarkets colluding to draw in children, there are many similar examples that are just as troublesome for kids' health, if not worse. Take Oscar Mayer Lunchables. The Pizza Stix is a children's product, of course, and you can tell by the colorful, animated package art. No trans fats, which is good. But Lunchables Maxed Out? This is just one ugly, shameful example of what the industry likes to call "convenience" food. If you read what's in Ultimate Nachos, you'll cringe (580 calories, 240 of which are fat).

And here is the ultimate irony—or hypocrisy, if you will. South Beach Diet products, produced by the same manufacturer, were directly adjacent to the Oscar Mayer kids' foods on the refrigerated shelf. There wasn't a single South Beach Diet package above 320 calories. So the message here is, it's okay for Mom and Dad to buy slimming products, but not your kids. Note that this type of "fast food" item for children is really being shelved in a way that the busy parent can impulsively put it in the shopping cart.

Despite the apparent science behind shelving, there is one thing that trumps all rules: money. Packaged goods companies, like Kraft's Oscar Mayer, pay for prime shelf space in every store, effectively leasing the best real estate from supermarkets to make sure that the products they want to sell are easy to find. The major companies forge deals with the retailers so they get periodic stand-alone displays and preferred positions on the ends of aisles near the checkout counters. These are carefully thought-out placements, and companies like PepsiCo and Kraft pay handsomely for the privilege of being up front. These are the high-volume, high-calorie "category leaders."

While we could benefit if the packaged goods companies chose to buy good shelf and display space for nutritious products, very often they spend their money pushing food that is less healthy, which in turn makes it harder for us to avoid those less-healthy products. On a separate trip to a Lowes supermarket, a popular chain in the southeastern United States, I calculated that 52 percent of stand-alone displays consisted of junk foods. The back-to-school displays featured a cardboard school bus hyping only Kellogg's presweetened offerings: Frosted Flakes, Fruit Loops, Honey Smacks, and Frosted Mini-Wheats. When I reached the Food Lion, I noticed that 68 percent of the displays (both premium stand-alones and in the aisles) consisted of junk food. These included cookies, soft drinks, potato chips, beer, and doughnuts.

It's bad enough to know that both the supermarkets and the packaged goods companies are working together to push these unhealthy products, but the larger question is *why*. Why do they spend money to keep you eating things that might be harmful for you? The short answer is the obvious one—money—but more important, they do it because it is necessary. The business models for both supermarkets and packaged goods companies are dependent on the idea that Americans continue to purchase these products. They need you to keep buying the 70-percent-margin boxes of sugar-laced Frosted Flakes at $5.49 a box because they're staples for the quarterly shareholder reports. This pays the bills.

Another reason for continuing to push established products is the high cost and risk associated with introducing new items. For instance, a new healthier product may cost millions—if not tens of millions—of dollars to ready for market and then support with advertising and promotions. If it fails, it costs big time. On the other hand, a smaller size of Oreos in a new package is a virtual lock if priced properly. So which course do you think the marketers are more likely to follow more readily?

Conglomerates—the multibillion-dollar companies that sell a wide array of foods and beverages—produce most of the products you buy in supermarkets. Consolidation in the food industry has long been a trend, just one that isn't as noticeable as the marriage and divorce of, say, Chrysler and Mercedes-Benz. Corporate mergers and acquisitions occur not only because CEOs are intent on upping their earnings and increasing their revenues, but also because they must expand in order to survive. The bigger conglomerates have more clout and get the best deals. There are basically three ways to grow in the food business: You increase sales or launch new versions of your cash cow brands; you introduce new products; or you buy a company, preferably a competitor.

This causes a large measure of corporate schizophrenia in which a company like Kraft markets a healthier, lower-calorie version of Capri Sun for kids, but it also makes hefty profits on their (truly awful) nonnutritious Lunchables. Nestlé is highly focused on child nutrition and baby formulas as well (it was the prime reason they wouldn't do a merger with Pepsi), yet they still sell a wide range of indulgent products like Toll House cookies and chocolate bars. General Mills sends a similar mixed message. On the same shelves you'll find whole-grain Cheerios and also Count Chocula. Pepsi serves both Aquafina water and Mountain Dew. The big food companies represent the good, the bad, and the abominable, depending on what you're buying.

The chief marketing guru at a big packaged foods concern wants to sell as much as he can of the company's entire product line, but he knows where his annual bonus is buttered, so to speak. Yes, there is a "health and wellness" link on the company's Web site, but let's be realistic, for the most part such efforts merely reflect image-conscious public relations. All large food concerns do this in one way or another. The shareholders and executives have historically been concerned more with profits than their customers' daily consumption of calories, and those profits point in one direction: unhealthy food spurred by creative marketing.

This is something that I've seen firsthand—not just in the grocery store but in my own food career. Even as recently as ten years ago, the major food companies were still ignoring anyone bold and creative enough to try to sell potential hit products with nutritional value. In the mid-1990s, I witnessed just such myopia when I pitched a new food idea to a number of executives at Pillsbury (now a subsidiary of General Mills). Pillsbury managed the fabulously successful Green Giant brand, which had so much shelf space and marketing momentum that it would be relatively low risk–high return to come up with new and healthy supplemental products.

My concept was very simple: the Green Giant's young companion, Sprout, was a symbol and trademark that could play well with kids. Not only was Sprout a character that kids could relate to, he also brought with him a healthy aura. By branding a line of products under the Sprout trademark and visual likeness, Pillsbury would have a vehicle to deliver foods with high nutritional content aimed at kids.

I was gunning for big game here. Specifically, I thought Sprout could launch a convenient portable kids' lunch product to compete against Kraft's Lunchables brand. Its point of difference would be that now kids could enjoy the same tasty and convenient food offered by Lunchables but in a far-healthier version. Knowing that animated characters appealed to children, this would be a great way to create demand for a better alternative.

To buttress my point, I had mocked up packages designed to help visualize how the Sprout character could be portrayed to prospective consumers. The warm green colors that had historically surrounded the Green Giant messages of the past came through and were very inviting. This was an excellent example of using battle-tested and successful marketing tactics to reach kids but for a product that would actually be good for them.

This was truly a no-brainer. First, Pillsbury had already made substantial investments in their well-known trademarks and would not have to spend the significant sums required to create new brand names. Second, I knew Kraft was highly vulnerable with its Lunchables line due to its high caloric and fat content; in fact, some of their individual lunch items contained almost 700 calories at a pop. Sooner or later, this kind of item would surely come under attack from the food police. By incorporating better nutrition and "stealth vegetables," Sprout would differentiate itself from the market leader.

Unfortunately, those executives I met with didn't feel that this was a big enough idea at the time. I was stunned. I looked at it like making the sequel to a hit movie. People are going to show up at the box office just because there's a "II" after the title. I argued that even if they weren't compelled by the health message, they could still effectively compete in a large market space using Sprout's cachet.

Exhausting all my persuasive options, I made my final plea to the senior executive at the meeting. I played the guilt card.

"This can be your legacy," I implored. "You'll make money and do the right thing for society," I said. "People will look back at this and see that the company had vision."

He promptly replied, "I don't care about my legacy."

Looking back, I'm still somewhat disappointed about the stillborn Sprout character. Childhood obesity had not even shown up yet as an issue, and using health as a mainstream benefit did not come across as enough of a breakthrough. Today, as then, I felt that Pillsbury not only passed on a business opportunity with tremendous potential, but they—and I—failed the American consumer.

As Goodale and I continued our walk, he explained why certain items were located a specific distance down the aisle. For example, sugar is not shelved at the end of the aisle. Why? It's located a third of the way down the aisle, because they want to pull the customer into the middle of the aisle so they are induced to traverse and travel the entire length of the aisle. The essentials are always at the middle to maximize your exposure to other, nonessential products. Once the supermarket gets you in the vicinity of these nonessential items, then they let the physical packages of the goods do the rest of the work that it takes to get you to buy.

But more than packaging is involved in landing a brand from the marketer into your cart. There are several components of a marketer's tool kit that are equally, if not more, important. Consider these:

**Product:** Does it taste as good as or better than the consumer expects? If so, they may have a winner. Usually the goal is to be preferred over the brand's competitors. How is the texture, mouthfeel, sweetness, or crunchiness of the product? If they hit upon the magic combination (like Oreos, Twinkies, Fritos, or Kraft Macaroni & Cheese) they've got a home run.

**Pricing:** The price of the product determines its perceived value to the buyer. Pricing is very tricky because the brand manager wants to charge as much as possible to capture the most profit. Then reality sets in and it generally takes some real-world market research to determine what the consumer is willing to spend. This creates a situation where the price is not necessarily proportionate to a product's cost or value. Many prices are tailored to achieve a target gross profit for the manufacturer. Cereal is a good example. Watch the price go up as ingredient costs increase. Coke and Pepsi have a tougher time due to their continual tug-of-market-share-war.

**Product Positioning:** How the manufacturer talks to the consumer is crucial. Marketers want to make sure that you clearly get the message *and* are sufficiently enticed to give their product a look. Advertising has extended into the actual supermarkets. In many chains you might hear public-address announcements about a specific product, view "on floor" product logos, or see an ad on your shopping cart.

Coupons and Other Promotions: Want even more incentive to buy my brand? Bring in one of the billions of coupons distributed via your newspaper, the mail, your e-mails, or even a dispenser right on the shelf next to the product itself. And just to make sure you Millennials won't be missed, here come text message offers right to your cell phone. Very targeted. Very precise.

As Goodale and I continued to canvass the vast sea of brands lining the supermarket shelves, I thought about the power of these forces. How elements like coupons, advertising, positioning, and pricing combined to stack the deck against the average consumer. The plethora of "buy me" cues would always win out. The forces were too powerful.

Goodale brought me back from my thoughts and suddenly asked, "Do you know who spends more, a person with or without a shopping list?"

The answer might surprise you: The one with the list. Why? Those with a list buy on average 30 percent more, because the list brings them into more aisles. The store is designed to make the list user hunt for several items that he or she might not normally see right away. There is usually no logic to his or her list because the items are listed on an as-needed basis, and are in no particular order; thus, it will take multiple trips around the store to find everything. Think about it. A person with a list is usually very organized and goal-oriented; he or she must find everything on the list before leaving the store.

My guide divided shoppers into three types:

The Perimeter Shopper: These consumers are in and out of the store very quickly. They average only ten to twelve minutes per trip and sometimes as little as six minutes.

**The Dipper:** These are perimeter shoppers who travel in and out of various aisles.

**The Weaver:** This is the grocer's favorite because this shopper buys everything he or she sees that captures interest, and then shows up at checkout with two completely full carts.

As we worked our way toward the far recesses of the store, we encountered bottled waters. Goodale explained, "Waters are buried, because they are a high-traffic section, and they pull you over to the frozen foods, which was right across that aisle." He noted that frozen foods had a good margin (25 to 30 percent). Finally, we came to the milk section in the far back corner—another power item that forced us to navigate the entire store to find it.

Goodale marveled at Harris Teeter's layout, which he hadn't analyzed in some time. As we came up the last aisle, we saw the eggs (yes, another power item) that forced us to traverse a large amount of real estate.

"The consumer is out of breath by the time he gets here," Goodale said.

As this master merchandiser examined the eggs, he noted that the cheaper commodity eggs were in the "coffin" or bottom of the cooler, whereas free-range eggs or eggs with omega-3s were precisely at eye level along with their threefold higher price per ounce. The retailer wants you to notice the $2.99 per dozen eggs *before* you can ferret out the $1.99 per dozen eggs.

We strolled by the ice cream freezers near the front of the store, and Goodale was careful to explain how this was the last item to tug the customer by the leash. "Shoppers are in the home stretch," he said. "And they don't want ice cream in their carts that is melting until they're ready to go."

On our way to the checkout, he delighted in Harris Teeter's merchandising philosophy by forcing us to walk past the health and beauty aids (HBAs) and the over-the-counter (OTC) drugstore products, both of which are high margin. He then pointed out, as we scanned the magazines, paperback books, candies, and loose cold beverages, that they were placed near the register because they encourage impulse buying.

The relatively new self-checkout lanes were on the end, and while they are proving to be quick and convenient for shoppers, this type of shopper loses the store some last-minute candy impulse sales. "I once tried to kick out the *National Inquirer* because I objected to an article they'd written, but I quickly found out that I would lose so many customers who would switch to another store. So I was forced to keep it. Ditto for tobacco."

This is how we are conditioned to sleepwalk through the aisles. We may have a shopping list, but it's only a rough guideline, isn't it? The Goodales of the supermarket world shrug off our best attempts at discipline when we fill up our shopping carts. Once inside, they depend on us to follow the cues and toss out our game plans. Not only do they get us to spend more than we plan to, they nudge us toward the comfort food displays and shelves where we know we're not going to make our best decisions regarding nutrition.

In the last several years, the food industry has witnessed a dramatic shift in power away from the more traditional supermarkets to more upscale grocery chains like Whole Foods. Low-end groceries thrive on price competition and cheap goods, while the middle-level chains are getting squeezed because they stand for neither value nor quality. These new "health-" and "quality-" conscious players in the supermarket competition have given rise to a new kind of supermarket paradigm in which the supermarket and the items on its shelves have nothing but the consumer's best health and best quality at heart.

While I'm the first to welcome the developments that Whole Foods and its ilk have to offer, it's important to remember that these are businesses in the same way that Kroger and others are businesses. Whole Foods is bottom line–oriented, too, and though they have set a good precedent on some health issues, it's dangerous to start believing in the current mode that a publicly traded food company is going to make your health paramount *all* the time. Littered throughout any of these "good for you" supermarkets are plenty of examples of how these stores use their image and brand to lull you into buying things that aren't actually as good for you as you think.

Bear in mind that every supermarket is slightly different in its approach because it's selling to a demographic and, subsequently, a neighborhood. It's putting items on "special" to reel you in, knowing that there's a built-in convenience in one-stop shopping. That's why you can buy your child a coloring book or a Hallmark greeting card in a store that basically sells meat and eggs. The psychology behind such an enterprise took a lot of thought, trial, and error. Basically, the supermarket purveyors need you to come back every week, and they want the atmosphere to be as comfortable and alluring as possible.

Let's take another supermarket tour, this time venturing to the Whole Foods in Chapel Hill, North Carolina, only minutes from where I live. On this particular trip, I entered and turned right to begin with the produce. Whole Foods, of course, is not Kroger, or Publix, or Vons, or Safeway—all popular national chains. It's upscale, expensive, and gives an aura of . . . well, wholesomeness and health. The people who shop here are not as price-conscious as the shoppers in most national supermarket chains. They know they're paying a premium; otherwise the store would never have earned the sobriquet "Whole Paycheck." They have grass-fed, free-range chicken and top-quality meats. They are doing some incredibly good things for customers. And yes, you pay for it. But you're also being lured into a false feeling of comfort and security of thinking that everything in the store is good for you. The words "organic" and "natural" are so ubiquitous that when you stroll past all that glistening produce being caressed by the mist from the water sprays, you feel like you're at a farm stand in Iowa.

Those irrigation systems you see in many supermarkets now? The person who came up with this idea is a genius. They can make any fruit or vegetable come to life, rescuing what might have been a wilted, week-old bunch of asparagus headed for the Dumpster. I'm not saying that the fruits and vegetables you see on display, especially in the upscale outlets, aren't fresh; you can see and feel this on your own. In fact, a business associate made several trips to Whole Foods in San Diego and Los Angeles on a recent visit and noticed a wide discrepancy in their famous produce sections. In some instances, he found unacceptable items. In one particular instance, he was searching for fresh limes, and he basically rejected every single one (69 cents apiece) in the bin. He concluded they were old. At a grocery store a few blocks away, the limes were much nicer and ten cents cheaper.

In Whole Foods and almost every other supermarket, there's usually nothing that gives you any information about how old the produce really is. We have no way of knowing how long it took to get from the ground or the tree to the store, so we have to place our faith and trust with our grocer. Whole Foods has worked hard to cultivate an image that makes you want to trust it when it comes to produce. You believe that because they seem to have their heart in the right place, they wouldn't thrust bad produce on you. So you squeeze a peach and make a decision. There's no label to guide you. My colleague who lives in New York snickered when he saw the sign next to the tomatoes in a Gristedes supermarket. "Locally Grown," read the placard. He wondered where. Central Park? Staten Island? Upstate? New Jersey? Connecticut?

Leaving the vegetables and fruits section of Whole Foods, you encounter the packaged goods, and suddenly you are awash in labels—everything has one, as is required by federal law. Let's check out the wares, and read the labels. I mean *really* read the labels, where the nutrition and ingredients are listed on the back or the side of the package in very small print. Of course, some of you do read the labels, but you're in the minority. Most of us do not have the time to absorb the fine print. Successful packagers know this. Why else would they put "No Carbs" on a product in large lettering when there were no carbohydrates in there to begin with?

This is where the credibility gap in the food industry needs reform. And this is why health food experts have generally proclaimed that the closer the food is grown to your refrigerator, the better off you are in consuming it. Packaged goods, frozen foods, and canned products are designed and produced to have long shelf lives. This is why, for example, the Hostess Twinkie has twenty-something ingredients in it. Steve Ettlinger, the author of *Twinkie, Deconstructed*, reminds us that we can bake our own Twinkies using only about a half-dozen ingredients, but it probably wouldn't taste like the Hostess original, and it certainly wouldn't last a month in our pantries.

The underlying messages in the aisles of Whole Foods are designed to make you feel comfortable. And not just for comfort food. Places like this understand that you *want* your children to eat healthier foods. They know that this desire is at least part of what pushed you in their doors today. They want you to *feel* like a responsible shopper. So unless it's a package of Oreos or goose liver pâté—to mention two extremes—they're telling you it's healthy. It's *good* for you. It's baby-safe, for goodness' sake.

In the produce aisle, we can largely assume this is true (especially if the goods are pesticide- and preservative-free), but when you go deeper into the store and over into the packaged goods aisles, the situation is markedly different. In the bakery section, if you closed your eyes and imagined yourself in Any Supermarket, U.S.A., you would notice the same high-calorie, large-size muffins, danishes, and cookies. On this particular Whole Foods trip, I picked up a carton of Whole Kids Organic Lemonade, the store brand, turned the carton over, and read the nutrition list. There I noticed the 31 grams of carbohydrates per 8-ounce serving, 30 of which were from sugar. You might as well buy your kid a Coke or a Pepsi. They have nearly the same nutritional value, or lack thereof, as this Whole Food's lemonade. But because it's a children's product—marketed to a parent who is trying to buy a healthy drink for his or her child—it has the aura of being good to consume. One can argue it's the height of hypocrisy. It's being marketed as a health product, but it has even more calories than a standard soft drink. Here's another example. Whole Foods 365 brand pomegranate juice had 160 calories and 40 grams of sugar per serving compared to Tropicana orange juice at 110 calories and 22 grams of sugar. Now, realistically, what's better for your waistline? Does a purported benefit to your immune system offset its high calories and sugar?

This is the Dark Side of the Force in the packaged foods industry. They say they want smart consumers who can make intelligent choices, but they don't mind if you remain ignorant either. (In fact, many count on it.) It's just one of the many conflicting messages that food sellers send us, and if you're confused, you're not alone. They're not consciously trying to confuse you, they're merely trying to *sell* you, or more subtly, lull you into just *giving up and buying.* They take out the trans fats, but they are still peddling saturated fats. They say they take away the carbs, but there weren't any to begin with. On the front side of the package you get your whole grains, and on the reverse, you find out how many calories the cereal will add to your waistline.

"Natural" or "organic" doesn't necessarily mean it's good for you, and it's surprising that so many intelligent Americans cannot grasp this simple fact. Do not feel bad if you didn't know this. You're in the majority. I really have to smirk when I hear the oft-told maxim: "If I can't pronounce an ingredient on a food package, I don't eat it." It's an impractical if ridiculous way to go about food buying. If you followed this adage, you'd starve in three weeks unless you had your own farm in your backyard and you never left home.

One colleague of mine told me that he saw an affluent-looking mother with a baby stroller enter an Upper West Side grocery store in Manhattan, only to ask a clerk if they had organic food. When the clerk shook his head, she turned around and quickly left. It was organic or nothing for her. While we may assume she was well-educated and wanted the safest and healthiest food for her baby, it's clear she thinks that organic is what's best for her family. To her the issue starts and stops there. I'm wondering, Did she know that organic is not interchangeable with "natural" or "free-range" or "hormone-free"?

Here's the corollary myth that comes from the word "organic," and one we've been consuming on a wholesale basis. If it comes virtually unfettered from the ground or a tree, we immediately assume it's great for being on a weight-loss diet and longevity. Eating "organic" has proven to be good for you—organic food has as much as 40 percent more antioxidants in it—but it will not necessarily get those last ten pounds off your midsection or help you live to be ninety. But look what happened to that magic word as it left rural America and found its way into mainstream, upscale emporiums. Wal-Mart is trying to eat some of Whole Foods's lunch now that the world's largest retailer has introduced organic products in its food section. And Kellogg's, Kraft, General Mills, and PepsiCo have announced plans to sell offerings that are "organic" (or already are doing so).

Many well-educated, affluent people seem more than happy to pay a significant premium—as much as 20 percent, and often as high as 50 percent—for food that's organic. Whole Foods's entire value proposition relies on this fact. The CEO has admitted it on financial talk shows. Yet the federal government's parameters developed under industry pressure that allow food sellers to label a product "organic" are now so broad they're laughable. Moreover, the food lobby is agitating to further loosen the labeling requirements. *What nerve*, you're thinking. I'd have to agree.

Beyond the vagaries of "Big Organic," we can't always count on large organic food sellers to be completely honorable. A large company in Colorado, Aurora Organic Dairy, which supplies private-label milk for several supermarket chains, was cited in 2007 by the Department of Agriculture for failing to meet the requirements for selling organic milk. These requirements range from raising cows that are free of antibiotics and growth hormones and are given only feed hay. The cattle must live in a pasture that is grown without chemicals, and they have to graze in a space with a minimum amount of acreage. Yes, some of this seems a little extreme. But if you know that a company is cutting corners, and you're paying a 50 percent premium for milk labeled organic, then this deception has an actual financial impact on you.

It's a fact of modern life that it's difficult to know what we're really eating. So many of our buying decisions are built on trust, and Whole Foods knows this. They're creating an atmosphere for the shopper in the hopes that the more he or she knows the more they'll *trust* the supermarket and buy into this idea that every single item in their store is inherently benevolent.

Local produce! Local bread! Freshly packaged!

It's not that their words are lies; on the contrary, they're certainly true. But these words don't always make the food better for you or help you get thinner. What they do is encourage you to spend, because they provide comfort, and an image that feeds into this idea that Whole Foods has your best interest (and the earth's) at heart.

Beyond these misconceptions about natural and organic foods, even a Whole Foods will capitalize on a lot of ignorance regarding the packaged goods they sell. Go on, read the fine print on the labels. While it's true that they support smaller, mom-and-pop companies, many of the products on the shelves of Whole Foods are manufactured by the same packaged goods companies that produce and market the food in your regular supermarket chain. General Mills has an organic line of tomatoes called Muir Glen; Kellogg's owns Kashi cereals; Coke has a minority interest in Honest Tea; Pepsi owns Izze beverages. There's nothing inherently wrong with this approach. It's simply one way to skirt the "big is bad" label that is often placed on major companies when it comes to criticism by nutritionists and green-oriented consumers.

Whole Foods knows this. They know that if you're shopping there you want to feel like your veering out of the mainstream offerings of Kroger and Wal-Mart. They know that large brands do not connote health the way that smaller, seemingly independent operations do. As a result, the labels and addresses that reveal true ownership of a company are written in small, hard-to-find addresses or not at all. Because most people don't read the fine print, they're willing to take a logo at face value, but in the end the same packagers who line the shelves of Harris Teeter are sitting there in Whole Foods with a different set of offerings.

Of course, none of this fundamentally makes anyone fat. Just because Kraft manufactures a product and Whole Foods shelves it doesn't make anything unhealthy. What it does, however, is show how food packagers have become more adept in their cajoling of Whole Foods customers. The companies know that Whole Foods shoppers rely heavily on this idea of trust. If you walk into a Whole Foods and immediately believe that a majority of the items on the shelves are inherently better for you, you're going to be much less likely to scrutinize what's actually in the products. This opens up the possibility that there will be a disconnect between what you think you are eating and what you are actually eating. And that disconnect may ultimately be dangerous for consumers' health.

When one considers the full picture of the shopping experience, whether it be the typical supermarket or a high-end chain like Whole Foods, you realize that it's not simply about going to market to buy the groceries. Shoppers are unwitting participants in a subtle theatrical performance. Grocers put on a show for the consumer's dollar, without the buyer being aware that he or she is among the cast of extras. All the bright colors and cues serve one single purpose: to get the consumer to buy.

Trusting that supermarkets and packaged goods companies have our health in mind 100 percent of the time was a big part of what made us fat in the first place, and we cannot continue to think that way if things are going to change. In order to quickly turn over their inventory, the Bob Goodales of the industry must keep us moving up and down the aisles, stuffing our shopping carts. It's the only way they can survive.

# 4

# the people behind the menu

Clara Peller probably did more harm to our waistlines than any single individual. Yet she likely had no idea what kind of an impact her work would have on the health issue. The elderly actress was never well known for any movie or television role. Peller was the star of the famous "Where's the beef?" commercials used by Wendy's in the 1980s to fence with its competitors who had shrunk the size of their burgers and enlarged the buns to try to disguise the fact that customers were getting less for more.

In the first spot, which aired in 1984, Peller looked at a burger with a massive bun (the competitor's slogan was "Home of the Big Bun"). The small patty prompted the gruffly behaved Peller to exclaim in mock anger, "Where's the beef?" No question, it was funny.

Sequels followed and also featured Peller yelling at a "Fluffy Bun" executive on his yacht over the phone, and coming up to fast-food restaurant drive-up windows that would be slammed down before she could complete the line. Wendy's burger sales spiked dramatically because of this campaign. The ads were such a success that Peller's memorably comic character soon gave the catch-phrase a life of its own, and it was repeated in countless television shows, films, magazines, and other media outlets. For years it was a metaphor for questioning the substance of any idea, event, or product.

Advertising, of course, is the food industry's most direct method to get us to buy their products. Go back in time to when McDonald's proclaimed "You deserve a break today" and Burger King let you "have it your way." Memorable advertising sells and has played a big part in driving consumers to the fast-food counter. The food sellers are spending record amounts to capture your attention. In 1980, a little more than $7 billion was spent on all food advertising, according to the U.S. Department of Agriculture's Economic Research Service. By 2005, that figure had more than tripled to nearly $24 billion. Only the automakers outspend the food industry in this category. Some of this can be explained by the natural growth in the population and the total sale of food ($672.9 billion in 2005). The remainder is the race for market share, especially among new product launches.

The classic approach on television ads is to make the food look so luscious, so appealing, so irresistible, that you run right to the refrigerator or your local Red Lobster, whose ad agency has managed to make a shrimp look so large and steamily delectable, it appears to jump off the screen. Over the last couple of decades food advertising has evolved in several directions, using characters like the Ronald McDonald clown (probably better known to children than the current president of the United States) and other icons to persuade us. Pizza Hut uses rock 'n' roll to reach young teens and even tweens. With segmented marketing a huge trend, it's not a surprise to see black actors smiling and saying, "I'm lovin' it!" when referring to McDonald's Dollar Meals. Is there any doubt that Mountain Dew is targeted toward the awesome baggy pants–snowboard kids ("Doin' the Dew!")?

Burger King's advertising is shamelessly aimed at the hungry guy who refuses to surrender to his yuppie self. In one ad for its

Whopper, a man abandons his date at a fancy restaurant, complaining that he is "too hungry to settle for chick food." Primed on the chain's famous burger, a slew of guys pump their fists, punch each other, toss a van off a bridge, and sing, "I will eat this meat until my innie turns into an outie," and, later, "I am hungry. I am incorrigible. I am man." And I am soon to be—if not already—overweight, largely because of these kinds of messages.

Of course, once all those ads have registered in some part of our brains, we instinctively head out to eat. The restaurants themselves are designed to subliminally seduce us into eating. Fast-food outlets use a high-stimulus decor to maximize the source of their profits.

"Specifically in fast-food restaurants, the use of bright light, bright colors, upbeat music, and seating that does not encourage lolling," Stephani Robson told smartmoney.com. A senior lecturer at the Cornell School of Hotel Administration, Robson said that this design "encourages faster turnover." I've always noticed that the fast-food outlets tend to favor inexpensive molded plastic seats, and in many cases they're attached to the tables, making it difficult to get comfortable.

Despite the encouragement to eat and leave quickly, Americans are spending an increasing amount of time dining out. Before the era of chain restaurants and fast food, dinner out was more of a privilege or reward than a given or a "right." Most middle-class families—especially the baby boomers—looked forward to a Friday or Saturday foray to the local family restaurant, an occasion to give Mom an evening off from kitchen duty.

The figures from the National Restaurant Association roughly confirm my recollection: only a quarter of a family's food budget was spent on eating out in 1955. Half a century later, nearly half of the family budget ended up on restaurant checks. In 2003 there was one restaurant for every 664 people in the United States; about three decades ago, there was one restaurant per 1,029 people. We eat out nearly twice as often as we did when Swanson first introduced the

TV dinner, and there has been a noticeable increase in the number of national chains to accommodate this growth. Restaurants expect revenue of more than $537 billion in 2007, a 67 percent increase in the last decade. There's a large likelihood that the restaurant you like best is part of a publicly traded holding company.

So if more people than ever are eating out, why is it that restaurants appear not to care about their customers' health? In the face of this massive growth in the last fifty years, the restaurant industry remains a business of high ingredient costs, large overhead, and modest profit margins. Even the most successful franchises have to cope with these issues. The wide expansion that has occurred in many of these national chains does not necessarily mean that they have a whole lot of money to invest in your health. Actually the truth is quite the opposite; because they're always trying to squeeze every last dollar out of their margins, they're doing whatever they can to make sure that none of their ingredients is better than is absolutely necessary. Nutritionists don't drive decisions; they listen to the cash register. If a product or offering is not working, it does not linger on the menu for long.

Most restaurants, from the national chains to the mom-and-pop joints, can't stand change for precisely these reasons. Even the smallest decisions to alter the look of your menu, your offerings, or your prices can have a profound impact on how well your business runs. This is true from the individual restaurant owners all the way up to the franchise headquarters. As a result it's not in a restaurant's interest to be concerned with the customer's health, unless doing so has a positive impact on the bottom line. Indeed, it would seem there are already too many things to worry about without allowing health into the discussion.

In the restaurant business more so than in packaged goods, this conservative, risk-averse mind-set has combined with unhealthy food and unspectacular profit margins to play a large role in making Americans fat. I think we'll all agree that eating out more often adds extra fat and calories to our waistlines. Even in high-end restaurants and mid-priced food chains (say, T.G.I. Friday's or Olive Garden), it's not readily apparent how the food was prepared or what ingredients actually went in it. In short, every dish has some mystery attached to it when it comes to nutrition. You don't know how much salt the chef used, what kinds of cooking oils were used, or how much butter was added to prepare that delicious sauce. And because you're paying a premium to eat outside your home, there is a direct or subliminal urge to leave nothing on your plate. (Another reason diets fail: How can you stay on one if you eat out?)

According to the National Restaurant Association, 4.2 meals are eaten each week in a commercial setting. There are several factors explaining why the typical family today eats out four times a week. The middle class and working poor are often holding down two jobs, and the heads of households are simply too busy or too exhausted to prepare a home-cooked meal. The alternative is to heat up something in the microwave, order takeout, or herd the family out to McDonald's, Wendy's, or Burger King. Many parents—even in affluent families—eat out or order in more often because nobody has time to cook a healthy dinner.

Restaurant owners and corporations know all this, and so convenience plays a big role in their marketing. Here the lessons and risks of Swanson are clearer than almost anywhere else. In modern living there's not as much time for cooking, running a household, fighting traffic, and getting work done. Something has to give, so why not just sit back, relax, eat out, and let someone else worry about your food? After all, isn't it all about "eatin' good in the neighborhood"?

Just as in supermarkets, everything in restaurants occurs by design. Even the most casual decisions are backed by vigorous thought and careful considerations. Everything from the mold of the chairs to the art on the walls to the way the hostess greets you is carefully orchestrated to ellicit a certain set of responses from the customers.

The use of aesthetics in a restaurant is intended to create a certain "feel" for the patrons and to signify how short or long a time one is expected to stay. Quick-service restaurants, or QSRs as they're called in the trade (McDonald's, Burger King, Kentucky Fried Chicken, for example), feature more plastic and metal seating and tables, which are also easier to clean, for quicker in-and-out. The generally spartan interior is intentional, meant to convey a slightly uncomfortable manner so you don't linger too long (they want to keep moving the customers in and out, or "turning" tables in industry parlance). On the other hand, casual dining (Applebee's, T.G.I. Friday's, for example) encourages you to stick around longer. You'll find booths and cozier wood decoration, memorabilia on the walls, and an atmosphere that gets you to keep ordering additional dishes as you linger. The Caribou Coffee chain has created a "lodge" concept, replete with couches and fireplaces to encourage you to loiter and spend.

To that end, the menu is one of the main staging areas for any restaurant—not just what's on the menu, but how the offerings are worded and laid out. This is often facilitated by experts in the restaurant industry, consultants who have studied consumers' eating habits for many years. Linda Lipsky is one such person who has advised restaurant owners.

Lipsky says that studies have shown that most diners do not spend a lot of time reading menus, so this puts a premium on how well laid out a menu is, and how well the menu writer uses language. This process is called "menu engineering." As Lipsky puts it in an article in *Restaurant Report*, "A flashy menu that doesn't generate sales is like a race car without an engine. Nice to look at, but it won't pay the bills. We practice the science of Menu Engineering, a design strategy that increases overall sales and profits by *promoting your low-cost and high-priced menu items*. Less is more. We list the item that makes the most profit first so it catches your eye," says Lipsky, "and bury the highest-cost item in the middle."

Next time you're at a mid-level restaurant chain, take a moment to carefully examine the way a menu is laid out. Good planners know that boxing certain specials will cause your eye to drift immediately to that item. Today, there appears to be some emphasis on listing ingredients in dishes, and in some cases it pays to entice diet-conscious patrons with information about fat, flavor, and food allergies. Lipsky says that "low-fat," "lean," and "fat-free" are defined by the FDA; currently "low carb" is not.

Still, the idea is to get you to buy the most profitable dishes on the menu—not the healthiest. To accomplish this, clever restaurateurs hire menu writers who pack in the adjectives to make the most mundane dish sound attractive. It's an art form and specialty that's not as easy as it first looks. The best menu writers use only the hype they think is persuasive. If it starts to sound silly and overwritten, it doesn't work.

The challenge is to avoid sounding bland. You can order a "steak" or an "Aged Rib Eye Black Angus Cut." You probably won't order "deer meat" but "Medallions of Millbrook Venison" might get you to take a chance. A "lamb chop" sounds pretty standard, but "Rack of Lamb au Sautoir" is another entirely different approach. In today's menu world you don't want to boast about frying anything. In an article in *Restaurant USA Magazine* from August 2000, restaurant consultant Isidore Kharasch recommends that instead you say, "It's hand-battered. That way you've told the customers the item is fried, without telling them the item is fried." On more than one menu I've seen a dessert called Death by Chocolate, a case where the hype is funny and almost always gets a customer to ask, "What's in it?" (This is now so common it's become a satirical sketch on *Saturday Night Live*.)

While the menu may give you a lot of information about what's in the dish, there's a lot hidden behind the florid language and appealing adjectives. With rare exceptions—health-food restaurants, for example—the descriptions are written so your mind doesn't wander to sodium or salt content, or calories or carbs. Some conscientious restaurateurs have made their menus more transparent in terms of content, but this is a recent development. The fast-food outlets, however, steadily continue to resist illuminating the "small print" (meaning nutritional disclosure) as long as it's legally possible. Fortunately, those chains in New York City must now display calories prominently on their menu boards. Resistance did not pay off.

We still live in a world where pictures make you hungry. The combo meals, for example, are always highlighted on the menu, and the photos you see of them are the crispiest fries and freshest lettuce you'll never experience in a QSR. The menu board is designed by experienced art directors and copywriters to get you to salivate as soon as you walk in and glance up. Its goal is to make you buy without worrying or even thinking about calories.

One thing that menus often go to great lengths to advertise is the size of the portions. Customers are generally willing to pay a little bit more money if they perceive they are getting a lot more food. This behavior collides with the restaurants' need to squeeze more profits out of their operations. Restaurant portions have played a tremendous role in getting us to the current obesity problem, and the answer for this harks back to a Business 101 discussion of profit margins. Think back to the bagel that we spoke about in chapter two. Since restaurants are a medium-margin business, increased portion sizes are an easy way to tilt that bottom line a bit higher. All of the ingredients are being bought in bulk anyway (more on that in chapter five), so it doesn't cost the restaurant much more up front to add more fries for a minimal price increase. While those extra couple of ounces are probably unnecessary for you, the customer, they work wonders for the restaurant's bottom line.

The restaurant industry's response to this logic has been nearly universal and can been seen in just about every national chain restaurant. Olive Garden promises customers bottomless salads. Fuddruckers, the burger chain, has unlimited soft drinks and condiment bar. Red Lobster has "endless shrimp." How many times have you been in a casual family-style restaurant where the waitstaff has been trained to ask you if you're interested in ordering a "few appetizers for the table" before you even look at the menu?

Are you ever not offered another cocktail before dinner? Waitstaffs are trained to increase their customers' bills by continually reminding them there is more to drink and eat. Your wineglass is constantly refilled for a very good reason.

The reason for all this is simple: The restaurants are making an investment that will pay off in higher checks and thus higher profits. This more than offsets the increased ingredient costs and some of the supposed giveaways. Their purpose in life is to get you to spend more and this is one way to do it.

Another way is called the "Sullivan Nod." The brainchild of restaurant consultant Jim Sullivan, the Sullivan Nod is a sales technique used to create a subconscious suggestion to a customer to purchase one of a list of items. Picture this: Your server approaches your table, welcomes you to the restaurant, and then recites a list of specials. At some point during the rundown, your server nods by about 10 to 15 degrees. This happens just when he or she wants you to choose a particular item. Perhaps the nod arrives at the very mention of an expensive cocktail or a slab of cake dripping in chocolate fudge. It won't be an overly obvious nod—the server doesn't want to distract you—but it will be subtle and, of course, suggestive. Beware: The nod, best implemented with lists of five or more items, is effective 60 to 70 percent of the time.

These not-so-subtle cues are very hard to resist. A big part of why massive quantities are sold to the public is through the concept of "value" and leading customers to believe that they are getting more than what they paid for. How do you think we got to consume so many chicken wings? It certainly didn't all happen on Super Bowl Sunday. The all-you-can-eat buffet has been a boon for many a restaurant. Why? It's priced so the typically hungry customer (who may feel that he has to sample every dish) returns a very nice profit. It's designed to make you eat more than you should. The only way they could lose money is if they were forced to feed the entire NFL roster every night.

But can portion sizes really be reduced, or are both consumers and restaurants so addicted to oversize portions that neither is willing to change? At the moment, the feedback is not encouraging. At least one restaurant chain took the risk that it could make more money by reducing serving sizes and thus lowering the caloric impact on its customers. "We had competitors who shrank portion sizes, and it's just been a catastrophe," Clarence Otis, Jr., told the *Shoals Times Daily* in March 2007. Otis is the chairman and chief executive of Darden Restaurants, whose chains include Olive Garden and Red Lobster. Most restaurants would like to make servings smaller, he said, because it's an easy way to increase your profit margin. "But customers are resistant to it." In theory, this could be a moneymaker for fast-food and other restaurants, but in practice the consumer is not buying it . . . yet.

They're giving us what we want, they say, and it's very hard to argue with them. Some portions at fast-food restaurants are now two to five times larger than those of the 1950s, researchers have found. Oversize burgers have been a key weapon in the battle to grab customer attention. Wendy's has the Baconator, which features two quarter-pound patties with six slices of bacon and two slices of American cheese. Not to be outdone, Burger King's Ultimate Double Whopper includes two quarter-pound beef patties topped with eight bacon slices and four slices of American cheese. There's nothing like the smell of fat sizzling on the grill, is there? But we all know there's a price to pay far beyond the cost of the meal. Hardee's Monster Thickburger weighs in at 1,420 calories (with 108 grams of fat and 229 milligrams of cholesterol).

Just how hard is it to figure out how many calories you're consuming when you eat? Very hard. Brian Wansink, a professor and nutrition researcher at Cornell University and the newly appointed food czar who will be revamping the federal Food Pyramid, put it this way in his book *Mindless Eating*: "Who really overeats—the guy who knows he's eating 710 calories at McDonald's, or the woman who thinks she's eating a 350-calorie Subway meal that actually contains 500 calories?"

When Wendy's took a little heat for calling its 42-ounce drink (the equivalent of three and a half cans of soda) the "Great Biggie," and its 32-ounce drink the "Biggie," it merely backed off by renaming the drinks large and medium. They're still the same size. The small size drink is 20 ounces, which actually replaced the 16-ounce size. Sugar water costs very little in the quantities purchased by fast-food chains, so it's in their interests to make sure they keep enlarging the cup size. It's an easy dime for them, but those calories add up for you.

Though most Americans assume that fast food is the worst offender, similar fare at casual sit-down restaurants can be even more caloric. The classic burger at Ruby Tuesday, for example, has a whopping 1,013 calories and 71 grams of fat. The McDonald's Big Mac, with its 540 calories and 29 grams of fat, seems downright diet-worthy by comparison. Many restaurants are still marketing the enormousness of their servings: Denny's Megabreakfasts and Ruby Tuesday's Colossal burger, for example. Chipotle advertises its one-and-a-quarter-pound burritos with this description: "The first half is fun. The second half is masochism." That may be one of the truest statements in all of food advertising.

The exceptions to these tried-and-true portion practices are the upscale restaurants that cater to a wealthier customer base and expense-account executives. Here, I'm referring to a destination restaurant in a large city, perhaps with a well-known chef, that attracts fairly well-heeled patrons. At places like these, the concept of value that drives people to large portions is all but forgotten. The appetizers are probably $10 to $15 each, and the entrées run $25 to $35—$40 or more in the nicer establishments. While these more expensive restaurants tend to use more expensive ingredients, they maintain their margins because their portions are smaller, which allows them to use less of those expensive ingredients. And wealthy gourmands tend to welcome the smaller amounts, eschewing the idea that they need to stuff themselves to get value from a four-star restaurant.

Let's take a look at two kinds of diners at these food emporia. First, there's the "ladies who lunch," say, a group of four or five women who meet regularly. They may order a glass of wine, a salad, and a bowl of fancy pasta. The lunch tab may run about $50 to $60 apiece. The second type is what I call the "carnivores," the four or five businessmen who meet after work for dinner out. No fish or pasta and salad for these guys. They're having a martini or two, a couple of bottles of wine, and they will order the calamari or shrimp cocktail, and follow up with a porterhouse steak or filet mignon. At the same restaurant, their tab will be $100 to $120 a person.

Now, which group would you rather have eating if you owned this establishment? If you guessed the guys, you're wrong. Though your gross will be higher with the guys, you're not going to make as much in profits as you will with the ladies. Here's why: The profit margins on a single glass of wine (menu price $8 to $12), a salad ($14 to $20), and pasta ($18 to $25) are far higher than a steak, which because it's expensive for the restaurant owner to buy, has typically low profit margins. When you factor in the rent and the high cost of kitchen labor, you can make a lot more money per diner if someone eats light, inexpensive dishes where the ingredients cost little. If you don't take into account the alcohol (almost all such beverages are huge profit makers in high-end restaurants), and if you eat healthier fare, you will not take in as many calories, and your host will still be happy and prosperous.

If you talk to connoisseurs who actually track the prices of these restaurants, they will tell you that restaurateurs are reluctant to go over the forty-dollar threshold for an entrée. They feel it's a price point that diners will resist. So instead you see cocktails running $15 to $20 at trendy places in high-rent districts. The result is: Raise the drink prices. Two glasses of wine or two cocktails per person keeps an innkeeper quite flush. But there's more bad news for us: Hard drinks are high in empty calories and they tend to make you hungrier.

So, you may have the notion that you're well off and can afford to eat at pricey establishments on a regular basis. But you're not really eating in a healthier way than the typical working-class folks who frequent fast-food establishments. When it comes to nutrition and calories, it doesn't make that much of a difference whether you're eating a forty-five-dollar porterhouse at Morton's or a $4.95 Angus burger at McDonald's. This is one of the great myths that we've perpetuated on ourselves when it comes to the nutrition and obesity issue.

While today some restaurants are increasingly going against these implicit restaurant industry "rules" regarding portions and margins, for many years these rules were what governed the business everywhere. No one gave much thought to the health of customers or the impact that having more people eating out would have on our nation's waistlines. Though the way people ate seemed to be changing, the restaurant business itself wasn't.

Recently, there have been increased grumblings from the restaurant industry—the fast-food industry in particular is being pushed by government and activists to make their menus more health conscious. The industry does not have a good record as the issue has become more prominent. As profits and revenues rose, the chains especially resisted changes in their menus. They claimed they are not wholly accountable for the eating habits of millions; they often point to providing healthy options for their patrons. And in some cases, they are. McDonald's has put salads on its menu. Their new Asian salad can be considered very progressive for a restaurant chain that has made its reputation on delivering the beef. This is a step in the right direction, but critics point out that it's not the salad, it's the salad dressing. The company's Bacon Ranch Salad with Crispy Chicken has 20 grams of fat. But when you add the Newman's Caesar or ranch dressing, that's an extra 15 to 18 grams of fat, for a total of 35 to 38 grams of fat.

Because the chain is ubiquitous, it's impossible for McDonald's to avoid being the center of attention and singled out for its practices (good or bad). By the same token, McDonald's does do some very good things, and the credit for this is often overlooked. The Golden Arches are everywhere, and they probably have a far greater influence on what we eat than anyone is likely to admit.

While an alternative of salads on the menus at the large burger chains seems to be a bulletproof dish as far as the health gurus are concerned (at least there is the alternative), the salads themselves rarely reach the mouths of the people who need them the most. In actuality they function more to lure customers' accomplices and family members who wouldn't ordinarily come in for the main menu. They're not really being offered as a health initiative; they're an accommodation item. At an obesity conference I chaired last year, the attending McDonald's representative said he hoped the chain could sell more salads and earn greater profits from them. But it's just wishful thinking on his part. The company's core business is burgers, fries, and soda, and that's not likely to change any time soon.

Indeed, burgers, fries, pizza, and Mexican foods are core businesses, and they comprise more than half the sales of food in restaurants. This kind of fare outsells vegetables and salads by a factor of five. It shouldn't surprise us that at Burger King customers order ten times as many Whoppers as salads and one hundred times as many Whoppers as vegetable burgers. Can you blame Burger King for giving consumers what they want?

Hardee's sales increased by 20 percent after the introduction of the Monster Thickburger. And guess where the bulk of McDonald's recent sales comes from? When it introduced its Dollar Meal campaign, the results were phenomenally successful. One reason was that the ads were targeted toward young African Americans and Hispanics. The message was simple: A "hearty" meal can be bought for just $1, barely a dent in your weekly allowance.

It didn't take long for the doubters to voice their views. "The problem here is that you're dealing with a segment where you have these huge obesity issues and you're making eating Big Macs and double cheeseburgers look like it's fun and exciting," said Jerome Williams, a professor of advertising at the University of Texas at Austin and an author of an Institute of Medicine report ("Food Marketing and the Diets of Children and Youth") on the marketing of junk food to children and teenagers. Others pointed out that African Americans and Hispanics are at much higher risk for obesity and diabetes than other population groups. One critic, speaking to the *International Herald Tribune* in April 2006, called the McDonald's dollar meal campaign a "recipe for disaster."

We clearly covet our hamburgers, flame-broiled or otherwise, especially when we don't have to cook them. It's hard for salads to compete with that and it's even harder for restaurants not to accommodate our taste buds. Consider the fallout from an academic study done in 2007 at Stanford University. Dr. Tom Robinson, the researcher, asked sixty-three low-income children from the ages of three to five in Head Start centers in San Mateo County, California, to become food critics. The study included three McDonald's menu items—hamburgers, chicken nuggets, and french fries—and store-bought milk or juice and carrots. Children got two identical samples of each food on a tray, one in McDonald's wrappers or cups and the other in plain, unmarked packaging. The kids were asked whether they tasted the same or whether one was better.

Care to bet on the results? McDonald's-labeled samples were the ones preferred by the kids. French fries were the biggest winner; almost 77 percent said they were better. The real surprise for me was discovering that 54 percent preferred McDonald's-wrapped carrots versus 23 percent who liked the plain-wrapped sample. These kids didn't even know that McDonald's doesn't sell carrots. Dr. Victor Strasburger, an author of an American Academy of Pediatrics policy urging limits on marketing to children, said on CNN.com (August 6, 2007), "It's an amazing study and it's very sad. Advertisers have tried to do exactly what this study is talking about—to brand younger and younger children, to instill in them an almost obsessive desire for a particular brand-name product." Only two of the sixty-three kids in the test had never eaten at a McDonald's.

This experiment was simply a testament to the power of branding. Given the power of the McDonald's arches and the influence of Ronald McDonald among children, they could market anything they want to kids, and it would probably be successful, including healthier items.

Let's take a look at another restaurant's offerings to get a broader perspective. Back in November 2003, Ruby Tuesday decided to take the initiative and do the right thing when it came to nutrition. The CEO was a hands-on manager—indeed, the company founder—who wanted to ensure that his customers would be able to choose low-calorie entrées. Ruby Tuesday has nearly a thousand outlets, and it's estimated that about 350,000 people eat there every day. It introduced "Smart Eating Choices" on its menus, accounting for about 30 percent of the items they sold. They revamped all of their menus to include the number of calories, grams of fat, net carbs, and fiber on every dish. For example, Grilled Chicken Salad is described as "fresh chicken with tomatoes, cheese and fresh mixed greens with light ranch dressing on the side" (380 calories, 15 grams of fat, 7 net carbs, 3 grams of fiber).

Ruby Tuesday was not surprised at the customer response. The great majority of their clientele did not comment one way or the other. They were menu-neutral, and didn't care. A small percentage welcomed the idea and applauded the company's forward-thinking change and their concern for their customers' health. An equally small percentage was somewhat hostile. "A number of guests said they didn't want to be reminded of it [the nutritional value of the meals] when they went out for dinner," said company spokesman Rick Johnson. "They said, 'If we want to know, we'll ask for it.'" Ruby Tuesday responded to these complaints by once again rewriting their menus so that the nutrition figures were posted only for the Smart Eating dishes. They do make available the figures for the remainder of the menu if a customer requests it. (On Labor Day weekend in 2007, they opened their first store in New York City, in the heart of Times Square. None of the menu items had nutritional information, although now they'll have to put the calorie information back, pursuant to the new law in New York City.)

Of course, when the restaurant chain once again changed its menus, it was widely reported that the experiment was a massive failure, a contention that the company disputes. Skeptics can rightfully claim that no other company has copied Ruby Tuesday's move. Had it been a rousing success, all the other mid-level chains would certainly have adopted the idea. But as Rick Johnson also correctly points out, America has gotten even fatter since the government mandated tougher nutrition labeling standards in supermarkets and grocery stores.

Throughout the food industry, stories of these "failed" attempts to go healthy abound, but none of them has dissuaded more restaurants from trying healthy food than the short-lived D'Lites fast-food chain. A former business associate of mine, Doug Sheley, founded it back in the 1980s, so sure of the idea that he practically risked his career on it. Sheley, who had previously owned a number of Wendy's restaurants, worried at the direction in which the fast-food industry was heading. He assumed the American public was ready to embrace smart, nutritious eating. He founded a new company called D'Lites. "We're pushing traditional [mainstream] fast foods," Sheley bluntly declared in *Nation's Restaurant News* at the time (July 22, 1985). But the big difference, he added, is that many D'Lites products have fewer calories and less fat than traditional fast food. Their mantra was "We're going to sell healthier food."

The Atlanta-based chain first opened its doors in 1981, offering lean burgers on multigrain buns and a large salad bar. D'Lites's regular menu was a potpourri of more than thirty items—perhaps the most extensive menu in fast food. There were several quarter-pound burgers; five sandwiches; baked potatoes and potato skins with toppings; two soups; fries; frozen yogurts with toppings; vegetarian pita sandwiches; and a large salad bar.

There were also three soft drinks, three sugar-free soft drinks, decaffeinated soft drinks and coffee; beer, wine, light beer, and light wine; sparkling apple juice; and low-fat milk. Mayonnaise, tartar sauce, and other condiments and salad dressings and cheese were low in fat. Hamburgers had a lower (20 percent) fat content. Sandwiches could be ordered on sesame seed or multigrain buns, each of which had 25 percent fewer calories than standard buns.

The best-selling items were the salad bar and hamburgers, each accounting for about 25 percent of sales.

There were several reasons why D'Lites failed. They did not run advertising; they never tested the restaurant concept; they never conducted research to determine the optimal taste-health ratio in their offerings; they ignored their core demographics (young, high-income, white-collar professionals in urban environments) by locating many units in low-income, blue-collar, downscale areas; and they never conducted guest satisfaction studies. In addition, there were other costly blunders. They sold franchise rights to many operators with little experience, and they overexpanded (to more than a hundred outlets by the time they went under), resulting in resources being spread too thin.

As I recalled listening to Sheley talk about his experience with D'Lites, I concluded that the concept might have been a bit early, but that it really failed due to strategic and restaurant location errors. If he had diligently stuck to placing units in cities and areas with the right demographics, and advertised in a focused manner to this target, D'Lites might have caught on at least as a specialty chain.

It is important to note that the major burger chains took notice and reacted to D'Lites. Wendy's soon offered a multigrain bun; Burger King tried a low-sodium pickle; McDonald's even tested a "Lite" version of its signature Big Mac. However, consumers didn't come back to D'Lites for seconds, and these competitive initiatives similarly disappeared.

This clearly shows how it takes an out-of-the-box entrepreneur to come up with a creative idea, like healthier fast food. But these big-picture guys run up against the industry, which is all about execution and operations. Seeing no further threat from D'Lites and not recognizing that D'Lites failed primarily due to poor execution rather than consumers disliking the concept, the industry has always pointed to this episode by saying "no one wants to eat healthier fast food."

If D'Lites had succeeded, healthier fast food might have celebrated its twenty-fifth anniversary recently. Had I met Sheley just a few years earlier (we lived within two miles of each other in North Atlanta), I might have helped him strategically to find a way to navigate his business in a more focused and targeted manner. The radical increases in obesity over that period might have been partially mitigated.

D'Lites's failure broadcasted a very significant signal to the restaurant industry as a whole, and the ripple effect was incalculable. The food industry stood back and saw the failure of D'Lites as a rejection of all things healthy. It reinforced everything that they thought they knew about the business: *There is no large target audience for this kind of food. The money to be made is with eighteen- to twenty-four-year-old customers. This group eats great gobs of greasy food and can seem to handle it all right. It doesn't matter what they'll look like or whether they're healthy when they're thirty-five. All that counts is that we want them now because they're in a desirable demographic.*

The wrong lesson was learned, and it has been incorrectly perpetuated up until today.

Failures like this make people in the restaurant industry *think* that every innovation and new venture will suffer a similar fate. They reinforce executives' entrenched views about change and their in-the-box thinking about profit margins. For the last twenty years, stories like D'Lites have been used to justify all manner of inaction on their part. If anyone questions the ethics of serving unhealthy food, the answer is simple: There's no money in serving healthy food because it's not what customers want. Just like that the discussion ends and they turn their minds back to practical everyday concerns like attracting more customers, never fully realizing that their behavior is harming the very people they rely on.

When you step back, you can see that the restaurateurs are trying to manage their business models. They're concerned about payrolls, the ever increasing price of ingredients, the cost of shipping, labor turnover, and whether or not their customers like what they're eating. They have to repeat what they do day in and day out.

This behavior is emblematic of the myopic view that people who go into the restaurant business traditionally have—and cannot alter. Food, like many an entrepreneurial endeavor, requires a substantial investment and countless hours of hard work. There's the need to deliver a return on investment to shareholders. So it's no surprise that it's difficult for restaurateurs to worry much—if at all—about their customer's health today, let alone ten years down the road. It's much easier to hold on to the ingrained horror stories of failed healthy food experiments than to change how they feed their customers.

# 5

# how purchasing agents make us fat

I know this may sound a bit strange at first, but one of the key people indirectly responsible for our growing obesity problem is someone you'll likely never meet when you dine at a Wendy's, Carl's Jr., Olive Garden, Applebee's, or P.F. Chang's. It's not a waiter or hostess. It's not a person in the kitchen, or even the head chef at the corporate headquarters who plans the menu. It's the guy who buys all the food ingredients these restaurants use in bulk. Meet the purchasing agent. I'm going to explain how he (or she) unintentionally produces more and more obese people every day he sits at his desk doing the job he's hired to perform.

Even if there were impetus to change a restaurant's product offerings to healthier fare, you would still be likely to run up against some very powerful resistance from all manner of behind-the-scenes players such as purchasing agents. It's easy to say that restaurant people don't like change, but to really understand the specific ways that this mentality has made us fat, you have to delve a bit deeper into the mechanics of the restaurant business and look at how specific ingredients find their way to your plate.

I'd like to introduce you to a purchasing agent, someone I've known and worked with for many years in the food business. He's now "reformed," and he agrees with many of my views of the food and health crisis issue. His name is John Kimber, and he's a consultant for food companies in new product development. In two key positions earlier in his career, he worked in product development for Burger King, and later moved into the purchasing arena for the chain until he was recruited by Hardee's as vice president of purchasing and supply logistics.

His background sounds a bit unassuming, yet Kimber, like most purchasing agents, was an executive who wielded a lot of influence over what his customers ate. As someone who ordered hamburgers and french fries by the tractor-trailer load, he knew what went into the food, what it took to prepare it, and precisely how much it cost to get the odor of a fried onion ring wafting into your nostrils as soon as you walk in the front door.

Perhaps more important, Kimber understands the personalities who work behind the scenes and the restaurant mind-set that has made health consciousness so difficult. He knows that the industry doesn't embrace change; on the contrary, it fights as hard as possible against it. When something "works" and makes money, the tendency is to leave it alone, regardless of its nutritional content (or lack thereof). You continue to feed the cash cow, and you don't fundamentally tamper with its DNA unless you can make it lead to a bigger payday. The mentality is this: No exec wants to be blamed for another debacle like the one that occurred in 1985, when Coca-Cola, the world's largest soft drink producer, introduced a "new and improved" version only to watch the public roundly reject it. Mistakes like that are certain to be career enders. This is why the Whopper will remain a Whopper and the KFC recipe for fried chicken won't change.

Understand, too, how a restaurant company operates. The marketing department plans new products to put on the menu, and sells the food. The operations side is running the day-to-day part of the business for corporate headquarters. The job is to make sure that everything works smoothly—everyone's fed the right product at the right time, the lights are on, and the bathrooms are clean. This is where an entire cast of characters like the purchasing agent come into play, setting up meetings with suppliers, forecasting future necessities, and making sure that no one overpays. He's strictly a behind-the-scenes guy, but without him, the restaurant can't even fire up the deep-fat fryer.

The purchasing agent in a large food concern has an unusual amount of power because the main part of his job is to negotiate long-term contracts with food suppliers on behalf of the restaurant. Since the purchasing agent for a national chain restaurant is buying in such enormous bulk, he typically works twelve to eighteen months out. Signing up suppliers for food that far in advance gives him the best price deals on the ingredients, but it also means that he has to anticipate the volume of ingredients his company will need a long time before it actually needs them. All the while, the purchasing agent must hope that his ingredient buys correspond with future sales projections. If he underestimates the appeal of a certain recipe, he'll have to pay more down the road to make up for the shortfall. If he orders too much, he'll be stuck with waste inventory that will exceed its shelf life.

Purchasing agents generally have long-term vendor relationships that lead to price breaks. Any small change can disrupt the relationship. The bigger the account, the more sensitive the relationship is to bumps and detours in the road. If you are a purchasing agent for a major restaurant chain, you are somewhat obligated to invest capital to support your supplier's business, and in return, you get a long-term commitment of high-volume food to pay off your capital investment. It's a very important quid pro quo, which is why you always hear large firms in any industry talk about their suppliers as "business partners," even though they're not partners per se.

For a purchasing agent, it helps to have the bargaining skills to negotiate the best prices, but by virtue of the huge numbers they're buying, purchasing agents for large chains are practically guaranteed competitive deals. When they're ordering in such massive bulk, it's critical for them to make sure their suppliers can deliver the contracted quantities. Their vendors had better be reliable. Failure to deliver supplies is not an option. The remainder of the job is relatively rote; you spend your days inside spreadsheets, assessing the above-line costs of your business. You're trying to save tenths of a cent a pound on products that you're ordering in tonnage. A dull but necessary task.

The way that the restaurant industry has evolved, the purchasing agent's position is essential, but it is not the most scintillating job in the business. The purchasing agent is not likely the person in a fast-food chain to suggest overhauling the menu with new ingredients or to introduce the idea of adding salads. In fact, he's the one executive in the company who loathes the idea of any kind of menu expansion or alteration. Why? More ingredients to order, and an ever-expanding spreadsheet. He likes simplicity. It helps to control costs. The head chef has just caused him headaches by telling him he has to now order lettuce, tomatoes, olives, alfalfa sprouts, and so on. He's typically a rigid conservative to the point of being labeled a bean counter.

The purchasing agent is not inherently a bad guy, of course; he's simply doing his job. Management recruits the type of person whose thinking and behavior never veers out of the box. The purchasing agent is never going to worry about your waistline. His boss doesn't want him to, and there are no bonus checks to incent him.

"It's all about supply and cost containment," says Kimber. The purchasing agent gets rewarded for keeping costs in check, so he never thinks about the company's bottom line four or five years down the road, and he certainly doesn't think about nutrition. That's for the CFO and the CEO to worry about.

Kimber once fit the role of purchasing agent quite well; indeed, he was very successful at it. Now that he has some distance and perspective on the food and health crisis, he brings some cogent views to the seemingly intractable problems in the restaurant industry. His comments highlight the long-standing reluctance within the restaurant industry to take any risks that are not guaranteed to preserve profits. Even if it means making the customer healthier.

When it comes to the ingredients that a restaurant chain must buy, there really is no such thing as a small change. The decision to switch brands of anything can have incredibly far-reaching implications, and as a purchasing agent you have to be convinced that the consumer will not be able to notice the difference.

While the major purchases for a restaurant chain include things like fries, meat, soda, buns, and ketchup, one of the most underappreciated items on that list that has a profound impact on your health is cooking oil. There are more than 25 billion pounds of baking and frying oil used in the United States annually. It becomes a key ingredient when you're frying a large portion of your menu.

"You need to become pretty intimately involved with cooking oil," Kimber said. "It is a high-volume item in a restaurant. Even though it's not on the menu, it's an essential ingredient to running the restaurant."

Here's a hypothetical scenario, actually based on my own travails. Let's say I'm a vendor with a breakthrough non–trans fat oil. Because of how restaurant marketing and operations run, usually, it's exceedingly difficult for any vendor to find an open door to pitch a new idea like this. But the purchasing agent is typically the person whose door is at least slightly ajar.

Suppose I get an appointment with a purchasing agent not unlike John Kimber when he was running such a department. I give him my ten-minute sales pitch. Suppose he's been buying cooking oil for fifty cents a pound, a line item that runs millions of dollars a year. I tell him that I have an oil with no trans fats, so it's healthier for his customers and will comply with government standards that probably will be mandated at some point in the next year or two, if not already. If he's an enlightened guy—and some are—then he'll welcome the idea of this new product. But he'll also wonder how much it's going to cost.

A little more, sixty cents a pound, I say. Then I see the disappointment in his face at the thought of heightened expenditures, so I counter this with some good news. He can have a lot more turns of french fries because my cooking oil decomposes at a slower rate than the one he's using now, so he'll use less of it. (Generally speaking, the healthier vegetable oils don't last as long as the high–trans fat oils.) In other words, it's healthier *and* it lasts longer, which will save money. Still, I admit that it might not net out for several months (he's already done the math).

The purchasing agent leans back in his chair and looks at these options. On the one hand there's the healthier, more expensive option that lasts longer. On the other, there's the oil that already works for a price that already works. Mulling this over, the purchasing agent knows his boss is going to look at the spreadsheet when the new fiscal quarter's figures are due and ask, "Why are we suddenly paying 20 percent more for cooking oil?" His boss isn't going to ask how long the oil lasts or how healthy it is. His concern is that it's more expensive.

Taking this idea one step further, imagine that I can convince the purchasing agent to buy at least enough to test out the cost effectiveness and customer response. (New, more nutritious cooking oils have been shown to be largely unnoticeable among consumers, but I'll get to that in more detail later.) There is room in the operating budget for this kind of test run in most large concerns, so this is not unthinkable.

But here is where another dilemma arises.

Kimber puts it this way: "I'm in charge of knowing to the cent what the input cost is going into the restaurants, but I don't have any control over how that restaurant runs. I don't know how they dump the oil, how they filter it, how they manage it. Now, if I am buying a more-expensive product, and they're going to be responsible for making sure the value gets delivered to the corporation,

I have a problem. My reputation is going to be all over the place because I'm buying this more expensive stuff and may have no control over how the cost savings are going to be delivered."

Put more bluntly, while corporate headquarters does maintain tight control of the products in its outlets—the Big Mac and the Whopper are prepared exactly the same way, whether in Boise or Baltimore—it may not be able to monitor how something like cooking oil is used and disposed. The added value that comes from an oil with an increased lifespan could therefore be easily wasted by the restaurant staff. In the front office, it could take months to discover where that waste is actually occurring.

"There is an inherent cynicism by operations officers within the organizations I've been part of—I can't say all, but the organizations I have been with—as to how much control they have over just some of these minute details at the restaurant level," Kimber said.

"It's kind of like, 'If you could just keep the restaurants clean and greet people with a friendly smile when they come to the counter and actually serve them warm food, we'd be really happy if you could just do those three things.' How often do you dump the oil? You know what? That's kind of down on the bottom end of my list of things that I worry a lot about."

Fast-food restaurants employ young managers, and they supervise an even younger staff; after all, it's the classic minimum-wage entry-level job for much of teenage America and immigrants who are trying to provide for their families. Without insulting the people who are running the fry operations, changing the cooking oil tends to be more of a low-level task in many restaurants as opposed to one that requires a great deal of skill. The people at the bottom of the chain responsible for a multimillion-dollar test run—whoever is changing the cooking oil—may not be inclined or relied on to adhere to strict and consistent standards.

This may be presumptuous and erroneous, but this is the way the purchasing agent *thinks*. Why take a chance?

In fact, I shouldn't immediately doubt—or even blame—the person working the frying oil. Changing hot oil that can easily scald you is one of the most dangerous jobs in the restaurant industry. Restaurants historically have had difficulty in measuring the throw-out point of fats. Determining the lifespan of cooking oil is more complicated than it first might seem. There are a lot of different techniques for doing this; some of them require expensive equipment that tends to get lost, discarded, or damaged in the hustle and bustle of a restaurant over a period of a few months. There are some measures that simply use comparison of the oil's color against a standard.

In the end, the only accurate way to do it is by analysis, and a restaurant simply doesn't have the wherewithal to do that. As such, it becomes more of a judgment call as to when oil is discarded because its endpoint has to be ascertained primarily by guesswork instead of a scientific measure. The employee who is vested with the responsibility of making that decision will vary widely from restaurant to restaurant. Local operators would rather err on the side of serving their customers something that tastes good as opposed to something that tastes too greasy. Given a choice, you jettison the oil early rather than let it linger for another day or two (unless you're really trying to squeeze out more profits). Now, imagine you have a thousand restaurants in your chain. You have a thousand different decision makers. The purchasing agent doesn't want to even think about whether they'll all be consistent. He knows it's next to impossible.

This helps explain why the purchasing agent unknowingly stifles any hope a company might have in, say, getting a new, healthier ingredient in all of its outlets. And this occurs despite any good intentions he has for his customers' nutrition.

We're talking specifically about oil, but the purchasing agent confronts similar conundrums and decisions whenever he is thinking about the cost—and future purchase—of any ingredient that the restaurant is using or considering using. Every item purchased in bulk is going to affect the health of his customers in some way.

The purchasing agent's dilemma begs us to confront an important issue: Does the responsibility for changing our restaurant menus to provide healthy alternatives—be it cooking oils or specific consumables—begin with corporate headquarters or with the franchise owners and individual single-location restaurants? Is it a top-down or bottom-up problem? Who has to take the lead?

Obviously, it's a complicated issue with no simple answers. Certainly, any restaurateur can do his part, though it's not going to make much difference unless it's done en masse. From my experience, it will take the power brokers of the industry—the CEOs of the companies that prepare the great bulk of what goes on the trays every day in restaurant chains around the nation.

Another restaurant industry trait that demands examination is its proclivity to extrapolate past experiences into the future. I can demonstrate the futility of much of this approach from my own experience. In their early days, many of the fast-food chains used beef tallow (beef fat) to fry their french fries. This gave the fries a wonderful distinctive taste and crispiness. In the late 1980s, beef fat was declared "bad" due to its saturated fat content and high levels of cholesterol. These oils were replaced in the early 1990s with so-called good vegetable oils. It turns out these "good" oils contained trans fats that were declared worse for the heart than saturated fats.

A firm I was involved with, Source Food Technology, actually developed a healthier cooking oil made from beef that had all the cholesterol eliminated and contained zero trans fats. It signified a marriage of taste with better health. On top of that it also lasted two to three times longer than the prevailing frying oils. The oil, named Nextra, was devised by K. C. Hayes, a Brandeis University research scientist.

When the product was ready to be test-marketed, our employees set up a booth at large industry trade shows and asked fairgoers to taste-test chicken and french fries fried with Nextra. The response was highly positive. The majority of tasters said the food was exceptional. And no one seemed to care about what it was made of.

But when the team presented the product to the large restaurant chains, a different dynamic took over. There were several chains where the product would have worked fabulously, but it was rejected due to its beef content or its premium price. It didn't matter that the fried products tasted as good or better, or that less grease was absorbed into the finished product, or that because the oil lasted longer a restaurant would actually save money despite a higher upfront cost. Our sales guys diligently presented the breakthrough oil from one chain to the next, and nearly everywhere they received the same feedback.

Source Food sales executives met with officials of Outback Steakhouse to pitch the product. They rejected the oil because it might highlight the fact that there is cholesterol in their *steaks* and other beef products. In other words, they were worried that making certain parts of their menu healthier would demonstrate the other parts of their menu that weren't so healthy. It's a catch-22: They were unwilling to offer more nutritious food because doing so would show how unhealthy their food was. As someone who sees any healthy change as positive, it's hard to come to terms with such irrational logic.

When McDonald's was approached, it was a similar story. Before the industry switched to high–trans fat vegetable oils, McDonald's used beef tallow with a small amount of cottonseed oil. This was considered the gold standard for french fries. Golden brown and crisp, the McDonald's fry was superb. When pressured by activists to get rid of the high-cholesterol beef fat, they did so but kept a bit of beef flavor in their french fries. This became controversial when they were sued by a group of Hindu customers because they had misrepresented the fact that they were adding the beef flavor. This hypersensitivity resulted in their avoiding beef like the plague. The Source Food oil would have allowed them to go "back to the future" with a trans-fat-free, no-cholesterol frying oil that mimicked their classic signature taste. However, they felt it would be a PR nightmare, and quite possibly, they might have been right. Nobody knows whether the food activists would have overreacted, despite the fact that it was a healthier product for customers. As it was, the small, vocal vegetarian community squawked so loudly, the company overreacted. The corporation was portrayed so negatively in the press that it was willing to make a significant change just to mollify its accusers and protect its public image.

At a dinner in Chicago in 2007, I actually met the McDonald's executive who could have made the decision to revert to a no-cholesterol beef tallow oil. She looked me straight in the eye and said, "There's no way I'm going to deal with the beef." There was no going back.

Things fared little better at Pilgrim's Pride, one of the largest chicken processors in the country (even though you may never have heard of the company). They sell to virtually all the major fast-food chains, in addition to supplying chicken for direct sale to the consumer. Our team had presented our frying oil to them as a means to improve their yield on oil, using less than normal. Following a successful meeting, the team received a call back from Pilgrim's Pride, asking to confirm that the oil really did contain beef. Of course it did—without cholesterol. They responded they couldn't fry their meat (chicken) in beef oil—the same excuse as Outback Steakhouse.

Following the 2006 announcement that New York City would be banning trans fats in its restaurants as of July 1, 2007, we embarked on a program to approach the leading steakhouses in New York with our new frying oil. This should have been like preaching to the choir. Any high-end restaurant that sold beef products should be our perfect customer. Better, tastier, healthier fried products made with the ideal ingredient. The oil lasts longer, but the upscale nature of the restaurants meant that you'd be able to have better reliance and oversight of your staff. Guess what the reaction was? Even though they would save money with a better product compatible with their offerings, higher upfront costs dictated their decision. No one was willing to pay a premium for the oil even though they sold premium steaks (where the sticker price is not usually a factor). Think about a forty-dollar steak; the minuscule extra cost for the oil would not even faze a diner.

In sum, there's no way the most visible restaurant chains will go back to a healthier version of beef tallow oil, because they feel there's no way they can overcome the negative image. It's too hard to explain, and risks embarrassment. It's a potential public relations nightmare, even if the oil yielded a superior product with an improved health profile. The risk/reward tradeoff didn't justify the switch. This was not the opportunity that would prevail over their engrained reluctance to change. There is no going back to the future in this industry.

So how can a novel product like Nextra be adopted to improve the nutrition profile of popular fried products? Could we persuade the army of restaurant purchasing agents to switch to a healthier oil? I asked a close business associate, Tom Ryan, what his take was. Tom has been in the restaurant industry for a number of years and he succinctly summarized the conundrum that large concerns have when smaller companies bring promising innovations to solve big problems such as making their foods more nutritious. The former chief concept officer for McDonald's, Ryan challenged me with a be-careful-what-you-wish-for scenario.

He asked, "What if McDonald's had said after test results came in, 'Hey, this stuff works; why don't we move to this? Oh, here's the problem: We've got a twenty-year relationship with Cargill and a commitment going forward with them. I'm going to send your oil to Cargill and tell those guys to do it. Only then will I change the frying oil worldwide. I know they're going to be able to do it at a better cost than you and produce it more efficiently.' "

I understood his point. For Source Food to accommodate a

huge order, I'd need my customers to make a long-term commitment to buy my product, and perhaps finance a manufacturing plant. Ryan added, "You have to acknowledge the fact that there was never a chance for McDonald's to convert to this oil unless they would have embraced the technology and codeveloped a large-scale production capability. You can't villainize McDonald's for not making a change because it was incapable of doing so."

Recognizing this built-in hurdle, I thought we should try a different route. Why don't we get some traction with an actual restaurant operator? So we interviewed Irwin Kruger, who owns several McDonald's restaurants in the New York metropolitan area—his store in Times Square is one of the world's largest—to make some informal tests using Nextra with some of his employees. Kruger has been associated with McDonald's for most of his professional career, and he's one of the more intelligent, enlightened purveyors of fast food. He understood the health issues in the restaurant industry long before most politicians and food executives. And because of his success, he has the ear of decision makers in corporate headquarters.

Let's not forget that the McDonald's french fry probably amplifies the scope of the health problem to the largest extent possible. McDonald's has more than 31,000 restaurants in 118 countries. While they have sold billions and billions of hamburgers, the number of pounds of fries they've sold is countless. It's major tonnage. And the taste of a McDonald's fry is seemingly immutable. It is perhaps even more of an emblem of the company than the burger. French fries are composed of cooking oil, potatoes, and salt, and the oil accounts for 30 percent of the mass after you fry them, so the flavor of that oil is an important factor. In short, it's the oil that seduces our taste buds and puts the smile on shareholders faces at quarterly analyst updates.

Kruger understood that we were trying to get some real-world data for our oil and he was intrigued that a healthier beef tallow with no cholesterol or trans fats had been developed. So he agreed to help us out. He was curious to see what it would do for his french fries.

Tests were run using Nextra and the existing McDonald's oil. Employees were asked to compare and contrast one french fry from another, and they were able to discern somewhat of a difference. Several actually preferred the new oil. But it was *different.* And herein lies another key factor in determining whether a new product should be substituted for an existing one: Even if the new oil yielded fried foods that were preferred over the current products, in many cases this was considered a negative. Why? Because restaurants fret that their customers want their products to *taste the same.* This is a classic deflector shield that any purchasing agent worth his salt would be proud of. Unlike the packaged goods crowd who persistently pursues a preferred taste over their competitors, the restaurant industry doesn't want to rock their customer's boat. Change is bad if it means different . . . even if the product is better.

I viewed these conclusions as a little disappointing until Kruger told me he used some common sense derived from years of watching consumers eat and listening to their feedback. He continued, "Then, when I asked my employees how many use ketchup on their french fries, they all said that they did. When you put ketchup on your french fries, guess what? The taste is the same; it's no longer about the oil. You have a variety of ways of actually consuming them, and certainly ketchup masks a lot of the flavor and taste. Some people think it improves it, some think it takes away from it, but I'd say the majority of the people today actually do use ketchup." (I'm sure you'll agree—people have very distinct opinions about their ketchup preferences, as well. And since ketchup contains a lot of sugar, maybe Heinz and its competitors ought to be thinking about a ketchup made with a safe, alternative sweetener.)

I think Kruger's employees gave honest responses to the taste tests, but knowing the boss was asking them to compare and make a choice gave them a built-in bias, as hard as they tried to avoid it. If somebody asks you to blind taste test any two similar items, your immediate thought is that they probably won't be the same. You're almost compelled to like one more than the other. At the very least, an error factor creeps in. It's human nature, and it doesn't take an advanced degree in science or statistics to figure this out.

The issue of removing trans fats from their frying oil was certainly discussed at McDonald's headquarters. McDonald's had been thinking about using a non–trans fat cooking oil for their fries as early as 2002. The company had made a limited test of reduced trans fat oil in a few stores in Janesville, Wisconsin, and based on the feedback, they decided to roll out the new oil on a nationwide basis. "New U.S. Oil to Bring 48 Percent TFA [Trans Fatty Acids] Reduction in McDonald's Fries in Early 2003," trumpeted the company's press release from the Oak Brook, Illinois, headquarters.

"Within days of making its announcement, and even before the new oil was rolled out elsewhere, McDonald's customer service lines were flooded with complaints," wrote Julie Jargon, a trade journalist for *Crain's Chicago Business.* "When the oil was introduced in Los Angeles a couple of months later, McDonald's got even more alarming complaints. The fries were coming out covered in a milky residue. They were pale yellow and turned soggy quickly. Customer surveys showed people weren't planning to buy the fries again."

McDonald's went public about moving to reduce trans fats—with all good intentions—but they had to back off because then–McDonald's USA president Mike Roberts moved too quickly. He committed to something when the data wasn't clear, according to a former executive who was closely involved with the decision. (Because he still has major business dealings with a number of people in the food industry, he prefers to remain anonymous.) He told me that he was opposed to a quick solution to the McDonald's cooking oil issue, and he was not hesitant to state his position. "I looked at the data and said, 'If you guys do this right now you're crazy.' The change in oil was not consumer-invisible." He thought management was acting without enough information, and that if consumers noticed a difference in taste, they would revolt, and revolt in a noisy way. This executive was correct.

The result was an immediate pullback, and while McDonald's did manage to avert a Classic Coke–type disaster with their customers, the competitive damage was done: Wendy's was able to make a global change by moving to a non–trans fat oil and jump ahead of McDonald's on this increasingly important nutrition issue. (In January 2007, McDonald's announced it was phasing in a new canola-based oil that includes corn and soy oils. The company did not say where the new oil was being used, but presumably it's already in its New York City restaurants to comply with the ban, which took effect in July 2007.)

As with the Ruby Tuesday and D'Lites fiascoes, the restaurant industry once again took the wrong lessons from McDonald's failed attempt with healthier food. The resounding attitude was that companies shouldn't be too hasty as they make their food more nutritious. This response ignored the fact that McDonald's had the right instincts to make America healthier and that they anticipated the coming wave of regulatory pressure to remove trans fats from frying oils.

The role of the purchasing agent is a crucial one, but his actions exemplify the kind of thinking that keeps the industry from making any meaningful, progressive changes in what we're eating when we eat in a restaurant. Until he is permitted to think less about cutting costs and more about reducing belt sizes, he unknowingly helps make our population less healthy every day. He's really only following the lead of his management, however, so it's hard to put the burden of blame solely on his actions. If corporate restaurant groups don't give their purchasing agents permission to graduate from the "cheaper is better" role, healthier restaurant food will be slow in coming. The impetus must come from the corner office, from executives who can appreciate the long-term implications of not offering healthier products to their customers.

# 6

# nobody wants to be told what to eat

*2) Any food establishment . . . shall not be allowed to serve food to any person who is obese, based on criteria prescribed by the State Department of Health after consultation with the Mississippi Council on Obesity Prevention and Management . . .*

—House Bill No. 282, in the Mississippi Legislature Regular Session, 2008

Two years before I began working on this book, there were rumblings within the industry and local governments that trans fats could ultimately be banned from restaurants. Frankly, I couldn't fathom this would ever happen, and neither did many of my colleagues in the industry. At the time, almost everyone I talked to scoffed at the idea, thinking it was short-lived. But of course they were, beginning in New York City in 2007, and similar laws were passed in other large cities in the United States, including Philadelphia and Boston.

The National Restaurant Association and the New York State

Restaurant Association's staunch resistance to the ban adopted in New York City illustrates perfectly the industry's intrinsic lack of foresight. The lobbying arms adamantly tried to avoid change, claiming the "costs" were too high and that many restaurant products would have to undergo a major reformulation. Yet the evidence against trans fats and their effect on heart health were overwhelming. The industry could have stayed ahead of the New York City Health Commissioner's demand to remove all trans fats from frying oils used in restaurants. If the restaurateurs had been proactive (as the food manufacturers had been the previous year) rather than defensive, they might have set their own ground rules for when and how they would phase in substitute oils. Instead, the terms were dictated to them by a zealous governmental agency.

It didn't take long, however, for the simmering trans fat discussion to heat up and become a national news story that symbolized both the food industry's hesitance to take preemptive action to aid the health of the public and the government's desire to direct what we eat. The characterizations of the government's efforts ranged from the laudatory to the derisive, and everyone, it seemed, had an opinion about whether or not it was the government's right to dictate what we eat. From where I sat, this ban was a frustrating case of good intentions gone wrong. Many people on the governmental side had their hearts in the right place, but there was a lot that they weren't considering about the larger impact that the trans fat ban would have on the food industry. I'm not talking about cost; I'm talking about whether or not this trans fat ban will actually make people healthier.

What the regulators involved in these pieces of legislation failed to recognize was that removing trans fats was not a simple silver bullet to clearer arteries. The reason that trans fat oils had become so pervasive in restaurants across America was that almost twenty years ago the restaurant industry had adopted vegetable oils containing trans fats largely in response to the public outcry against cooking oils that were high in cholesterol and saturated fats. Because they were low in saturated fats and had no cholesterol, the trans fat oils were seen as a relief, but as nutritionists later discovered, the trans fat oils came with their own set of drawbacks.

Many substitute oils would take the place of trans fat cooking oils, some of which would return to the higher levels of the previously demonized saturated fats. If you want your baked goods like biscuits to be nice and flaky, this would be the only course industrial bakers could take. Simply put, one evil would be exchanged for another, and just protract the problem. The cycle would continue with little sense of how any of this would actually help consumers control their weight.

In the end, there may be something intrinsic in the nature of government regulation such that the regulators simply can never be nimble enough to imagine even the most likely unintended consequences. One-size-fits-all solutions like trans fat bans don't reflect the diversity of problems that the food industry and consumers are up against. This shortsightedness renders the purported solutions ineffective at actually changing the way that people consume unhealthy food. When people outside of the industry (such as politicians) advocate for change, it should come as no surprise that the collateral damage from their decisions only exacerbates the obesity problem in this country. However well intentioned efforts like the trans fat ban may be, it's often what our regulators don't consider that leads to weight gain for everyone involved.

Despite the flaws of this regulatory approach, there seems to be no shortage of politicians who'd like to control the things we eat. As the food industry has grown over the last fifty years, the government has stepped up its regulations to match, and though some of these regulations mean well, they haven't necessarily made us healthier. In fact, government regulations designed around nutrition have a pretty poor record of actually making the American public healthier. Witness the fact that the last twenty years have seen more government food statutes adopted than ever before, and yet during that time we've also seen the most dramatic increases in obesity.

The end result of all this is that while food companies have certainly done their share to make us fat, they aren't the only contributors to this broken system. In the last fifty years, the failures of federal, state, and local governments in the United States to create a workable guidance and regulatory system have played an important role in making Americans fatter. Every level of government has tried, to no avail, to make a contribution to our nutritional health. On the federal level, we've seen efforts to design and redesign a plausible food pyramid—trying to cajole us to eating more of the right foods and less of the bad stuff. Ask the typical American what the four major food groups are and he's likely to answer, "Italian, Mexican, Chinese, and Southern Fried." We've also seen our national government buckle to the big farming interests, tossing needless subsidies to the corporations that not only don't need taxpayers' handouts but also provide the bulk of what's wrong at the dinner table. School districts allowed vending machines to infiltrate cafeterias, and state legislators reacted by saying, "That's why your children got fat." States' attempts to regulate school board behavior have caused ugly turf battles across the nation.

These policies are not working, and yet we continue to pursue them with the misguided belief that some combination of laws and oversight will bring our national waistline to the size of previous generations.

Food regulation in this country began some 130 years ago, when the Department of Agriculture recommended a national food and drug law. The bill was defeated in 1880, but it laid the groundwork for more than a hundred bills that were introduced in Congress over the next quarter-century. Adulterated imported tea came under scrutiny just before the twentieth century, but it wasn't until 1906—a watershed year for the government—that we first took the safety of our food seriously. That year Teddy Roosevelt signed the first Food and Drugs Act, prohibiting interstate commerce of misbranded and adulterated food, drink, and drugs. Later on, the Meat Inspection Act, perhaps a direct result of Upton Sinclair's famous muckraking novel about the deplorable conditions in the Chicago stockyards, *The Jungle*, also was signed into law. Food regulation on the national level followed with various statutes ensuring that we don't eat anything immediately harmful or dangerous.

Primarily, federal actions surrounding food concerned food *safety* with little to no mention of nutrition. Except for the pesticide bans in the mid-twentieth century, it has only been recently—in the past decade or so—that our lawmakers have begun to step in and tinker with the long-term health effects of what we consume. Government's role began expanding beyond ensuring we didn't ingest pathogens or unknown substances.

It became *parental.*

It's hard to say when exactly this shift began to take place, but somewhere along the line, as the food industry grew, the role of government oversight took on a parental tone. Safety and nutrition began to be one and the same, and just like that, the government pulled up a chair to America's dinner table. Since this behavior began, there have been plenty of examples of the government screening our groceries and our menu orders, but some of the most recent (and most egregious) examples provide the best look at how these flawed policies get implemented.

In 1992, the FDA combined its recommendations for nutritious eating into a single chart when it created the Food Guide Pyramid, one of the most altruistic and least intrusive efforts to help us improve our eating habits. Offered as a replacement for the simplistic and widely understood Four Basic Food Groups, the pyramid was designed to graphically illustrate for consumers which products to eat more or less of. When the pyramid was first published, it grouped foods into four categories, starting with fats, oils, and sweets (at the top, to be consumed most sparingly). Going down from the top, the sweets were followed by milk, yogurt, cheese, meat, poultry, fish, dry beans, eggs, and nuts; then fruits and vegetables; and finally bread, cereal, rice, and pasta.

You can see the problem with this paean to ancient Egypt right away. First of all, how could anyone remember what foods went where? The original four food groups were memorable (milk; meat; fruits and vegetables; grains). Nothing fancy and no confusion. Every baby boomer had this drilled into their heads in grade school. Contrast this with the Food Pyramid. On the one hand, there are too many products listed to serve as an effective educational tool. On the other hand, nutritional variances among products within the same category are not highlighted. For example, fats and oils were grouped together with no distinction between good fats and bad fats or good oils and bad oils. The third category lumps so many products together—with hugely varying nutritional differences—that it's virtually useless as a guideline. Even the base of the pyramid, where we're allowed the most liberal number of servings, is problematic. It doesn't distinguish between refined carbohydrates (like white rice) or unrefined ones (brown rice).

Further compounding the problems with the pyramid is the notion of serving sizes. Has anyone yet figured this out? How many carrots must I eat to get five servings a day? Besides, consumers don't think in terms of consuming a "serving size." They eat a *collection* of items at each sitting. The pyramid looks at eating in a vacuum. It is not practical for the way people eat today, but because it was a government initiative, it's regarded by many as the only road map needed for nutrition—follow the guidelines and everyone will be healthy. The problem is that Americans have only become more overweight and have been eating less nutritiously since the pyramid's inception. Clearly something is being lost in translation, and we're all getting fatter as a result.

And that's just from the science. When politics entered into the debate, you can bet that the various food trade groups all weighed in on that initial Food Pyramid with a vengeance. The National

Cattlemen's Beef Association complained that they were too close to the top and that would stigmatize beef. Dairy manufacturers were equally displeased.

In 2005 the pyramid was made over, showcasing new vertical lines for each food category, but the revision still did little to make Americans healthier. Today the same debate is being waged as government officials once again begin to rethink and redesign the Food Pyramid, and it's obvious that the result will be a hodgepodge influenced by special interests. The U.S. Potato Board, already smarting from the frenzy surrounding low-carb diets, desperately wants to be included in the vegetable category. After all, spuds can claim that they are vegetables. The meat folks certainly don't want to move up the pyramid either; it could adversely affect hamburger and steak sales. "Every aisle of the supermarket has a lobbyist in town," Jeff Nedelman, a food industry consultant, told the *Wall Street Journal.* "The pyramid has crumbled. The industry groups are warily circling and eyeing one another."

The newly appointed executive director of the U.S. Department of Agriculture (USDA) Center for Nutrition Policy and Promotion, Brian Wansink, is now the point person on managing the effort to revise the pyramid. Wansink is a respected food scientist with no ties to lobbyists. He has said the new guidelines will "give people latitude but still tell them exactly how much latitude they have." There's been some speculation that there will be a new pyramid specifically assigned to senior citizens. That begs another question: Should there also be one for children and teenagers? Wansink has said that the current pyramid has had some four million hits on its Web site. Yet this is only a minuscule percentage of the adult population.

I'm sure the new version will be bold, contemporary, accurate, and more complicated than the old one. It will mean well. But I wonder, after the first weeks' flurry of hard-earned, positive publicity, will the American consumer pay heed to the government's well-meaning advice? If you understand the psychology of people and food, the new pyramid can only help a small part of the population.

The Food Pyramid saga gives us a good look at what happens when the government tries to do more than it is capable of. While meaning well, the government took a simple idea (the four food groups), added some new science, crafted a teaching device negotiated with lobbyists, then introduced guidelines that are virtually impossible to follow and comprehend. It's not enough just to be well intentioned. What's missing is real knowledge of the food consumer, and what it takes to reach them. Without that, there can be no genuine effectiveness. What the Food Pyramid introduced was an impractical system that was incompatible with how people shopped. What makes it worse is that because it comes from the government, it holds the appearance of usefulness and objectivity; meanwhile, it does little to actually change unhealthy consumption patterns.

The Food Pyramid is not the only place where these governmental shortcomings become apparent. Because there's so much at stake, food industry groups use their resources to appear everywhere there are decisions to be made about what we eat. The lobbying is continuous, and the machinations behind food policy often occur behind the scenes, where influence peddling is all part of a day's work. We don't generally get to see this, especially the horse trading that goes on among members of Congress when they're divvying up the pork on something like a farm bill.

The farm bill demands our attention not just because so much is at stake in terms of crop growth and subsidies, but because it harks back to the days when families tilled the soil for generations. Sadly, this humble, heartland agrarian ideal has long since lost its allure. As you're probably well aware, the country farmer, the small-time grower, has all but disappeared. The hardworking families so quaintly depicted in Hollywood films have long been replaced by Big Agribusiness, where sophisticated seeds and fertilizers (continually tweaked by Big Pharma) maximize crop yields.

If you do not farm big, you do not farm at all anymore because it isn't profitable. And big growers in recent years have been very profitable, mainly because they concentrate on the commodity crops—rice, soybeans, cotton, wheat, and corn. Often a large concern concentrates on a single crop. Ironically, the food growers refer to everything else—the stuff we actually eat, like fruits and vegetables—as "specialty" crops. So much of what we eat we owe to the heartland of America, in regions like the Midwest.

In the long, complex arc of the food chain, every stalk of wheat, every kernel of corn, and all those amber waves of grain, are touched in some way, both good and bad, by government—from comprehensive regulations drafted by federal agencies to those ordinances adopted by local authorities.

But this is where public policy becomes critical. Through farm bills, the federal government earmarks very large appropriations to subsidize the commodity crops. Most of that money goes to food stamps and nutrition programs, but a large chunk goes to wealthy farmers. Over the past decade, 70 percent of all farm subsidies—totaling $120 billion—has gone to 6 percent of the farms. These payouts were originally adopted during the Depression to help those tilling the land who were struggling to make a living. But under the law, payments can continue even if the farmer is earning windfall profits. There are so many loopholes in the legislation that some medium-size entrepreneurs have been embarrassed by the windfalls. However, the checks are rarely returned.

Such structural idiocies cost us a fortune and also indirectly contribute to the obesity issue. In a *Washington Post* series (nine stories, running from July 2006 to December 2006) on the farm bill, reporters discovered that $1.3 billion in farm subsidies went to farmers who didn't farm. A 2002 program aimed at helping those facing a serious drought gave $635 million to ranchers and dairy farmers who had moderate or no drought. Some recipients of taxpayer largesse lived in counties declared disaster areas after debris fell to earth from the space shuttle *Columbia*.

All of this means that carrots, apples, and other fruits and vegetables are getting more expensive every time you visit the grocery store, and junk food remains relatively cheap in comparison. The farm bill does almost nothing for farmers growing fresh produce. As a result, the real price (inflation adjusted) of fruits and vegetables between 1985 and 2000 increased by nearly 40 percent, while the real price of soft drinks (sweetened by high fructose corn syrup) declined by 23 percent. And the situation is getting even worse. In just one year, as of March 2008, the price of fruits and vegetables went up 20 percent.

This is, of course, the opposite of what should be happening. Though almost all nutritionists agree that Americans don't eat nearly enough fresh fruits and vegetables, the lack of government incentives to farm such produce means that they are simply not available in many parts of the country. Think back to the story of the woman from chapter one who said it was easier for someone to buy a handgun than an organic tomato in her neighborhood. After hearing numbers like these, you start to see what she's talking about, and how the inadequacies of this mammoth legislation have made us all fat.

The farm bill directly affects all of us and our subsequent nutritional health, like it or not. It doesn't matter what your food preferences are, from ardent carnivore to the strictest vegetarian. Because of our federal policies, the least expensive food in the supermarket is the food with the highest caloric content and the lowest nutritional value. In aiding commodity farmers, the farm bill creates added sugar by subsidizing corn and added fat by subsidizing soybeans.

Highlighting this absurdity, Jack Hedin, a small organic vegetable producer in southern Minnesota, shared with the *New York Times* in March 2008 that his efforts to expand his vegetable acreage were thwarted by government farm policy. After planting tomatoes and watermelons on acres reserved for federally subsidized corn, Hedin learned he was out of compliance with the commodity program. "I've discovered that typically, a farmer who grows the 'forbidden' fruits and vegetables on corn acreage not only has to give up his subsidy for the year on that acreage, he is also penalized the market value of the illicit crop," stated Hedin. He noted the penalties only applied to fruits and vegetables! If he grew another commodity crop or nothing at all, there would be no fines.

In early 2008, Congress was heavily debating a new farm bill that had so many add-ins to satisfy special interests—including "healthy" special interests—that it grew to a gargantuan $290 billion. President Bush vetoed it on the grounds that it was too expensive and too generous with $40 billion in subsidies for farmers who are already enjoying record high prices and incomes. Almost $30 billion would go to farmers just to idle their land. Congress overturned the president's veto on May 22, 2008.

The result of this kind of bureaucratic foolishness is that the government ultimately promotes the consumption of food that is high in calories, sugar, and bad fats, and low in almost everything that's good for us to eat. The consumer ends up paying more money for less available healthier crops.

The lessons of the farm bill are straightforward. As long as the government controls which foods are farmed, there is little reason to expect any improvement in the overall nutritional value of the nation's food supply. Fats and sweeteners are in. Fruits and vegetables are still out. Hold on to your waistlines.

One of the most noticeable and arguably successful food regulations that the government has introduced in the last twenty years occurred in 1990 when the Nutrition Labeling and Education Act (NLEA) was passed. NLEA required all packaged foods to feature nutrition labeling, and all health claims for foods to be consistent with terms defined by the secretary of health and human services.

The law superseded state requirements regarding food standards, nutrition labeling, and health claims, and for the first time, permitted some claims for so-called health foods. The food ingredients on the package panel, serving sizes, and terms such as "low fat" and "light" were standardized.

On the surface, it looked as if this would be a win-win for the consumer—an added amount of transparency for them about the contents of their food and a new way to gauge the nutritional value of what they were buying. This was even helpful for the industry, in that it gave them a set of universal guidelines to adopt, so that they didn't have to deal with different labels in different states. Of course, the fine print made the information difficult to read, comprehend, and dissect. I've watched many a baby boomer squinting at a package in a crowded supermarket aisle, shaking her head in disbelief.

While labels have served some purpose in educating shoppers about what is in their food, they remain problematic and only go part way. They're on the sides or backs of packaging, and they're difficult to read. That's not good. One could also argue, however, that even if they were printed in larger type and more prominently displayed, consumers as a whole would not be enamored of spending their time in supermarkets "educating" themselves on nutrition. But there are other flaws. Consumers often confuse the ingredients and calories in a "serving" with the entire contents of the package. The side panel of a Kraft Deluxe Macaroni and Cheese Dinner notes 320 calories. Then you see that you are supposed to get four servings per box, for a total of almost 1,300 calories! There's no indication of how many calories are in a box. (In late 2007, the FDA held hearings on nutrition labeling, no doubt thinking it was time to revamp the requirements. I'll comment on this development in a subsequent chapter.) Ultimately, perhaps the biggest flaw with the labeling is that—like the Food Pyramid—it simply does not cater to the practicalities of how people shop and eat. As a result most of the labels are ineffective.

Of course, that doesn't stop the periodic scrambles to label whatever the prevailing food concern of the moment is. To address the rising attention surrounding trans fats, in January 2006, the FDA instituted the requirement that a product's trans fat content would have to be disclosed on food packages. Given the potential impact on heart health, the government felt that providing details of a product's trans fat content would be a good thing. Up until then, you could only recognize its alias, "partially hydrogenated oil," on the list of ingredients.

Despite some initial grousing about the cost to change all the packages and the need to reformulate a whole host of products containing high levels of the demonized fat, the packaged goods companies pretty much complied and went about their business. At the end of the day, they recognized that the evidence on trans fats was stacked against them and it was wise to just suck it up and deal with it.

The same could not be said about the restaurant industry's reaction when various municipalities proposed listing ingredients in restaurant food. Following the trans fat ban, the New York City Board of Health passed a regulation requiring restaurants to list calories on handheld menus and menu boards. But the edict would apply only to restaurants that already made calories available voluntarily on brochures, Web sites, or elsewhere. The restaurant industry promptly took the city to court to overturn the requirements. While the case was pending, some chains, notably Wendy's and Chipotle, took down nutrition information from their Web site or stopped making it available in New York City. Irwin Kruger, the New York City McDonald's franchisee whom you met earlier, mentioned to me that the city fathers hadn't given much thought to the actual logistics of such a move. Was it even practical? He was only being slightly facetious when a reporter from *Restaurant News* asked him how he felt about displaying nutritional content on the menu board. Kruger said, "Well, you know, it's pretty hard to get all that stuff up there; customers are going to need binoculars. We have so many items, and who wants to read that stuff? You want to get in and out of a restaurant."

Kruger has a point. And so do consumer advocates who want easy-to-find food information in restaurants. I've been in so many restaurants where the nutritional information is posted in such an out-of-the-place way that it's difficult to even find, let alone read. However, it seems doubtful that government legislation mandating the display of nutritional information is really going to solve the problem. Of course, it might make things more transparent, but transparency does not necessarily cause people to lose weight. Chuck Hunt, the head of the New York State Restaurant Association, has mounted serious counterattacks against the city's health advocates, citing the fact that labeling in the packaged goods industry has done little to curb obesity. "For the last fifteen or so years, they've been required to have nutritional statements," Hunt said on CNN.com (September 30, 2007), "and that hasn't caused obesity to decline."

The controversy ignited in April 2008. Over the objections of the New York State Restaurant Association, a federal appeals judge ruled that the City of New York could proceed with ordering certain chain restaurants to post calorie counts alongside prices. Under the ruling, any chain with at least fifteen outlets nationwide must now display calorie counts on menu boards, menus, or food tags. The mandate applies to roughly 2,000 restaurants, or about 10 percent of the 23,000 in the city. (In 2007 King County, which covers Seattle, also adopted such a law.) As of the date of this book's writing, the New York State Restaurant Association is challenging the ruling.

Following the calorie mandate, the Center for Science in the Public Interest (CSPI) joined in the fracas. Said Margo G. Wootan, director of nutrition policy at CSPI, "The restaurant industry isn't concerned about defending the First Amendment, as its lawsuit laughably claims. It just wants to keep its customers in the dark.

People need nutrition information to exercise personal responsibility and to feed their children healthy diets."

While changing over all their menu boards can be costly, time consuming, and generally a pain in the behind for restaurant operators, their advocates could have gone ahead on the menu nutrition issue and offered a program that would work for their members and at the same time placate city health officials. Understandably, they don't want the large chains to be penalized by being singled out to list the calories for all items. But their ingrained culture worked against them this time. Anticipating the extent of the problem or compromising in any form of give-and-take once the conflict unfolded was not in the restaurant industry's vocabulary, and it hurt their position in the long run.

The New York City menu-labeling case provides insight into how the government and industry should not work. Rather than declare an outright ban of trans fats and require the change to menu boards for only a select group of restaurant chains, the city officials didn't work with the restaurant industry to come up with practical solutions in advance of the proposed changes. This way they could have made clear their intentions and given the restaurant industry time to digest the situation and formulate a plan of action.

Changes mandated by government can create a whole new set of problems, and they often don't do anything to address the main issue in the first place. Will calorie counts on menus drive patrons to order meals with less calories? Will restaurant sales really suffer by posting calories? Will the initiative make a serious dent in the rate of obesity? Only time will tell.

The subtle correlation of the New York City ban on dangerous food ingredients (in the form of trans fats) with the smoking prohibition in restaurants that took effect a few years earlier seems to have opened a sort of Pandora's box for the food industry. It's as if a signal has been sent out to all forms of government that it is open season on the public health dangers of food: If an industry can't responsibly regulate itself, in an echo of the message to the tobacco industry, government should have every right to intervene and protect the public.

On the surface something like labeling or the Food Pyramid seems useful enough, even if it doesn't get our national weight down. After all, just getting people to focus on nutrition in some way seems valuable, right? Even if government initiatives are impractical, what in the end is the real harm?

And yet regulations like these do actual harm because they offer the appearance of a solution, a Band-Aid to something far more complicated. Though there's little track record to support these initiatives' efficacy, they continue to pop up on political dockets around the country. Looking to the legislative successes of labeling, trans fat bans, and the Food Pyramid offers a smokescreen solution that obscures the more entrenched problems of healthy eating—issues like the farm bill. As a result, people in government and in the food industry avoid having the kind of meaningful dialogue that would actually result in a healthier America.

Frustratingly, these unworkable solutions also have a way of bringing about ideas that are just plain bad. One side effect of this emerging trend is the advancement by city and state governments of some questionable proposals to address the obesity crisis. We are seeing a host of dubious recommendations start to float into the arena of public discourse and political activity. For instance, in San Francisco, certainly a progressive city, the table is being set to tax "sin" foods, such as sodas containing corn syrup. In Chicago, foie gras was outlawed and then decriminalized, in the spirit of Prohibition in the 1930s. The height of ludicrous government behavior perhaps revealed itself in Mississippi, when there was a proposal to refuse service to obese people in restaurants. Who's going to be the arbiter of fat in the obviously panicky Magnolia State? Imagine having the hostess ask you to step on a scale after checking your reservation.

Can the government save us from our own bad habits, especially what and how much we eat? The questions remain: Which interventions work? Which don't? What is too much government? What's too little?

Perhaps we can get a clearer picture of the role government plays when we look down the hallways of the nation's schools.

# 7

# let them eat cupcakes

Can you imagine anything more innocent than a cupcake? Inherently hand-size, easily gripped so that even a small child can carry one around a classroom. The cupcake's delicate crowned top and circular shape lend themselves perfectly for a touch of frosting and a little charming decoration. The simple treat can easily symbolize all that's right in the world for a small child, or even certain adults.

Almost everyone loves cupcakes but few people covet them as much as Rachel Kramer Bussel. She is the cupcake queen. On her Web site she appears to be demure and serious, wearing studious black eyeglasses, and until her Cupcakes Take the Cake blog became a sensation among foodies, Bussel was better known as a sex columnist for the *Village Voice*, New York City's iconoclastic weekly.

If you cruise her blog, you notice a few added comments by the devoted minions who log on to it on a daily basis. ("Yum!" and "I love your cupcake blog" were the only two I found during one such search.) But that's no surprise because there's really no need to say anything. Mostly, the blog consists of photos of cupcakes and occasional YouTube videos (why moving footage of a dessert is necessary is anybody's guess) posted by enthusiastic professional and amateur bakers from every corner of the country. The toppings and icings are, of course, thick and creamy and smooth, and they convey the moods of their creators—dominoes, R.I.P. headstones, hearts, flowers, cherries, snowmen, teddy bears, panda bears, stripes and swirls, lollipops, sailboats and life preservers, billiard balls, even an uni sushi topping.

Bussel started the Web site in December 2004 "on a whim and it just kind of exploded." She guessed that it really picked up momentum after cupcakes got a publicity boost when they were shown at Magnolia Bakery during an episode of *Sex and the City*, the long-running television series about career women in Manhattan. "It's almost like the new popularity of the cupcake snuck up on us," Bussel said. "Now you see them in merchandising, clothing, and other cupcake-themed items."

If anything, Cupcakes Take the Cake is a "food porn" site, celebrating the essence of the most egalitarian of comfort desserts. All the pictures of cupcakes have one thing in common: They immediately make you want to jump into your computer screen and wolf one down. Just doing the research for the above paragraphs made me hungry.

Cupcakes are everywhere, especially in politics. New York senator and former presidential candidate Hillary Clinton jokingly made the cupcake part of her campaign. On *Late Night with David Letterman* she listed it as number nine of her Top Ten promises: "Each year on my birthday everyone gets a cupcake."

What is it about the once-lowly-now-sort-of-chic cupcake? "People like brownies and frozen yogurt and other desserts but it's not the same," Bussel said. "It makes them happy, and there's an excitement you see with them that you don't see with other desserts."

My guess is that it's an iconic product, a symbol of Americana, much like Coca-Cola and chocolate, part of the realm of feel-good comfort food where people who make them and eat them have an emotional attachment. There's something in this self-contained dessert that appeals to our senses and gives the typical home baker a way to be a little creative. The cupcake is to our country what the croissant or baguette is to France. And until now the cupcake hasn't faced a crisis since first appearing in cookbooks in the nineteenth century.

Given the nearly universal adoration of this favorite indulgence, it seems strange that the cupcake now finds itself squarely in the crosshairs of food policy makers around the country. Some parents and school administrators welcome it; others have scoffed, wondering whether they're going to bring out cupcake-sniffing dogs to detect them in third-grade classrooms. "Step slowly away from the baking pan, ma'am." When your cellmate asks, "What are you in for?" you simply say "cupcake felon."

Okay, so maybe that's a bit extreme, but the cupcake has become a source of real contention when it comes to the subject of childhood obesity in America, making it an unwitting participant in the battle over government's role in controlling our kids' stomachs. It is perhaps the most sensitive front in the war against obesity taking place in the hallways of our nation's schools. How did this happen? The cupcake has simply become a metaphor for all the issues related to what our children are eating and drinking while receiving their education. The fact that it's found itself at the epicenter of the nutrition debate was not exactly a surprise to me. Once, cupcake wars referred to personal "snack downs" among aficionados who claimed they made the best batches. No longer innocent fun in the kitchen, it's now a war between the food police and the libertarians. And the kids are caught in the middle.

In December 2007, the *Chicago Tribune* reported that several area elementary schools were ditching the cupcake in favor of healthier snacks during holiday season. Down in Florida, one county banned cakes, cupcakes, and other low-nutrition foods as a response to a federal mandate that required school officials to develop stricter policies for the school districts. The controversy over contraband foods was touched off by a federal law that took effect in the 2006–2007 school year requiring every school system in the National School Lunch and School Breakfast programs to write a "wellness policy" in 2006.

To be fair, the issues that have produced these and other cupcake controversies are completely legitimate and vital to the discussion of childhood obesity. In a variety of ways, our kids have been subjected to far too many sweets and calories at their schools where parents don't have the ability to help kids self-regulate. In marketing parlance, children in school are a "captive audience." If they need something to eat or drink, they can only buy what's available at the school. It's kind of like being in the movies. You can only choose from a very limited number of items.

This setup is a food marketer's dream, and that's precisely the problem that has occurred in many of our nation's classrooms. While these issues of junk food in the classroom are vitally important to our understanding of why our country is so fat, vilifying the cupcake is not the answer. Though it may sound good to some lawmakers, these cupcake criticisms fail to grasp the entire problem of the highly caloric food being put in front of our kids during their hours at school. The cupcake has become yet another smokescreen issue, something that grabs headlines for both supporters and detractors while obscuring the real forces and problems at work.

By focusing on cupcakes and demonizing the role of this specific dessert at school, legislators and school administrators overlook the host of decisions that they've made that have contributed to a generation of childhood obesity and set precedents for how an entire cornucopia of unhealthy foods find their way into the classroom. From vending machines to cafeteria options, local governments and school boards around the country have been complicit in allowing the biggest names in junk food to waltz into their school districts and set up shop. The end result has been an entire generation of students who grew up consuming hundreds if not thousands of excess calories a day—calories that simply were not there twenty years ago. It's not the cupcake's fault. After all, kids have been eating cupcakes in school for a long time. M&M's and 20-ounce Pepsis from vending machines—well, that's a different story altogether.

Children by nature—even teenagers—are defined in part by their lack of impulse control. And because kids are renowned for their inability to say no to sugar, it would seem like an illogical decision that school districts around the country began allowing vending machines stocking little of nutritional value on their premises. One would think that the kids would behave, well, like kids in a candy store. Despite this logic, however, this is precisely what local governments and school boards started doing over the past two decades.

How can we be sure that school vending machines have specifically had a negative impact on America's girth? Consider the example of soda. Somewhat surprisingly, researchers are *just* beginning to study the effects of soft drinks on teenage obesity. The early results of small-sample studies are far from conclusive, but they indicate that sugared beverages are causing our youth to become fatter than in the past, and certainly to unhealthful levels. The more they've become widely available in schools, the more teens have consumed them.

Boston Children's Hospital's David S. Ludwig said that these drinks are almost impossible to avoid. "They're basically everywhere," he said when interviewed for the *New York Times Magazine* (March 7, 2006). "Schools, cafeterias, vending machines." According to Ludwig, in the 1950s, kids drank three cups of milk for every cup of soda. Today, the ratio is reversed. Think of the overall impact: a typical 12-ounce can of soda is 10 percent sugar, or ten teaspoons. Three sodas are almost 450 calories of sugar. The typical American drinks a gallon of soda every week.

Vending machines now are ubiquitous in our high school cafeterias. According to the Centers for Disease Control, vending machines and snack bars are in 98 percent of high schools, 74 percent of middle schools, and 43 percent of elementary schools. While it's hard to pin down precisely when this trend began, the reason why it began is not so elusive. Vending machines and corporate-sponsored snack bars started because they offered pay-for-play corporate subsidies that eased the tax burdens in local communities. Snapple alone paid $106 million for the rights to supply New York City schoolchildren with beverages over a five-year period.

In the short term, these soda- and snack-filled machines appeared to be a win-win for the local governments and food industry. The local governments could put off raising taxes for public education, thereby making it seem to the voters that they were doing more with less. The food industry not only gained a profitable new revenue stream from the thousands of new machines in schools across the country, it also was able to cultivate a new, entrenched form of brand loyalty. Trapped in a school with no other options, kids were forced to drink either Coke *or* Pepsi *or* Snapple, depending on whose machine was placed in the hall. If a high school student drinks a Coke while he's at school, the likelihood that he'll turn to Coke again when he's outside school and actually has a choice becomes much greater. Thus in the end, the goal is not just about getting kids to spend money, it's about getting kids to choose the right brand.

And choose they did, unfortunately for them. Kids and teens across the country were the only real losers in this equation because almost no one—not in the government, not among most school administrators, not in the food industry—considered the long-term implications of what having vending machines in schools could do. The budgets were balanced, more sodas and snacks were sold . . . and our children got fatter.

To its credit, the American Beverage Association has announced that through voluntary initiatives by its largest member companies, sales of sugared drinks to schools dropped in the three-year period between 2004 and 2007. But it doesn't overshadow the fact that two-thirds of the drinks still sold in high schools contain considerable amounts of sugar and calories. (It could be considerably less by the time this book is published.) Nevertheless, Coca-Cola, Pepsi, and the other giant drink makers have promised to rid the vending machines of everything but diet sodas, bottled water, sports drinks, unsweetened juices, and milk products by the 2009–2010 school year.

Which raises another important question. Should vending machines offer only artificially sweetened rather than sugared beverages to our kids? This question arises because some of the beverage companies said their research revealed that adults had no problem with diet sodas, but they were loath to serve the same drinks to their children. This was a direct result of the fallout from early concerns about NutraSweet, saccharin warnings, and the banning of cyclamates a number of years ago. Do you put your child at a future risk for cancer or some other disease because of artificial sweeteners (if this is indeed the case), or do you put him at risk for obesity (and diabetes) by feeding him traditional sugared sodas? It's a Hobson's choice, isn't it? *The scientific jury is still out. We just don't know.*

There's more work to be done.

Of course, vending machines were not the only nutrition problem taking root in our kids' schools. The other big problem is right where we should expect it: in the cafeteria. In most cases school lunchrooms operate as stand-alone businesses that cover salaries, benefits, maintenance, and fixed costs. But cafeterias are plagued with a "financial albatross" around their necks: the National School Lunch Program.

The School Lunch Act, first passed in 1946, established federally subsidized or free midday meals to 30 million children at an annual cost of about $7 billion. Some 187 billion plates have been served in the past sixty years or so, and certainly many needy students and families have benefited from this program. For states and local school districts to qualify, the cafeterias must meet minimum nutrition standards drafted by the federal government. The point is to provide a wholesome, healthy lunch so students can perform at their best.

At least in theory that's the point. In practice there are much more difficult hurdles to success. Take for instance the experiences of Donald L. Knode II, the food service coordinator for Calvert, Maryland. In a 2005 article in the *Washington Post*, Knode recounted that his school district loses $1.88 on the average high school lunch and another 60 cents on federally subsidized meals *after reimbursement* by the government.

"The more meals you sell, the more money you lose," Knode said. Yet his program makes a modest profit. The only way to balance the budget, according to Knode, is to sell à la carte items, such as stuffed-crust pizza and onion rings, products known in education circles as "competitive foods." These foods account for half of the program's revenues and all of its profits. Each à la carte item carries a markup of at least 100 percent. "Junk food is subsidizing the school lunch program," Knode added. Linda Burns, the cafeteria manager of Huntingtown High School in Prince Frederick, Maryland, who was also interviewed for the article confirmed this: "Of the 2,079 food items sold à la carte one day last week," she said, "1,384 (67 percent) were junk foods, such as nachos smothered in cheese, sugar-loaded smoothies, and chicken nuggets."

In other words, high-calorie junk foods are just about the only thing propping up the school cafeterias' economics. Without them, they would be in a serious financial bind. It is actually in their best interest to sell more of these nutrition-busting foods, since, as with the vending machines, these junk foods eliminate the pesky problem of having to ask for more money.

How did this happen, you're wondering?

Again it all comes back to taxes. School boards across the nation are caught in a bind. When property taxes rise (the biggest part going to support schools), communities look for ways to balance spiraling budgets. The food and beverage purveyors know this, so they offer up-front payments to school districts to allow fast foods into school cafeterias and vending machines in corridors.

Who would have thought that one of the biggest pizza shops in America was in the kitchens of a school cafeteria? Some days, they make more than a thousand pizzas for students in the Corona-Norco school district in Riverside County, California. Though the cooking staff resembles any other, if you saw them ladling the tomato sauce onto the dough every morning, you probably wouldn't think they're really a subsidiary of Pizza Hut. As the nation's only school district licensed to make pizza under the Pizza Hut name, Corona-Norco gets all the supplies from the company: frozen dough, sauce, cheese, pepperoni—even the oil. (Other schools in the area bring in pizza from brand-name suppliers such as Domino's.) Corona-Norco was not the first district to produce fast-food-label meals. Capistrano Valley High School in Orange County was the first in the country to do so when it opened a food court in 1992 with a limited menu from Taco Bell, Pizza Hut, and KFC, all then owned by PepsiCo.

The Corona-Norco school district made the agreement in 1995, soon after fast-food chains began appearing in the nation's schools. The district had forged a similar agreement with Taco Bell, but that ended when the chain stopped allowing schools to make its food.

By 1999, nearly all of California's high schools surveyed by the Public Health Institute were offering branded fast foods as part of their menu during lunch. At three out of four of these schools, fast food dominated revenues. And 72 percent of the high schools allowed fast-food and beverage advertising on campus.

California school districts were particularly susceptible (or innovative, if you want to take a more cynical view) to making these deals, but the rest of the nation's school boards, suffering budget cuts, followed soon thereafter. The federal guidelines governing food in school cafeterias have been harshly criticized. As nutritionist Ms. Margo Wootan said to the *New York Times* (September 5, 2007), "The national policy is so pathetic that states who [*sic*] follow them should be ashamed of themselves." Jellybeans and popsicles are banned, but Snickers and Dove bars are allowed. This kind of inconsistent rulemaking is not the way to go to adopt a wellness plan for kids.

What this means is that children are subject to more tempting, fattening food than ever before, and their parents aren't entirely to blame. When I was a student, you had to eat in the school cafeteria (or brown bag it), and there were no pizza or fries on the menu. The idea of vending machines in schools was just a gleam in the beverage companies' eyes. In my time it was that little white carton of milk or the water fountain, and no snacks. Today, teenagers in schools across the nation can grab a Snapple or M&M's out of a machine, or enjoy a Taco Bell burrito in the cafeteria—all without much extra effort. In fact, it's encouraged by the very local administrators you entrust your children's health to.

Which brings us back to the cupcake. With the ubiquitous vending machines packing high-calorie snacks and sodas, and the cafeterias pushing overstuffed meals on our children, why are we pointing the finger at such a perennially favorite dessert? Simply put, it's an easy target. It's pretty hard to argue that a cupcake is good for you, even if it is a once-in-a-while indulgence. It provides the perfect alibi for the real problems and factors that have contributed the largest collective weight gain ever seen in America's children.

The innocent bystanders in all this are the kids. While some school districts have banned cupcakes altogether, others are trying to find a middle ground that has led to confusion on all sides. Sheila Gallagher remembered the sweet confections she brought to her daughter Olivia's kindergarten classroom in 2005 to celebrate her fifth birthday. There were a couple of dozen cupcakes, piled high with pink-and-purple frosting. In first grade, it was a different celebration. The ban on cupcakes in her school district meant no more of these sweet concoctions for class-celebrated birthdays. "I understand the thought process behind it," Gallagher told the *St. Petersburg Times*. "I'm in nursing school right now learning about diabetes and obesity. But you can't put a birthday candle in an apple."

Others have been less draconian in response to the call for healthier snacks. Many have decided to issue recommendations or optional guidelines rather than mandates. In other areas there has been a mixed bag of responses, and not all of them are consistent. School officials in San Francisco allow sodas and chips for classroom celebrations but strongly urge nutritious treats. The Des Moines, Iowa, school district has barred sugared sodas and candies but still allows cupcakes and cookies. The Hillsborough County, Florida, school board adopted a policy that asked its principals to find ways to reward schoolchildren with something other than food and drinks.

That there has been a palpable backlash to the cupcake bans was not unexpected. One school superintendent reportedly received a threatening e-mail after her school district supported the ban.

"I think the wholesale banning of parents' bringing cupcakes as a legal issue is over the top," said cupcake maven Bussel. "Banning cupcakes from school doesn't eliminate the problem. Part of the problem with childhood obesity and nutrition is that if you forbid it, they're just going to want it more. A cupcake is supposed to be an occasional treat. I eat them about twice a month, and only occasionally do I eat more. I'm still shocked that cupcakes are controversial."

Apparently, a number of officials agree with her. When the Texas Department of Agriculture announced a crackdown on junk food in schools, parents from the panhandle to the cities vehemently protested. It led to the "Safe Cupcake Amendment" of 2005. Texas said it would abide by its nutrition guidelines but excused any school district from having to eliminate any high-calorie desserts from birthday fests.

Last fall, Michael Benjamin, a New York State assemblyman from the Bronx, drafted legislation (Bill A09446) that would make the cupcake the official children's snack of New York. Benjamin admitted that he is trying to send a message to New York State school districts that are attempting to institute cupcake bans. This, of course, is a ludicrous action and overreaction, reminding me of a gun controversy some years ago. In June 1981, Morton Grove, Illinois, passed a local ordinance banning guns, the first such village in the nation to do so. When officials of Kennesaw, Georgia, a suburb of Atlanta, heard about the ban, they passed a law *requiring* its citizens to own a gun.

Benjamin apparently disagrees with his wife (who thinks his bill encourages childhood obesity), but when speaking to the *New York Post* (September 28, 2007) he said that this is an issue he won't back off. "It's a personal peeve of mine that everything that brings warm memories, the muffin mullahs want to cut out of our diet."

When the cupcake controversy began to fester, the comments from respondents reached epic numbers. Food Web sites featured long strings of impassioned opinions from every viewpoint. When CNN's Dr. Sanjay Gupta uploaded a story about it, viewers hit the Internet in droves. Dozens of parents and teachers weighed in, many supporting a ban on cupcakes in schools, others arguing that the idea was ludicrous. Some wrote that they felt the problem wasn't cupcakes at all, but the lack of sound diet and exercise programs constructed by school districts. Most, however, acknowledged that obesity among young children was a serious problem that has not been adequately addressed by health authorities and parents themselves.

New York University nutrition professor Marion Nestle has heard the hysteria from both camps, and she cuts through the noise: "Cupcakes are deal breakers. It sounds like a joke, but it's a very serious problem on a number of levels. You have to control it."

What does Nestle mean by "control it"?

"The operative word is 'occasional,'" she said in an interview.

"Reasonable people might have different opinions as to what that word means, but I'd say several times a day for a cupcake or other sweet treat is not occasional.

"The problem is not qualitative; it's quantitative. Cupcakes are the tip of the iceberg. Parents complain to me that the real problem is that kids get sweets in school multiple times a day—from teachers rewarding them for performance, from classmates having birthdays, from school celebrations, and from similar foods at lunch. I'm not a banning type but I do think there should be some guidance and some policies."

I'd have to side with Nestle on this. Her take is logical and rational, and certainly one that could lead to sensible solutions in every school district. Cupcakes may be at the crux of the issue, but they obfuscate the larger problem of what, when, and how much we feed our kids. I'm pro-cupcake, and I always will be. But it's important that we don't overstuff our children with them, birthday party or not. And I do have some ideas how to appease those on both sides of the cupcake wars without adding unnecessary pounds on our kids.

Hidden below the surface of the debate are a number of specific items that might be useful to discuss. First, there's portion size. Like the bagel we mentioned earlier, the cupcake has gone through an expansion phase over the past several years. This has occurred both in and outside the home kitchen. On one level, bigger baking pans are now encouraging bigger cupcakes baked at home. Cupcakes used to be not much larger than a golf ball. Today, some are the size of softballs. Step inside any gourmet specialty store, and you'll note huge cupcakes with an inch or more of icing. At one Starbucks I noticed that the megacupcake was priced at $2.25, and I've seen them as high as $3.50 at Sprinkles, a high-end bakery in Beverly Hills. I'm not sure if these are making their way into classrooms, but it's certainly a dangerous trend.

The bigger cupcakes produce much heavier calorie content. It's not just at the gourmet bakeries and other specialty outlets. When you visit the supermarket after having a grande latte and are eyeing the megacupcakes, you'd think that the packaged goods manufacturers appear to have maintained a modicum of control over size. You'd be wrong to think this. Most packaged cupcakes run in the neighborhood of 175 to 225 calories; the Hostess Golden Cup Cakes check in at 200 calories. Little Debbie Creme-Filled Chocolate Cupcakes are 200 calories apiece. (Little Debbie is sold primarily in the southern crescent grocery stores, and is usually on display, making them highly visible to prospective purchasers.) They also are very high in fat content. They are popular because they are store-door delivered (rather than going first to a warehouse) and are fresher than other packaged cakes. Specialty cupcakes can run significantly higher. The Coffee Bean & Tea Leaf Pumpkin Cream Cheese Cup Cake is about as bad as a large fast-food burger: it's 531 calories.

If you're shopping for the school birthday party, there are some lower-calorie versions you can choose, such as the Hostess 100 Calorie Cupcake pack. It's encouraging to note that Hostess and Tastykake are doing a better job of managing the fats in their cupcakes (generally less than 30 percent of calories). But some others are not health conscious on any level. Little Debbie's Coffee Bean–flavored cupcake has 43 percent fat calories while Tea Leaf brand totals 66 percent fat calories.

Frosting is, of course, a usual feature of most cupcakes, and this is all about sugar and cooking oils. Most Betty Crocker frostings still contain trans fats (and are loaded with sugar and/or high fructose corn syrup). If Betty Crocker is still laden with trans fats, I'd be very surprised that frostings made from scratch are any better, unless they use Crisco that has been reformulated to have zero trans fats.

Packaged cupcakes are likely used as a snack item compared to the more indulgent cupcakes that skew more toward adults or special occasions. I suspect a number are going into lunch boxes or being sold in convenience stores and vending machines. I'm not sure if there are certain sizes that are used in schools. Probably they vary unless the teachers are asking parents to bring in reasonable-size treats. My guess is that they are not humongous, but also not likely to be consistently low in fat per 100 calories.

Bussel, the food blogger, and I are on the same page here. She specifically mentioned that we shouldn't be serving Crumbs Bake Shop cupcakes (a New York City bakery, whose jumbos cost $3.50 each) to elementary school kids.

"It's an extra-large cupcake with a lot of frosting with candy on top," she said. "I think it's totally ridiculous because you reach a saturation point. It's too much sugar, and it detracts from the enjoyment of it. For the average person, the normal-size cupcake is fine, and even mini-cupcakes for small children. There's a bakery in Los Angeles that does only mini-cupcakes, and there's one in Williamsburg, Brooklyn, that does the same thing. And it's two bites worth of cupcakes, and that's enough."

In reality, cupcakes are something of a victim, the poster child for all that's gone wrong in our attempts to regulate what our children eat when they are at school. The cupcake has become a cause for the shrillest and most unreasonable voices within the food controversy, but instead of creating a useful dialogue, all it does is ratchet up emotions and distract from the real problems that are making our kids the fattest in the world.

The Cupcake Controversy captures everything good and bad about how government can affect what you and your children eat. It demonstrates how government can intervene and potentially restrict what they should or shouldn't be eating. It also highlights government's shortcomings in getting to real solutions for our collective health and obesity problems. School policies cause our children to get stuffed with high-calorie junk food while ever more complicated food pyramids simply confuse the consumer. Trans fats (bad) get banned, causing saturated fats (just as bad) to proliferate. And while Washington ponders its next program, Americans keep getting fatter.

Meanwhile, the cupcake languishes. Once the special treat for that third-grader's birthday party, now the demonized symbol for the fattening of a generation. Will the cupcake survive the obesity wars, or will it suffer the fate of other, less worthy, food casualties?

# 8

# the nanny state versus the restaurant lobby

Rick Berman must have known he'd arrived when CBS *60 Minutes* broadcast a profile of him in April 2007. Morley Safer made sure his viewers knew that Rick was called "Dr. Evil" by his legion of critics, that he was a pit bull for the restaurant and beverage industry's point of view, and perhaps the ultimate libertarian. Berman didn't even wince. He's the guy the food police love to hate. You can't miss him in a crowded room. He's an imposing person, a hefty six foot four, 245 pounds (he happily admits he's overweight), and he has an imposing manner. He drinks at lunch and enjoys his cigars. And with his mostly bald pate, you might think he was the model for the Mr. Clean character.

Berman wears two hats: public relations man at his Washington, D.C.–based firm, Berman & Co., and lobbyist. As a PR guy, he's hired by companies to get positive press, and in this endeavor he has been deft and quite successful. You could say he's the Sultan of Spin. As a lobbyist, he flies a little bit below the radar—and this is what gets his naysayers overly agitated. Berman is the head of a nonprofit group called the Center for Consumer Freedom (CCF), whose charter, according to the Web site, is to defend "the right of adults and parents to choose . . . what they eat and drink, . . . and how they enjoy themselves." The opposition complains it's almost as if Berman wants to reinvent Sodom and Gomorrah, but with better restaurants. His CCF Web site declares that it is "devoted to promoting personal responsibility and protecting consumer choice." The CCF is a tax-exempt 501(c)(3) U.S. nonprofit organization, which allows food companies to make hefty donations to the group without requiring it to disclose the list of its donors.

Through the CCF, Berman attacks the groups that attack the food business for its unhealthy behavior. Financial support for the group has come from such giants as Philip Morris, Cargill Processed Meat Products, Anheuser-Busch, Coca-Cola, Tyson Foods, Perdue Farms, Outback Steakhouse, Wendy's, and White Castle. The list, of course, is not comprehensive, and it obviously changes with the seasons (Berman's firm likes to claim it's inaccurate, but in general, it's close enough). The CCF gives the food companies a way to protect their image, if ever so transparently. Because he draws such a minimal salary from the foundation, it's as if he's giving a pro bono boost to his major clients, past and present, in the food industry.

His opponents claim that he all but extorts donations by telling his clients, "they're going to go down the tubes unless they pay him to fend us off," as one nemesis put it in *USA Today* (July 26, 2006). Berman has taken out full-page ads in newspapers and magazines attacking zealous health groups for what he deems extreme positions on food safety and fat content. When he really wants to go on the offensive, his messages also appear on billboards.

He probably relished the comparison when *BusinessWeek* wondered, "Why shouldn't business have its own Michael Moore?"

But a debate isn't really a debate unless there are two sides, and Berman's principal foe in all this is Michael Jacobson, the head of the Center for Science in the Public Interest (CSPI), perhaps the oldest and most visible watchdog group and advocate for consumer nutrition rights in the United States. As you might suspect, Jacobson is a marked contrast to the restaurant and food-processing advocate. He has a PhD; he looks professorial with his salt-and-pepper hair and studious eyeglasses. Jacobson is trim, fit, and an avowed vegetarian—he won't even touch a cookie, it's been reported—and he won't let his employees go near "bad" foods in the workplace. He apparently backed off his plan to eliminate the office coffee machine when a third of his staff threatened to quit.

In fact, legend has it that the term "junk food," a ubiquitous label to describe everything that begins with Coke and potato chips, originated with Michael Jacobson. It's no surprise to his critics that Jacobson began his career alongside Ralph Nader in the days when the famous consumer advocate was railing about the Ford Pinto and auto safety. Nader was, and still is, a true believer, and he gets our attention. Jacobson is cut from the same mold.

He's the Top Cop of the Food Police. Like Berman, he relishes a good food fight, and he often makes more noise than the FDA, the Federal Trade Commission, and the surgeon general combined. He has no problem with threatening to sue restaurants and food companies. "We used to file all sorts of complaints with the government," he told the *New York Times*. "Sometimes we'd get a response, but usually nothing happened. Now, when we have told companies that we're going to sue them, they show up in our office the next week." And he has been quoted as saying he envisions a day when there are additional taxes on butter, meat, potato chips, whole milk, and cheeses.

In 2006, Jacobson's group sued Kentucky Fried Chicken over the chain's use of trans fat oils in the preparation of their chicken. In a press release he explained why he didn't sue McDonald's instead. KFC's crime was that it was producing a main dish, whereas McDonald's was only guilty of cooking a side dish, french fries.

That same year, Berman's group posted a number of videos on YouTube, one of which was the trailer for the children's movie

*Charlotte's Web*, claiming that the movie "encourages" kids to "say no to bacon."

Looked at casually, Berman and Jacobson can be viewed as caricatures of two extremes, but they both play their roles very seriously and are passionate about their positions. At any given moment, you can listen to their bromides and nod in agreement to a point either of them is selling. Both sides periodically accuse the other of fabricating facts or playing fast and loose with the research conclusions. It's not surprising that they've stood toe-to-toe on food issues. It's good theater. Media producers feel compelled to get both of these guys on camera, sparring with each other and spinning their points of view.

Food is far from immune to the spin that defines so much of our modern discourse, and all this talk makes it incredibly difficult for consumers to hold the food industry and the government accountable in an effective manner. We think that healthy food is all about the choices we make at a grocery store or in a restaurant, but the truth is that much of our conception of what constitutes nutritious or indulgent eating comes from people like Berman and Jacobson. The government may be involved when it comes to mandating labels and advocating intelligent consumption, but when the discourse moves out of legislatures and into the public arena, Berman, Jacobson, and their legions of supporters and detractors take over, making it hard if not impossible to discern what information is actually helpful and what is merely lip service to change. Theirs is talk that makes you fat because it prevents a legitimate dialogue from taking place. Just as the food industry has avoided change and the government has promoted the wrong change, the spin doctors have hijacked the language of change and made it hard to see what we really need in order to eat healthfully.

The nannies want too much change and set lofty benchmarks that are impossible to achieve for any company with a bottom line to feed, while the pro-food advocates spend their time reflecting upon the importance of maintaining the status quo and defending their actions, past and present. Now that the nannies are breaking through, it is finally sinking in to the food industry that some change needs to take place. But this change—this move to healthier food—is not universally recognized.

Food advocates like these two enjoy using the domino theory, a strategy that leads people to worry that pretty soon we'll be banning everything we eat. *Goodness' sakes,* Berman seems to be saying, *one day it's trans fats and foie gras, the next it's some other ingredient that puts warts on rats, and pretty soon, you won't even be able to buy a potato chip!* If you got rid of every food that had "chemicals" in them, Berman seems to say, then we'll have nothing left to eat. And he does have a point. Jacobson figuratively rolls his eyes at these comments and suggests that Berman would be happiest without any government regulation whatsoever. *Oh my, why bother even inspecting beef? So what if we have a few cases of mad cow disease?*

Once you analyze the rhetoric, what's left? It's not simply a choice of A or B. While Berman and Jacobson polarize the food and nutrition crisis with their scorched-earth approaches, they do get the consuming public to begin thinking about some of the important issues. They are vigorously debating problems vital to our ultimate wellness that deserve to be among the top items on our national agenda. The point-counterpoint style of most television news programs guarantees disagreement and maybe even a good shouting match. A little scream fest never hurt a broadcaster's ratings. As Kelly Brownell, founder of the Rudd Center for Food Policy and Obesity at Yale University, said, "When I'm on *Nightline* with the head of the grocery lobby, it is going to be about debate and conflict."

I'm not solely blaming the messenger here, though the messenger should bear some of the responsibility, since the folks who get the most ink are the ones with the most extreme views. Berman and Jacobson are "good copy" when it comes to the food wars, and they know this. Reporters and newscasters also are aware that they are a good first stop for a snappy or startling quote when it comes to any simmering controversy surrounding food or nutrition. Their positions are well known and they're accessible on deadline. Berman would allow almost anything bad on the menu because he believes in personal choice and responsibility. His argument is just say no to the regulators. Jacobson welcomes sanctions that will result in healthier food and would jettison anything remotely harmful, if it were possible.

The entire food chain, from seed to table, is made up of for-profit businesses. Most of the critics on either side have no real food-industry experience. As such, none of the talking heads on this matter can really appreciate what business executives must deal with. As operators of their own nonprofit organizations, perhaps health activists can't really appreciate what a for-profit business has to go through on a day-to-day basis. They don't have a feel for managing to the bottom line and the responsibility of keeping tens of thousands of workers employed. They have never felt the heat of Wall Street pressure to exceed quarterly profit promises.

The back-and-forth arguments make great theater, but the extremes don't offer practical solutions. Low fat, low cholesterol, low carb, low sodium—over the last fifty years we've heard every passing idea about what kind of intake reduction will make us healthier. We've seen almost every food demon attacked at least once if not twice, and yet in spite of all this "knowledge" we find ourselves more overweight than at any other time in history. Perhaps it's the data, not the food, that's to blame. In a half century, the two sides have grown to give us more info than ever about our food, and that hasn't made us any healthier. Clearly something is wrong with the information.

A big part of the problem here is that it's not just the libertarians and the food police who are in disagreement; even scientists can spin the truth and sometimes unwittingly create consumer panic. They often caution that one study doesn't make for policy, but as soon as their findings are all over the Internet, it's too late for them to issue caution signals. Look at what happened over the appearance of acrylamide, a potentially harmful chemical that has been under scrutiny for the past few years. For some time, we've been consuming acrylamide in french fries and potato chips, but it hasn't been an issue until recent scientific studies suggested it might be a problem. Swedish government scientists first disclosed findings that a possible carcinogen from acrylamide is formed at exceptionally high levels in fried and baked starchy foods. These results were then replicated and confirmed by other health agencies here and in several other nations. Notice I used the phrases "potentially harmful" and "possible carcinogen." Now, in the hands of the spin doctors, it's become an immediate and volatile battleground.

Acrylamide is known to cause cancer and birth defects in lab rats and mice. That's all we know so far. Reasonable people can question the leap from this to humans, of course, and while we should be cautious and aware of the possible problem, we should be careful before we sound an alarm. It's certainly important to conduct further research studies to determine just how dangerous the chemical is in humans, and in what quantities. (In 2005 the state attorney general of California sued eight major food companies in the hopes of getting them to label certain products as potentially causing cancer—acrylamides were the impetus for the litigation. While this was a huge legal stretch—the suit was based on a 1986 state law requiring companies to label products with warnings if they contain known carcinogens—it quickly heightened the debate about nutrition labeling.)

"The food in which it is most abundant is french fries, sorry to say," noted Jacobson in a CNN interview, adding that his CSPI group is "recommending that people reduce their consumption of french fries." (Nothing wrong with that idea, but for reasons other than acrylamides.)

Berman took the immediate offensive by claiming spinach will also cause acrylamides to form. Why was Jacobson singling out fast foods? Why not tell people to eat reduced amounts of other fried healthy foods with acrylamides? "I don't think Michael is going to go after 'Spinach Amalgamated,'" Berman said. (Then again, how many prepare spinach fried in a cooking oil?)

Sometimes the science itself is not unbiased. There's an increasing amount of research being done into food and ingredients and what they do to us. Some of it is funded by the food industry, and some of it is funded by taxpayers' dollars. When it's funded by the industry, there's a double-edged sword. A company can quietly fund a study, and if it doesn't like the results, it can bury them. On the other hand, even if the results are legitimate, they're questioned. This is unfortunate, because industry has the ability to fund many necessary studies to improve our lot nutritionally.

One way to deal with this cumbersome issue is to convene a panel of experts with no links to the funding company. With the support of the Unilever Food & Health Research Institute in The Netherlands (Unilever owns Lipton Tea), a panel of health and nutrition experts was convened and published a "Beverage Guidance System" in 2006, in hopes of getting people to stop drinking their calories when those calories contribute little or nothing to their health, and may actually detract from it. That panel was led by Dr. Barry Popkin, a professor of nutrition at the University of North Carolina in Chapel Hill, and a widely quoted scholar in the field, a researcher with a stellar reputation worldwide. Under disclosure, it was revealed that "Unilever had no power to influence or veto panel decisions and did not attempt to make changes."

But this hands-off honesty remains the exception in nutrition studies. As the food and nutrition debate gathers more momentum, it will be harder for all of us to recognize what's real and what's imagined and what both sides want us to believe. There will continue to be a gap between the facts and the "truth," though we can hope that it narrows before it widens. We're all impressionable, and it's difficult to step outside of our emotional selves and remain somewhat objective when it comes to scientific findings in regard to food studies.

When we read a food-warning article in *USA Today* or in a service magazine in an airport lounge, we should ask ourselves the following questions (but rarely ever do): Was it just a single research event? Who funded it? How many people participated, and how in-depth was the study? Were the results reliable, and more important, repeatable by other scientists? And the most critical question: How much further research is necessary before we can draw a definitive conclusion?

One problem revolves precisely around this last question. I'm wondering how we ever have a definitive conclusion in *anything* in the research regarding health and nutrition. We are creatures of an absolute nature and tend to divide the world of eating into black and white. We want to know: This is good for you; that is bad for you. I'm just as guilty of this neurosis as anyone else. But even good science is fuzzier than we want to believe. Let me give you a couple of examples. The health community has weighed in on trans fats in a conclusive manner. Basically, all trans fats are bad because they raise the bad (LDL) cholesterol and lower the good (HDL) cholesterol. Medical experts agree that no amount is good for you, and you're reminded of this every time your doctor orders your blood work. So we're starting to ban trans fats.

Among the frying oils fast replacing them is what's known as interesterified (IE) oils. While devoid of trans fats, these new oils may help create a new demon. Recent research by K. C. Hayes, the noted expert on fats at Brandeis University, reported in *Nutrition and Metabolism*, a science journal, that IE oils resulted in elevated fasting glucose levels and reduced insulin values compared with naturally structured fats. In fact, according to his research, they were even worse than the partially hydrogenated (high–trans fat) oils they replaced. As more cities pass laws and restaurants convert to these new types of oils, consumers may be at risk for higher rates of diabetes.

Does it make sense to "reduce" heart disease and "increase"

diabetes—if that's indeed the trade-off? The short answer is, *we don't know.* More work has to be done.

But even that might not get the answers to help us make informed decisions.

Reductive science has its limitations and always will. The story of twentieth-century food is a story of continually updating and refining what we believed was necessary for a healthy and happy life. All of which serves to obscure the simple truth that even to this day we really don't know what's going on in our bodies when we eat. On any given day we have a lot of very good, highly educated guesses, but the definitive truth on many of these issues remains elusive.

Michael Pollan made this point quite well in a seminal 2007 essay in the *New York Times Magazine* entitled "Unhappy Meals." In the piece, Pollan wrote about a scientist named William Prout who had been doing food research, saying, "When William Prout isolated the big three macronutrients, scientists figured they now understood food and what the body needs from it; when the vitamins were isolated a few decades later, scientists thought, O.K., *now* we really understand food and what the body needs to be healthy; today, it's the polyphenols and carotenoids that seem all important. But who knows what the hell else is going on deep in the soul of a carrot?"

Man has always consumed food in one form or another, but it's only been in the last half century that we're really beginning to understand what's in it, and what it does to us. And at the same time we're growing it differently and altering it in many ways, and feeding many millions more people. It takes a lot of deep thought (and subsequent testing) to conclude whether the risks are outweighed by the benefits of any food. We appear to know a lot about nutrition, but in the grand scheme of man's existence we actually know very little. Food is part of our evolutionary development, and its effect on our bodies appears to be in constant flux, especially as our own life span increases. But that doesn't stop the talking heads and by extension the scientists from speaking in clear-cut absolutes that contradict one another and make it hard to pick out the right selection of products when we get to the grocery store.

Consider this: Researchers have discovered that people who live in countries where high-starch diets are common produce a greater quantity of the enzyme that converts starch to simple sugars like glucose. The explanation appears to be evolutionary, according to the journal *Nature Genetics*. The authors of the study said those in the population with the extra copies of the enzyme seem to have been favored by "natural selection." So our bodies metabolize food in different ways, scientists seem to be hypothesizing. And some of this probably occurs because of mere chance, and not necessarily what our mothers fed us when we were babies.

Scientists are also putting in late hours in the labs wondering if violent behavior is somehow connected with poor nutrition. They're looking into whether a diet rich in fatty acids found in seafood and vitamins will have an effect on prison populations. When a story about this appeared in the *New York Times Magazine*, the headline asked, "Does Salmon Lower the Murder Rate?" Catchy, creative work by the editor, but certainly nothing we can yet take too seriously.

In the summer of 2007, the *New England Journal of Medicine*, the august magazine revered by most doctors, reported that "social networking" might have more to do with weight gain than your genetic makeup. A respected scientist at Harvard Medical School headed the research team, so there was no surprise when the story spread quickly to the mainstream press. By the time it reached the *Wall Street Journal*, the headline read, "Can Your Friends Make You Fat?" It's hard to fathom the implications of such a suggestion, isn't it? And the skeptic in me wonders, "Do heavy people tend to simply be more apt to adopt a social network with other heavy people?" How do we really know what is the cause, and what is the effect?

It's no wonder that our brains, let alone our digestive systems, seem totally confused, and all the while we continue to gain weight. Almost all food is a complex construct, and it will take a lot of hard lab work in the future to understand precisely how it affects what goes on inside our bodies.

Nevertheless, these are the kinds of stories that send us to the supermarket with a different mind-set, and make us susceptible to the current fads promoted in food advertising. The food manufacturers play on these weaknesses and our willingness to jump on the latest magic elixirs in the aisles without giving much thought to whether or not they'll really make a difference. This glut of information makes it hard to know what really is healthy, which brings up an awkward reality: What's healthy might not cause you to lose weight, so it benefits the culture and industry of dieting to keep selling the idea of an attainable weight.

When it comes to diets and food, we're a nation of lemmings. We engulf every trend, no matter how ridiculous it sounds or potentially harmful it may be. Why? When you've tried everything and failed, you continue to search for the Holy Grail. Every year, the dizzying number of diet books competes with the cookbooks in the bookstore chains. When Atkins was all the rage, you couldn't walk down a supermarket aisle without the phrase "No Carbs" boldly displayed on dozens of labels. Low-fat or no-fat stickers (on items that never had any carbs or fat to begin with) became ubiquitous. And there were those labels that promised one-third fewer calories, though they left the consumer to ponder what one-third fewer actually meant. (We are still arguing over the proper size of a "serving." Does it distinguish between a 102-pound ballerina and a 260-pound linebacker?) Certainly, much of it was hype or close to downright bogus. But the food industry could at least say it was trying. When pressed, the typical response is, "We're offering the consumer choices." Or, the health issue is squarely a matter of "personal responsibility."

Ultimately the diets become just a part of the background noise that makes it difficult for most Americans to discern what's really going to be healthy for them, equating weight loss with healthy eating. For years the industry has capitalized on these conflicting messages, alternating between embracing and condemning findings, studies, and trends, as it seems to fit their needs. It's a vicious cycle that constantly repeats itself. First, we'll see a pronouncement about a food or ingredient—it's either good or bad for us. Second, we'll get the spin. The advocates line up on either side, and then there's the consumer reaction. When consumer reaction reaches a critical mass, the food companies then step in and fill the emerging demand. Then, the existing products are modified or repositioned, or new ones introduced, to take advantage of this phenomenon. The result is: increased revenues, higher profits, and more fat people. This pattern keeps repeating itself. Everyone wins in this model except the consumers who don't really know whom to listen to.

What makes this issue even harder for Americans to dissect is the fact that there are plenty of company tie-ins with diet plans. Kraft has taken advantage by offering foods allied by with the famed South Beach Diet. Jenny Craig, a diet plan well known throughout the United States, has been acquired by food giant Nestlé. Disney discovered the danger of these tie-ins when they encountered a backlash from coupling their children's films with McDonald's Happy Meals. When criticized for the move, Disney wisely backed away. None of these relationships, in and of itself, is a completely doomed idea. Weight Watchers is highly respected among nutritionists and dieticians, and they have branded products. But the philosophy behind this program is more about portion control—how *much* you should eat—rather than *what* you should eat. Again, none of the marketers who concocted the alliances thought they were doing any harm. Still they create consumer confusion when it comes to nutrition. People rightfully wonder, is this product part of the "plan," or is really just a prompt to ensure that I'm buying the preferred products of a food firm with a vested interest in selling them? In short, is this approach about our health or about our money?

Despite my effort to be reasonable and somewhat objective about this, I'm not about to let the food companies and the fast-food restaurants get away with their standard excuses: "We offer plenty of healthy options" and "It's about consumer choice." This is an attempt to duck responsibility (denounced by Berman) and rationalizes the industry position rather than doing something proactive.

Of course, the more ubiquitous a product, the harder the healthy choice is to make, no matter what the health concerns. I spent much of my career perfecting the art of persuasion. Could I be called a spinmeister myself? Looking back, it would be difficult to wriggle out of the accusation.

For example, my experience with the soft drink giant Coca-Cola leaves me with mixed feelings. In the early 1980s, I served as the group brand manager for the company's U.S. division. I had a coveted corner office in the old Coke building in Atlanta, and I had a bird's-eye view of Georgia Tech and the company's new headquarters, then under construction. I didn't have much time to reflect on the future of the famous script logo with the red background and its contoured bottle, a trademark embedded in the minds of consumers all over the planet. I was too busy figuring out how to advertise and market my cola brands.

So yes, I suppose I was a spinmeister, albeit not to the shameful levels of others who weigh in on this issue. After all, I never claimed to be unbiased; I was working for the largest beverage marketer in the world. A large part of my strategy was to market the new soft drink, Diet Coke, that used NutraSweet. When CBS did an exposé on the potential harm of NutraSweet, I wrote a memo explaining to my vice president that it wasn't a big issue in terms of marketing and advertising. We'd stay the course—it's all about the "taste"—unless the CBS story snowballed. It never did (later research proved the safety concerns to be unfounded). Diet

Coke was certainly a healthier drink weight-wise than Coke—it has only one calorie—but my motivation, and the company's in general, was just to sell more bottles. America was at the predawn of health consciousness, so we gave it little attention. Was I, in fact, doing reverse spin? Was I actually trying to do media control on my own bosses?

As I recall that era two decades ago, the marketing mandate was defined by a single word, "ubiquity." Our goal was to make Coca-Cola ubiquitous. At all times, at all places, even in the Amazon forest (though this was technically not in my territory). It was the Real Thing. Coke was It. My job was to keep this logo in your face, and present it in the most positive light. And I had access to a huge war chest with which to accomplish this: a $250 million annual marketing and advertising budget. As you might imagine, this wielded a considerable amount of influence in the supermarkets of America. The nutrition-minded corps of activists could not compete with us. As nutrition expert Barry Popkin put it: "If I got a dollar that Coke spent on advertising to spend on fair trade advertising, then I would be able to level the consumer playing field. It's no different from tobacco in that sense."

What did worry me back then? What kept me up at night? My flagship brand's image. Image is that total satisfaction index that consumers have when they're asked about your product. It not only should taste good, and be refreshing, but it should make you *feel* good. In my notes, I wrote about Coke's image: "Overall declines continue, relative to Pepsi, particularly among males and females under twenty."

Uh-oh. Teenagers were drifting to Pepsi, a somewhat "younger" sounding brand. I remember doing a tie-in with an au courant rock group, Duran Duran, to help stave off this trend. Among teens at the time, Coke was slowly being viewed as "your father's" brand of soft drink.

The Coke of today is more aware of the health and nutrition movement and, subsequently, consumer backlash. Last year I attended a meeting of high-level marketing executives who were intent on finding out where the company stood in the public's consciousness. Keep in mind that this is a company that can afford focus groups and market research at any price. But on this morning in Atlanta, the eight or so executives and marketing gurus were interested in what a couple of outside experts were thinking. One was a prominent public health care researcher.

We were in a twenty-sixth-floor conference room—leather chairs, wood-paneled walls, a spiral staircase connecting floors; elegant but not too plush or ostentatious by any corporate standard. Also in the group was a Coke guy from Washington, D.C., who was a government affairs liaison. One executive had to admit, "We feel like we have a target at our back." This didn't surprise me. Soccer moms were revolting every time they read another story about obesity among their kids. In fact, right around this time, the Center for Science in the Public Interest (CSPI), along with other advocacy groups, spearheaded a new campaign to "dump soda" on a worldwide basis. The initiative was directly aimed at Pepsi and Coca-Cola, and the five-pronged attack included banning sodas in schools and taxing sugared beverages. The group of Coke executives had to be thinking about this.

It didn't take long for one of them to ask the crucial question of the public health expert, "What's our image like among your peers?"

"Not too good" was his response.

The Coke execs probed a bit deeper. They wanted to understand this groundswell of concern among the growing flock of health-conscious consumers. The researcher brought up their new product, Enviga, by way of example. Enviga is a carbonated green tea with antioxidants, a joint venture of Coke and Nestlé, the world's largest food company. At the end of 2006, it was being test-marketed in Philadelphia and New York as a "functional food" that burned more calories than the user consumed. The health marketing claims were a little too bold, complained the researcher.

He didn't even have to mention that when Michael Jacobson saw the claims, the Center for Science in the Public Interest went, well, sort of ballistic. A Coca-Cola corporate press release suggested that drinking three cans of Enviga would burn between 60 and 100 calories. Coke and Nestlé funded the short-term studies that were the basis of this claim.

Jacobson, the arrows in his quiver at the ready, said in a December 2006 press release, "It's ironic that Coke, a company that has been a major promoter of weight gain, is now pretending that it is coming to the rescue of overweight people. They should have called this drink 'Fleece,' since that's what they're trying to do to consumers. Plain old tap water has zero calories, five calories fewer than Enviga, but unlike Enviga, tap water doesn't cost 15 bucks a gallon." Note the anticapitalist spin here. Even when Coke tries a little bit, they're vilified for being in business.

The health expert at Coke headquarters that morning was far more diplomatic and polite, I should add, but he made his point. After lunch, I left with a number of brochures that Coke had prepared to trumpet its move toward more healthy beverages. They sell 1.3 billion drinks a *day* in 200 countries around the globe. One brochure said, "We are dedicated to listening to consumers, understanding their health and nutrition concerns, and addressing their needs through the beverages we make and the ways we market them."

Coca-Cola is a different company today than it was during my tenure. When I worked there, two-thirds of the product line came from sugared beverages. Today, this is down to half of the portfolio. And they continue to acquire brands with healthy pedigrees, such as Vitamin Water and Honest Tea. While they are making progress in the right direction, they, like so many food companies, are still the beneficiaries of consumer confusion.

As visible a company as Coca-Cola is, it generally finds itself dealing with all kinds of publicity issues. Spin works both ways for Coke. As a marketer, it presents its brands in the most positive light it can. Nevertheless, it is going to continue to be the frequent recipient of some harsh press, some of which might be unjustified. But that's the way it's going to be for the food industry until obesity trends turn around.

The doctrinaire positions on either side will never accommodate the majority. We're mired in a media blitz of sensational headlines that in the end helps none of us come up with sensible approaches to a difficult problem. The block-and-parry politics of these interest groups can't move this nation, so we just keep getting fat without any real progress. Nutrition isn't easy. If it were, there wouldn't be any need for intelligent discourse. Again, nobody wants to see a fat America continuing into the future, but if we can't rise above the din, we'll never be able to hear the collection of reasonable voices with real solutions that have been drowned out for the last fifty years.

# 9

# the consumer conundrum

It is late May, a windy Midwest spring day, and I'm standing in the middle of McCormick Place in Chicago at the National Restaurant Show, as I've done many times over the past thirty years or so. It is one of the biggest trade conventions in the United States, and the hangar-size booth and exhibition space, covering 600,000 square feet, is daunting in its scope.

This show is sponsored by the other NRA, the National Restaurant Association, and it is a four-day food and cocktail party—if it's not the world's longest it is certainly one of the world's largest. Some 74,000 people in the food business cruise the aisles and get free tastes from the 2,100 companies that feature their wares. It's one serious finger food fest. Up and down every aisle, you see fair-goers holding little plastic plates and cups. In every booth there's somebody beckoning you to drink their concoctions and eat their hors d'oeuvres.

Spareribs, Asian noodles, pizza, meatballs, chicken wings, tacos, wraps, tortes, tarts, cakes, gelato, popcorn, every kind of bottled water imaginable, every kind of coffee imaginable, hot dogs large and small, pork rolls, scallops, shrimp, french fries, crackers, dips, sauces, olives, cheeses from everywhere, aisle after aisle of nibbles. Cinnamon pretzels, cream-cheese pretzels, jalapeño-cheese pretzels, and, if you search hard enough, even the classic hot pretzel. One or two aisles alone are enough to stuff you for a week.

Soft drinks, weird drinks (Clamato blended with Budweiser, chili powder, hot sauce, and salt), and, yes, the hard stuff. Experienced conventioneers know that you must be especially careful when you cruise the sake and vodka lanes before noon. And once your taste buds start responding, you no longer pay much attention to the featured entertainment: the ice-carving classic, celebrity chef cook-offs, or even the keynote speaker, who in 2007 happened to be actor-turned-senator and onetime Republican presidential candidate Fred Thompson.

The show space is dominated by large companies with mega-displays; Coca-Cola, Pepsi, Archer Daniels Midland, ConAgra, Nestlé, Tyson Foods. Mostly, these companies are pushing their core products. This year there is a mild effort to appease the health interests with the move to safer cooking oils. Tyson's booth, for example, has a large sign with "zero grams trans fat."

"No artificial ingredients"
"100% all natural"
"No added hormones or steroids"
"Enhanced Flavor Technology—EFT"

ConAgra urges us to "Take the Wesson Challenge! Trans Fat Free Frying Oil—How Does Your Oil Stack Up?"

These cooking oil displays are a good thing, I'm certain. And I'd like to believe that they signal some kind of trend toward positive change and healthier products from the food industry, but it's probably wishful thinking. As one reporter put it on the *Chicago Tribune*'s Web site (Chicagotribune.com, Monica Eng, June 1, 2008), "Even when some new high quality fruit drinks packed with antioxidants are being offered, people will still stand in a long line for a cup of Pepsi. If you offer free hot dogs and fried chicken, they will come." The lines for the pomegranate juice are short.

Some of the conventioneers looked like they had never stopped eating, with the midsections to prove it. At the NRA show, I realized it's impossible to avoid food cues. We're all subject to the weight—forgive the pun—of the industry's massive marketing and advertising muscle, and our own inability to resist these temptations.

It certainly doesn't surprise me that the restaurant industry has made only a feeble effort to help us eat better. Consumer response to the restaurant industry's initial attempts at selling "health" on the food menus has been fickle. Many of us just don't want to be reminded of calories, sodium, and fat content when we're out to eat. Nobody wants to be on a diet on his or her birthday or anniversary. Let's face it, so much of eating out is the "experience," or, as the restaurant industry likes to say, it's about "hospitality."

At one time or another, most of us have been indiscriminant eaters, and we shouldn't be ashamed to admit it. It's natural. I'm certainly one of those folks. I confess to eating too many richly prepared feasts, and consuming more than was prudent on some occasions. I'm not a saint. I like good food and eating in nice restaurants as much as everyone else with the resources to do it. I exercise sporadically, but not as much as I should. I know most of you feel the same way. Even ten minutes a day could make a difference; twenty to thirty minutes is ideal. You know that, too. But it's hard to do something that isn't fun, even though *you know* it's good for you.

The reality is that consumers say they want healthy foods, but what they say and do are two different things. We're just talking the walk. The food industry is merely reflective of our hypocritical views on food.

And nowhere is this hypocrisy on greater display than the NRA show. While the show focuses on restaurants, it is an industry-wide event, one that displays the full breadth of manpower and machinery behind the food that has made America fat. It is perhaps the clearest demonstration of the vast array of forces that all converge in our stomachs and convince us to consume the good, the bad, and the even worse. The efforts of the group gathered here have made denial and self-control with the knife and fork tougher every day. It's been their job to do so because it's how they've learned to make money. As such, the food looks better, smells better, tastes better, and it's harder to resist than ever before. If there is one theme to this convention it's choice—every kind of culinary choice imaginable, all hidden behind a curtain of industry lingo, smooth marketing, and grandiose salesmanship.

The food companies say the onus is on the consumer. They say it's up to the individual. But to place blame so squarely on the customer is to overlook the forces that have been pushing the food industry forward for the last half century, the forces that I've been writing about since page one of this book. You can't make more fattening food, sell it in bigger packages, and then tell people not to eat too much. This is not logical. It collides with my convictions about human behavior, based on the research I've done and reviewed.

The conventional wisdom among the food industry, activists, and government is that we consumers should act in a rational, disciplined manner. If something's bad for me, I'm obliged to say no. If it's good for me, then it's okay. But life doesn't work this way, as witnessed by our increased belt sizes. Every January, millions resolve to eat healthier and take better care of themselves. Diet books abound. New exercise programs proliferate. So we get off our couches and give it a shot. But a funny thing happens on the way to the (Fat) Forum. We don't stick with it. In fact, less than four out of a hundred of those who start a diet ultimately keep it up.

Despite the public consciousness about "dieting," research shows that for all but a few of us it's an exercise in futility. Scientists say that it's difficult to complete a rigorous controlled study on how effective any particular diet is because so many participants drop out. Statistics are scant because there are so few reliable studies. One such 2004 effort, however, conducted by the Weight and Eating Disorders program at the University of Pennsylvania and funded by the National Institutes of Health, looked at nine different commercially available programs with 1,500 participants. The results revealed that as many as *half* the dieters quit within months of starting a program. (Only the Weight Watchers regimen, which is more of an integrated food and lifestyle program, appeared to be acceptable to the researchers.)

Dieting is easy to pledge, tough to do.

Why? Because it's hard and you have to think about it—all day long. Who wants to do this? A typical diet plan requires you to eat a certain amount of calories, fats, carbohydrates, or protein. Okay, but then out comes the thirty-day diet planner that specifies what you can eat for breakfast, lunch, dinner, and snacks. Ouch!

So by the time the "Male Potato Type" hits day three of his Perfect Weight diet and is told to eat a breakfast (preferably at 7:30 a.m.) of kefir, extra-virgin coconut oil, raw honey, and goat's milk protein powder, the shades are on the way down. Turn off the lights, the party's over.

The problem is, most consumers glaze over when confronted with these intractable, unbendable programs. Not only is the dieter challenged with eating new and often less-tasty foods, but he is also being asked to spend a significant amount of time purchasing and preparing such wonders.

The way these diet and weight management programs are designed, it's no wonder we fail. Fitness maven Jack LaLanne is still fit as an active nonagenarian, but that's because he maniacally exercises every day and hasn't had a scoop of ice cream in probably half a century. He is our poster child for this kind of person. If everyone were like Jack LaLanne or the Navy SEALs, there would be no need for diet books, or even *this* book. Everyone would manage what he or she eats and be in total control.

To be successful over the long term, perhaps the hardest thing is to limit one's intake as a lifestyle decision—which is what good doctors and nutritionists recommend. "Delayed gratification" is how one cardiologist (Garr's heart doctor) puts it. The problem is that it's not delayed gratification, it's *no* gratification. Ever.

A few years ago, there was a spate of news reports about how extreme low-calorie diets were an antidote to premature aging and the onset of life-ending diseases. Aging, happily rail thin senior citizens who swore off comfort food with a Spartan-like resolve were trotted out on newscasts. But while studies proved that several animal species benefited from heavily restricted caloric diets, there was little or no conclusive evidence that it did the same thing for *Homo sapiens.* Evolutionary biologists were quite certain in their analyses that what would help rats and spiders live longer would not necessarily help us. Exceptions? Certainly. Athletes, soldiers, and the few very disciplined creatures of exercise habit. Most of us do not live these kinds of lives, nor do we exhibit the kind of willpower to stick with this kind of discipline.

On the other hand, the notorious documentary filmmaker Morgan Spurlock did just the opposite to prove a point. Who could ever forget him? In his movie *Super Size Me*, he ate nothing but McDonald's three times a day for thirty days, just to make the statement that the hamburger chain provided unhealthy food. Halfway through his stunt, doctors became alarmed at his high blood pressure and cholesterol levels and urged him to stop. Did we really need to have someone prove that if you ate 5,000 calories of that stuff every day, it will eventually kill you? (During the filming, he suffered from depression and liver dysfunction.) Spurlock's message was delivered ten minutes into the film. In the end, it was nothing more than an odd but predictable piece of performance art. Perhaps entertaining, and certainly funny at times, it did nothing for public service other than arouse the opposition (not to mention also providing a huge career boost for Spurlock).

Most of us live and eat in that vast gap between Jack LaLanne's lifelong commitment to health and Morgan Spurlock's strange monthlong experiment.

Why? We like food. We like to eat out. We want things to be convenient. It doesn't matter whether we're eating low-priced junk food—Little Debbie's range of treats—or gourmet meals at Le Bernardin. It's the same issue whether you're at McDonald's or a four-star destination restaurant. It's become chic in fashionable circles to be a "foodie." Let's grab our *Zagat* or *Michelin* and go to Italy and eat our way through Tuscany. Then, let's hit the South of France and eat our way through Provence. Look at how upscale the nation's newspapers have become on Wednesday—traditionally "food day" at the supermarket. Spaghetti Day has become Pasta Day. Before cable TV, the concept of a slew of television cooking shows was unimaginable (except for a handful of marquee chefs like Julia Child). What hath Julia wrought? Now we have celebrity chefs and regularly scheduled competitive cook-offs. Flip through TV channels and someone's chopping in the kitchen at any time of the day or night.

How can you reasonably be expected to watch your weight with all these external food cues?

If, under normal circumstances, consumers are challenged to eat well or stick with their diet plan, what do you think happens when they collide with Weapons of Mass Consumption (WMCs) offered by many food, beverage, and restaurant corporations? What happens when they look a Monster Thickburger or super-size soda in the eye? It's not a pretty sight. Only the most Jack LaLanne–ish among us are fully equipped to either say no or to just eat the right size portions every time.

So when industry plays the guilt card and proclaims that the consumer must make his own responsible eating decisions, it does not take into account that when confronted with mass quantities of nonnutritious food sold at value prices, a large portion of the populace will have trouble saying no even if they want to.

It is this dynamic that I believe lies at the core of the obesity crisis: *Too much high-calorie food that's marketed too effectively to too many who can't resist.*

And therein lies the consumer conundrum: though we desire to be healthy, the current system as we know it has made it impossible for most people to eat well. The ways marketers market, government governs, spin is spun, and consumers consume all contribute to our dilemma.

So although I would love for all consumers to step up and Be Like Jack, the reality is that it won't happen any time soon. Most can't, and that's the problem. The only solutions to solve the national obesity crisis have required consumers to change their behavior and habits. This is extremely difficult to do as illustrated by the diet plan failures. And even if an honest attempt were made to change, the typical American lifestyle with all its time pressures and stresses intervenes.

Over the years my research and observations have confirmed that there are different ways people approach eating. Some make more decisive choices about what they eat. They know what they want, have a clear understanding of what foods are good (and not so good) for them, then manage themselves and their families to eat properly. Again, Jack LaLanne is your poster child for this kind of person. These folks are clearly in the minority.

Most of us do not approach food in this manner. Even those with the best of intentions or a good appreciation of which foods are nutritious are challenged to pass on an overstuffed plate. The food and marketing cues are too powerful to overcome and the majority succumb. We adapt to the situation instead of sticking with food we know is better for us. That's why Morgan Spurlock's story struck a nerve. It wasn't just about eating fast food 24/7, it was that we saw a part of ourselves playing a role that was familiar. This fundamental inability to stand firm makes eating right that much more difficult.

This behavior set shows up when trying to lose weight. Diet plans are not adaptable. Each plan brings its own "my way or the highway" set of rules. Follow this or else. Only someone who is more "locked and loaded" can be successful on these diets.

The same holds for everyday food situations. If we have trouble saying no, then we order as much as our friends do, get the dessert even if we're full, or just let the kids pick out whatever they want instead of continually mud-wrestling with them. You can see how easy it is for us not to control what we or our families eat.

With this mind-set, we're prone to become "serial overeaters." Understanding this mind-set provides the missing link in uncovering the reason why all previous solutions have failed. Every approach, every fix has had noble intentions but cannot overcome our inclination to give in to what's on the menu or on sale at the grocery store. All the diet books, newsletters, blogs, weight-loss commercials, appetite-suppressant drugs, decrees from the surgeon general, and government nutrition mandates have failed to change this mind-set. This is the reason the problem hasn't been solved.

We've been asking the consumer to change, and it's never going to happen. People have been lectured and hectored, pilloried to the Stairmasters, but to no avail. They're hard-wired for dietary failure; they just can't say no to the wrong foods. So why should we expect things to turn out differently?

Our society is a leftover of an outdated food model that no longer serves us well.

When I was a boy, we spent our afternoons at the playground, came home exhausted, and ate whatever mom cooked. It's different today. We're living in a sedentary culture where suburban teenagers drive three blocks to the movies, rather than ride a bike or walk. Computer and video games like World of War Craft and Grand Theft Auto mesmerize them. They exercise their thumbs and little else. Snacks and game controllers seem to be an inseparable pairing, from urban apartments to suburban basements. More and more, kids continue to avoid exercise and do the kinds of things that cause unwelcome weight gain. Physical education requirements have been slashed across the nation's schools, largely because of budget cuts.

I know that the battle with your kids is just one front in the struggle. The battle that you have with yourself over what to buy, what to eat, and how to stay healthy is even more difficult.

I am reminded of all this just by walking the aisles of the NRA show.

I could blame the obesity crisis on lax parents, ignorant school boards who cut vending machine deals with overzealous soda sellers, Washington lobbyists, high-pressure advertising, government ineptitude, or desperate CEOs in the food business.

Because it's really everyone's fault. There isn't enough *shared* responsibility. We are all complicit in this drama. If you're looking to point a finger, the finger goes *everywhere*. Me, you, the activists, the spin doctors, the government, the packaged goods marketers, restaurant chain operators, and the supermarket merchandisers.

Although the responsibility for this problem lies on everyone's respective doorsteps, in the end, every workable solution leads to one place: the corner offices of the food industry's power brokers. The food industry can offer healthier and safer products, and still make a comfortable profit. I know because I've seen the figures. Will it be more expensive? Perhaps in some cases, yes. But not always. It will be affordable more often than not. And because we are a nation of fat people who are already taxing the health care infrastructure, we have no choice but to make massive changes in the way we manufacture, market, and sell food. The food companies must think about investing in the future of their customers.

While it might appear that all these companies are touting healthy products and alternatives, what is there to make us think that these will have any more of an impact now than last year or the year before that? This isn't an issue that will be solved by one or two products. We need to look at the entire spectrum of restaurants and packaged goods companies to see what it will take for them to really make fundamental changes.

Let's think about those restaurant opesrators. We can't expect the restaurant guys to lead the charge. They're all about defending the castle and resisting change. However, if we can show them how improving their products and practices can also make their operating model more efficient and profitable, they will listen. Don't expect any altruism; if we can demonstrate that adopting a healthier direction can increase store traffic or improve food profits or bring back their customer more often, they will go along.

On the other hand, the consumer packaged goods companies like General Mills are closer to their consumers and watch consumer trends intently. They take a longer view. They are more likely to be receptive to marketing healthier products as they anticipate the surge of demand for such items. But don't expect them to abandon their cash cows, even if they're not as good for you. We just have to show them, as with restaurants, how to change and still earn decent profits.

There are a number of things both the restaurants and the packaged goods companies can do right now. One of the first changes they can make is to alter their mind-sets. Food purveyors must absorb the notion that without a future customer, there is no future for them.

One of the first tenets of marketing—any kind of marketing—is that once you secure a customer, you want them coming back as long and as frequently as possible. This is called a repeat purchaser. While this holds true across the food industry, it is a particularly vehement mantra for the fast-food guys. Their stunning growth over the last three decades is a testament to the fact that they know how to sell burgers and fried chicken and instill loyalty in their customer bases.

In the long term, this strength will also prove to be a weakness, however, as people come to attribute a generation of weight gain, obesity, and the ensuing health risks to these companies. What the food industry does not yet realize is that by continuing on the current path of selling high-calorie, high-fat products, it will be slowly, unintentionally killing its best customers. The current propensity toward national gluttony will eventually catch up to the food companies. It's up to the food sellers to solve the health crisis, not because they're totally to blame, but because they are our last best hope. They alone can make the difference, and it's in their own interests. Rather than resist change, the food sellers have to embrace it. Otherwise, they're going to run the risk of being vilified in the same way another industry was that also killed their customers. (Yes, I do mean the tobacco industry.)

What may have begun as a moral imperative will soon become a financial one as well. If altruism doesn't work for them, survival will. This more than anything else should help us see that food companies lie at the heart of the solution to our health crisis. There will be public pressure for better, healthier products, and those companies that are slow or recalcitrant to provide them will be put under financial pressure. They will perform or perish. So they'll end up doing the right thing because it's required, and not because a group of right-thinking executives sat around a boardroom and asked, "What can we do to ensure that our customers live long enough to return to the checkout counter?"

Here's an example of what I mean:

The auto industry has successfully built much safer cars, prodded somewhat by government fiat. A generation ago, there were only seat belts in cars—air bags and antilock brake systems were expensive "options" that few people were willing to pay extra for. Today, those features are commonplace in almost every vehicle sold in the United States. They're simply priced into the cost of the car. We don't think twice about it. We demand it. Would you shop for a car today and even consider asking the dealer to remove the air bags and antilock brake system?

And guess what? The auto industry is helping themselves with safer cars because their customers live longer, and are around to buy more cars. To add to that, the more safety features they build into their cars, the less attractive they become to nuisance lawsuits from accidents. Fewer lawsuits will mean more profits.

The same analogy can be extended to food. Safe food—healthier food—can be made available at little additional cost. For those of us in the food industry, we can either pay for it now, or we'll pay dearly for it later. There is a robust future in healthy food, and there is a way to offer safer products that taste just as good as the bad stuff. This can be done without you, the consumer, having to give up your favorite foods and snacks. Food can be made far less harmful, and you won't taste the difference in all the stuff you love to eat. And most important, this can be done without having to make a marketing issue out of it, or even without your being aware of it.

Ultimately, we have to force-feed the American public healthier food, without threats, and without telling people they have to diet all the time. It can be done, but each side has to know its place. Here's the way today's food battlefield shapes up:

The Food Business: Let's never lose sight of the principal fact that the food business exists first to make money and second to feed our bellies. If up-sizing and fatty foods help them make more profits, guess which path they will be inclined to follow? This is the primary driver. Most are public companies responsible to their shareholders, aiming to give them the highest return possible on their investment. Thus, their position has been one largely of defense: We'll offer you some healthier options; after that it's your responsibility. This is, frankly, a punt. When this model was first promulgated, obesity was not a problem. The game is different today, and business must change to fit the times.

Government: Now focusing on the problem with greater scrutiny, governments position themselves to take control over a downward-spiraling situation and examine new rules and regulations to impose on the industry. The reality is that governments don't think about delivering results like a corporation, and are structurally poor at implementation.

Government actions, like most well-intentioned actions, run the risk of unanticipated consequences that are bad for both the industry and the consumer. But unlike more nimble individuals and for-profit organizations, governments are inherently slow to correct for those inevitable unintended consequences. That's why legislating away certain bad fats can invite worse fats into the food chain, and years can pass before anything corrective can be done.

Consumer Advocates: Hardcore-activists smell blood. Pushing "Dump Soda" campaigns and "sin tax" agendas will not yield sensible long-term solutions. (Witness Chicago giving up on its foie gras ban and repealing a law it passed just two years earlier.) While their ostensible intent is to "save" the consumer, their motives are perceived as getting tough on big businesses.

Human Beings Who Eat Food: Finally, the Consumer. Yes, we too must take our share of eating responsibly. We need to pay attention and appreciate that our actions influence not only our own well-being, but others' pocketbooks. We need to get the kids off the couch. But we also need help from the food industry so that we are not continually blasted with cues and messages to eat galactic-size portions of nonnutritious foods.

In the end, we're all complicit in what's gotten us to this point—the food industry most of all. But though we've all played a role in creating this problem, we're not all in a position to fix it. The solutions here must come from the food industry, not because they are to blame, but because they are the only ones who can do it.

And I will show you how.

# 10

# foodonomics

*"On a dollar-per-nutrient basis, healthy food is not more expensive."*

—*Time* magazine, June 21, 2007

*"Healthy eating really does cost more."*

—*The New York Times*, December 5, 2007

Okay, we have a little dispute here. In the same year, within six months, two respectable publications disagreed on whether eating healthy costs more or doesn't. So who's correct? The reporter for *Time* or the *New York Times*? They're actually both right. We do know this: Junk food has higher calorie content and less nutrients—known as "empty calories" by health authorities. Fruits and vegetables have fewer calories, more nutrients, and are "better" for us to eat though they provide "lower energy" than other foods. And it's more expensive to ship and distribute fresh fruits and vegetables because of the simple fact that they're highly perishable. The shelf life of frozen foods, canned goods, and boxed foods is longer and thus they're cheaper to keep in inventory. Because junk food is inherently less expensive to buy than healthier food, the actual "cost per nutrient" is not more expensive. Junk food is low on the good stuff and fruits and vegetables are high on the natural chemicals that keep our bodies in good condition. The *Time* writer was referring to a *ratio*, and the *Times* reporter was talking about what we *pay* at the cash register, or the retail costs.

If you're going to try to provide a solution that can effectively solve the obesity crisis, understanding the costs commonly associated with healthier food is paramount. One of the most frequent critiques lobbed at healthy-eating advocates by the food industry is that it costs more to eat healthier. For years this has been the go-to rationale behind food executives' risk-averse behaviors: that it would cost them too much money to produce food that's healthier for the consumer.

It goes without saying that *Time* and the *New York Times* are not the only ones with differing versions of how to do the math. Discrepancies abound throughout the food industry and its many critics. Still, some aspects of the price of some foods are absolutely clear: Healthier fresh products are scarcer in low-income neighborhoods, where residents pay a greater percentage of their income for what they eat. In more affluent neighborhoods, the percentage is much lower, so people do not pay as much heed to how much their food ultimately costs. If you commute to work every day, the price of a gallon of gas is significant. If you drive occasionally, and your gas bill is a small part of your expense budget, the difference in the price per gallon does not materially affect your standard of living. The same thing goes for food, but to a greater degree because everyone has to eat, but not everyone has to drive.

The math that I'm talking about here is "foodonomics," or how food purveyors price their products, and how the profit model is constructed. I'm not out to bore you with figures, but I'm hoping to convey the point that when you strip away the layers of expenses in the food chain, there is no reason why the food industry can't produce healthier products across the entire nutrition grid—and still ensure that the restaurants, producers, and grocers do not suffer on their bottom line.

In fact, selling healthy food can actually increase their net profits. The food industry has been far too complacent about the long-term well-being of their consumers. In order to keep their customers healthy—and turn them into repeat buyers—they should be thinking along the lines of doing the right thing. If all the companies were similarly motivated, they would be acting with unselfish motives. But they're not. So my challenge to them is, "If you can't do the right thing merely because it is the right thing, then do the right thing because you'll make money." In short, if you can't reformulate your thinking out of altruism, then do it out of greed.

The goal here is to get the companies to think about their enlightened self-interest, or, put another way, to think along the lines of "altruism-based profits." I want them to look at their businesses on both a micro and macro level. On the micro side, they can run the numbers on individual products to see how healthier versions might be profitably implemented. Obviously, there will be some items that are more amenable than others. Should one ever change an icon like Coca-Cola? I think we know the answer, but there are plenty of opportunities. On the macro side, they should look at big-picture solutions. Can we improve the healthiness of a certain portion of our brand portfolio? Should we modify our marketing tactics to promote healthier products? Ultimately it's their entire line of offerings that will make a difference.

To understand how healthy food can be more affordable, it's important to understand the rationales behind how the food industry currently prices many of its products.

First, let's take a look at the restaurant business and deconstruct their numbers. Gross margins (or gross profits) are extremely high for beverages, french fries, and salads because of low ingredient costs per serving. However, the gross margins are lower for the namesake items like burgers and fried chicken. A hamburger like the Big N'Tasty from McDonald's was reported to cost $1.07 to make, and sells at a price of $2.25. This yielded a gross margin of 52 percent. But if a chain wants to drive more traffic into the restaurant, they may feature that product at 99 cents, a steep discount that dips below cost. Since the chain loses money on that promotion, they end up either "eating" the loss, or recouping profits by increasing the sales of other menu items.

What do they usually turn to? If you guessed soft drinks, you're correct. A large Coke or Pepsi (32 ounces) has generally been priced at $1.59 in many fast-food outlets. Here are the costs built into this $1.59 price:

| | |
|---|---|
| Ingredients are 1 cent per ounce: | 32 cents |
| Cup/lid/straw: | 4 cents |
| Total: | 36 cents |

The retail price of $1.59 yields a 77 percent gross margin, so it's easy to see why it's in a fast-food restaurant's best interest to sell a lot of soda. (This also explains why movie theaters make more money selling popcorn and soda than they do renting you a seat.)

Let's take a softer drink than a soft drink. Sweet Tea was introduced by McDonald's at 32 ounces for $1.00. The cost of the ingredients, including the sweetener, is 15 cents, resulting in an 85 percent gross margin. (This is just an estimate; the profit margin if you include the packaging costs may be about 80 percent—still quite high.)

The famous—or infamous, depending on how you look at it—combo meal deserves its own special consideration. While combo meals offer a price break versus ordering items individually, they do provide additional benefits for both buyer and seller. Customers choosing the combo add incremental sales of higher-margin fries and beverages and increase the check size (which increases overall revenues). Two out of three items in the combo meal are high margin, while one (typically the "main course") is lower. For instance, if I separately buy a McDonald's Quarter Pounder with cheese and a medium fries and a medium Coke, it will cost me $5.03. According to a National Alliance for Nutrition and Activity report, if I buy the combo meal containing all three items, the cost is down to $3.74, a 26 percent savings or $1.29 (about the cost of the soda). This is a serious deal that encourages customers to buy the combo—*even if they don't need or want all three items.* The chain basically gives you a free soda when using this approach. That's why some astute customers buy the combo meal, throw away the soda, and still come out ahead.

The combo meal is promoted in ways you haven't imagined that begin long before the point of sale. For example, Unilever, parent company of the Knorr and Hellmann brands, provides specific advice to restaurateurs and food-service operators on "comboing your menu" and offers a "combo profit calculator," in effect doing all the work for their clients. Here is a verbatim look at their suggestions, taken from the firm's own marketing materials:

### How to Maximize Profit Opportunity in Soups, Salads, and Sandwiches

*Bundling items improves total check and profits!*

*We provide you with useful information about "comboing" your menu and the download of the Soup, Salad & Sandwich Combos Profit Calculator.*

**Why Combos?**

***Combos Increase Sales Volume***

*If a typical sandwich costs five dollars and the salad is five dollars, these items can be menued as a combo for $9.50. Thus, the combo has a high perceived value to your customer.*

*The benefit is that your customer may have intended to buy only the sandwich for five dollars, but was drawn by the value of the combo meal and therefore spent an additional four dollars more than they would have otherwise.*

*Soup, salad and sandwich combos have significant menu penetration: featured on 24 percent of QSR [Quick Service Restaurant] menus, featured on 36 percent of FSR [Full Service Restaurant] menus.*

*By bundling soup, salad and sandwiches into combo options you are helping to:*

1. *Simplify the ordering process for your customer*
2. *Streamline the menu with pairing recommendations that will best deliver the optimal food experience*
3. *Increase sales check average and potential profits by capitalizing on an impulse decision to add soup or side salads.*

If you thought there was a financial incentive to buy a combo meal, "supersizing" gives you an even better deal. Let's look at the supersizing pricing from Kangaroo Convenience stores, owned by The Pantry, the largest group of independently owned convenience stores in the Southeast. I recorded the prices in their Chill Zone beverage section:

| Size in ounces | Price | Price per ounce | Calories |
|---|---|---|---|
| 22 | $0.99 | $.045 | 267 |
| 32 | $1.09 | $.034 | 388 |
| 44 | $1.19 | $.027 | 534 |
| 64 | $1.59 | $.025 | 776 |

To a consumer, it is economically compelling to upgrade to larger sizes due to the discounts as one supersizes, since it costs only 60 cents more for an additional 42 ounces. The consumer is thinking, *Even if I drink only half, I'm still getting a good deal.* (If indeed he'd only drink half, his waistline also would be getting a good deal!) Going from a small drink to a supersize netted a 44 percent savings on a price per ounce basis. Despite the savings though, he nearly tripled the amount of calories.

A University of Wisconsin group has studied the effect of supersizing on society. They calculated that for paying an extra 17 percent (on average 67 cents) to supersize an order, you have the potential to eat or drink 73 percent more calories. Those "impulse" decisions that Unilever refers to are piling up the poundage across our nation. If you're operating such a restaurant, it is easy to see how it makes so much economic sense to upgrade the sizes on drinks while providing a discount. Can I blame these franchisees? Hardly. I can't believe that anyone sat in their offices and said that the first thing they wanted to do was get their customers fat. They just saw an opportunity to make more money and they took it. The problem is that in doing so, they didn't think about what the ramifications of their action would be. Now that it's clear what the health implications of such decisions are, the food industry needs to rethink the business models that got us here.

I believe it's important that the folks who run convenience stores also rethink how they're stocking their shelves and charging their customers. Small independent owners, operating as a sole business or franchisee, dominate convenience stores. It's a core value of the American Dream, so it's hard to fault. But it's tough to make money. They rely on food and beverage sales to get them over the hump.

Of the top ten in-store product categories (in terms of consumer sales and exclusive of gasoline), six of ten are food related:

Cigarettes

Packaged beverages (nonalcoholic)

Beer

Food service

Other tobacco

Candy

Salty snacks

General merchandise

Fluid milk products

Packaged sweet snacks

It's worth noting that the convenience store–gas station combo makes larger margins on food and beverages than it does on gas. Even with the price of gas going up, that money isn't going into the pocket of the convenience store owner. As a result, he's got to take steps with the items in his store to make sure that they boost him out of the red. Out of necessity, the store operator must slow you down long enough to contemplate other purchases. And, of course, the bigger the size, the less per ounce you'll pay. And the more profit he will make.

Offerings such as combos and supersizing are embedded marketing practices for the restaurant and food-service industry. Not only are they clever sales devices, but they may be a necessity as well. Given their modest profit margins, many restaurants rely on savvy pricing and bundling meals together to create real—and imagined—value for their customers. It's essential so that they keep coming back. None of this bodes well for those of us who should be limiting calories.

When it comes to consumer packaged goods, you will see many of the same pricing models that you see in the restaurant industry. Historically, many of the more popular foods that have been labeled "bad" are highly profitable. Examples include: carbonated soft drinks (gross margins exceed 90 percent); chips (gross margins are between 60 and 70 percent); and presweetened cereals (gross margins of about 70 percent).

The industry has generally been creative in adding profits to its products when it has offered healthier versions. When Stonyfield Farm organic yogurt first became available, 8-ounce cups of Dannon were selling for 70 cents. Stonyfield was priced at 99 cents for a smaller 6-ounce serving and quickly found a clientele.

Granted, Stonyfield's cost of goods were higher since their ingredients were organic and they incorporated special bacterial cultures with unpronounceable names like *Lactobacillus rhamnosus*, which were shown to boost the immune system and improve digestive health. But their pricing more than made up for this extra cost—and they were able to charge almost twice as much per ounce as Dannon—because the demographic that buys organic cultured yogurts has money to spend on a higher-priced item. In most cases, the manufacturer charges more than the extra ingredient costs and therefore makes more absolute profit. (Note: Dannon's parent company, Danone, is now the majority owner of Stonyfield.)

Here are some other examples of healthy alternatives that produce greater profits:

**Butter and Spreads**

| | |
|---|---|
| Land O'Lakes Butter | $.32 per ounce |
| Benecol (cholesterol-lowering) | $.62 per ounce |

**Beverages**

| | |
|---|---|
| Coke Classic (2 liters) | $.03 per ounce |
| Dasani Bottled Water (20 oz.) | $.07 per ounce |
| Glaceau Vitamin Water (20 oz.) | $.07 per ounce |

**Energy Bars**

| | |
|---|---|
| Quaker | $.27 per ounce |
| South Beach (Diet/Protein) | $.58 per ounce |
| Special K (Lose the weight) | $.62 per ounce |

The results are easy to compute with just a casual scan of the above retail prices. Benecol is almost twice as expensive as Land O'Lakes on a per-ounce basis. Glaceau and Dasani are more than double the price of Coke/Diet Coke/Sprite. South Beach and Special K bars are more than twice as costly as basic Quaker bars.

In other words, packaged goods makers are charging *double or more per ounce* for a "healthier" alternative. They get away with this because a core group of more affluent and health conscious consumers are willing to pay for it. As a result, many companies are embracing the shift to healthier fare because they see it as an opportunity to grow their brands and to make more money. The key for the producers is to become the leader or a strong player in a category, generally the number one or two brand. Being a leader gives the company more clout—higher sales means more profits, which means more marketing and advertising spending, which means more awareness, which means even more sales. Also, leading brands sometimes get to "set" the grocery shelf layout for their category, so that they secure the more desirable shelf locations and positions on the shelf.

When a company has more control over pricing, the impact on the consumer cuts both ways. If a company wants to sell a ton of its products, it will skew its pricing lower, which is good for the consumer. This is attainable because the more product it sells, the less it pays per pound of ingredients and the less it pays per pound to ship those products. Soft drinks and orange juice are examples of such high-tonnage items. Conversely, strong brands can also artificially keep prices up. Witness the cereal aisle or Grey Poupon or Häagen-Dazs. Corporations have a lot of flexibility with their leading brands, but the goal is always the same: the bottom line. Ultimately, they will employ whatever strategy works best for delivering profits. Sometimes the consumer wins, and sometimes he doesn't.

Let's talk just briefly about the 100-calorie packs that are finding their way onto supermarket shelves. Many popular brands such as Oreos and Goldfish now come in these small packages. It's the industry's most recent effort to limit the size of junk-food snacks. There are two ways to look at them. Consumer advocacy groups such as the Center for Science in the Public Interest have accused the industry of making obscene profits on these—from as little as 16 percent to as high as 279 percent—over the regularly packaged items. Clearly the higher end of this range is egregious, but the concept of a premium price per se is not an issue for me. I believe it is better to pay more and eat less, especially if we're snacking on high-calorie junk food. I don't mind that the manufacturers make a reasonable premium selling these items.

Here's the key point: 100-calorie packs *cost no more per eating occasion* than regularly packed items, which is okay by me. The goal is to have people *consume less calories per occasion* and these packs do the trick without a higher absolute cost to the consumer. There is no harm to those who can't afford it—they just take in fewer calories per sitting. Disciplining consumers to eat out of the big box and manage what they eat is not a solution. Even if you eat two 100-calorie packs, you'll still likely consume fewer calories than if you ate out of the regular-size box. The bottom line: The 100-calorie pack is a good idea if we can get the extremists on both sides to meet on common ground. It's okay in a capitalist society for companies to make money, but low-income consumers should be priced into this trend, not out of it. Isn't there a reasonable figure between 16 percent and 279 percent?

The critical fact that junk food is cheap magnifies the problem. If you really think about it, to stem the calorie overload, *the cost per calorie should go up.* People are not undernourished—they're taking in too many calories. So if we cut them back—portion control on the shelves, if you will—we're doing them a favor. This way, for the same dollar spent, the consumer will take in fewer calories and the food companies will make more per calorie. This is a win-win and reflects a core principle of my thinking regarding how things need to change in the right way.

. . .

So now that we have a clearer idea of what things cost, what can we do to get healthier foods to have a greater impact on our overall well-being—and still keep the food industry healthy as well?

We can start with the beverages in restaurants. My first suggestion is, if supersizing is so important to the profit picture of restaurants, begin supersizing the *right* products. It's possible to limit supersize beverages to zero- or low-calorie drinks like Diet Coke, Coca-Cola Zero, bottled water, and lightly sweetened iced teas. Currently, a medium-size Coke is 210 calories. This is a reasonable caloric ceiling for any beverage offering in such a mix.

The large concerns like Coca-Cola and PepsiCo need to play a role in designing programs in connection with these efforts to promote lower-calorie drinks. Not only can they provide discounts on these items, but they can also package new consumer promotions with retailers built around these better-for-you products.

Consumers will always look for (and some really need) combo or value meals, and as we already discussed, these combo meals have proven to be profit centers for the restaurant industry. There's no reason why combos can't be reconfigured to give consumers a financial incentive to choose the healthier options. Here's a possible example: A new Subway sandwich combo includes a Coca-Cola Zero and Baked Lay's potato chips. Programs can also be designed to create special meals or discount pricing behind these healthier items in lieu of sugared sodas. Why not put a cap on the number of calories offered in a combination package? They could base the calorie cap on a percent of the daily calories needed for an active adult male (2,000 as recommended by the Nutrition Facts Panel; calorie requirements vary by age, gender, and activity level). Nutrition experts and industry consultants could come up with a reasonable number. Companies could then design healthier combos that do not contain more than 50 to 60 percent of the daily caloric requirement. It's certainly a better option than loading up on a 2,000-plus-calorie combo consisting of a Monster Thickburger, large fries, and a giant soft drink. (By the way, the Thickburger is pretty tasty.)

This is still a win-win proposition. The consumer will get a price break without being steered to a superhigh-calorie meal, and the restaurant can make its extra profits by promoting these group-item sales. They will earn more profits than they think with low-calorie, low-cholesterol, lower-fat meals.

Here's a simple template for a healthier fast-food combo:

**Beverages:** Only use no- or low-calorie items (Coca-Cola Zero, Diet Coke, Pepsi One); limit to 50 calories per serving

**French fries:** Limit to small or medium portions only; no larges allowed

**Meat:** No "monster" or "quad" burgers like the BK Stacker as part of the package; say, 700 calories maximum

Also, fast-food and casual dining restaurants alike should offer the option to substitute healthier sides instead of fries. Side dishes generally have a better profit margin than the main course. Why object if someone wants a salad or apple slices instead of french fries? Pricing can be set to yield a handsome profit.

Restaurants aren't the only businesses that can safely adapt to this brand of thinking. This can also work for the packaged goods companies—including those with vending machine operations. We can expand the 100-calorie (or less) packages to more categories, such as soft drinks. Coke just introduced a 100-calorie can. What's wrong with a "small" Coke sold anytime, anywhere? And let's not worry about evacuating Fruit Loops and Cocoa Puffs from the shelves. We should put 100-calorie colorful "fun" packets inside the cereal box for presweetened cereals to limit the serving sizes for these less-nutritious cereals. This would be a huge plus for everyone. Parents are happy that they're limiting calories to their children, while manufacturers earn higher margins.

Let's take a trip to the school cafeterias and install mini vending machines—those that only carry the mini cans (8 ounces or less). These machines can now go anywhere since none of the items in them would be more than 100 calories apiece. And no one has to give up his favorite brand.

Here's a real-world situation that proves that bold, logical thinking can lead to creative solutions: Faced with the alarming statistics about childhood obesity and overweight statistics, Assistant Principal Bryan Bass of North Community High School in Minneapolis took a look at the school's vending machine program. He didn't like what he saw, so he called on the district's Coca-Cola representative to help him make some changes. They increased the number of vending machines from four to sixteen and stacked thirteen machines with water or juice, two with sports drinks, and one with soda (with limited hours of sale). They also instituted pricing differentials to give incentives to students to buy healthier products. Water is 75 cents, sports drinks and juices are $1.00, and soda and fruit drinks are $1.25. Water machines were placed in high-traffic areas and students were allowed to drink only water inside the classrooms. The result? Soda sales declined but vending profits went up by almost $4,000 a year. Water, as you might suspect, was the best seller.

The Minneapolis program reflects big-picture thinking. It may actually cost a little bit more to produce those healthier beverages, but the way the pricing and number of vending machines were established made the initiative work for the school, the bottler, and, most important, the students.

The best part of this program is what I call "Digestion Pricing." Digestion Pricing places a premium price on foods that may "clog" your arteries or otherwise be unhealthy to eat. This is simply a page out of the playbooks of London and other large cities that have placed heavy tolls called "Congestion Pricing" in high-congestion locales in order to reduce traffic. Drive your car or truck into these areas during rush hour and you pay a premium price to do so.

It's a disincentive to adding to overly clogged roadways, and it's worked in many of the venues it has been applied. New York City mayor Michael Bloomberg proposed the same idea, although his plan failed to win approval in the state legislature.

Beyond vending, corporations can also skew their marketing, promotional, and public relations budgets to healthier items. Why not spend more on Coke Zero and less on regular Coke to try to help tip the scales of fatness in the other direction? This is a huge opportunity to make a serious impact.

At the point of purchase, groceries and supermarkets could create prime shelf space in several aisles that are designated for some of these ideas, much in the way that they currently showcase the overly sugared foods. Instead of the eye-catching displays featuring junk food, they could cordon off a section for "Healthy Kids," and use that existing successful practice to drive kids to healthier alternatives. A highlighted section for "Healthy Kids" could include brands like Cheerios (but not Honey Nut), Quaker Oatmeal, Special K, and Kellogg's Corn Flakes (but not Frosted Flakes). These sections would be clearly identified, perhaps by shelf color or ceiling signs. They would be located in the middle of the aisle, in prime real estate territory. The section would need to have a "cool" effect to attract the kids. Animated displays, cartoon characters, and other media devices could be used to accomplish this. If this idea achieved some traction, we could develop minimum nutrition standards (calorie limits, portion sizes, and so on) for inclusion in these sections. Companies could be expected to pay location premiums to retailers for including their products in these areas, but they would still retain their existing space allotments. This way the "good" brands in question would have two permanent locales. This is a plus for everyone—grocer, manufacturer, and consumers.

I also see no reason why we couldn't create "school-friendly" menus for any fast-food outlet that is located within one mile or walking distance of an elementary, middle, or high school. Let's not mandate it; let's ask the fast-food guys (nicely) if they couldn't see the long-range value in such a plan. I obviously borrowed this idea from the folks who created the drug-free zones near schools. In areas where there are large issues with obesity, I would take the proposal one step further. Why not consider restricting the sales of high-calorie items on the fast-food menus during certain hours? Parents, pay attention: Should we encourage our kids to buy Whoppers and Big Macs after school (and before dinner)? Alternatively, fast-food chains can reward students for purchasing selected products. Kind of like the frequent-flyer programs for coming into the stores.

Think about this: Video gaming outlets with responsible managers have tried a similar approach with some excellent results. Truancy is diminished when the kids can't get into these establishments during school hours. In New York City, at least one game loft denies kids entry before 3:00 p.m.

Some of these ideas may work, others may not, but many of them have more than a fighting chance because they work with the existing systems and success patterns that the industry has in place. In one sense we can't force-feed healthy food on the American public just because it's healthier. On the other hand, we can't let the food sellers complain that they've tried to provide healthier alternatives in the past with no financial success. It's a cop-out on both sides.

The largest food, beverage, and restaurant corporations are generally well run, with large marketing budgets—meaning that they can afford to put money up for the development and promotion of healthier food platforms, especially the packaged goods companies. Part of the foodonomics at work here is that the marketing budgets of the "healthy alternatives" tend to be small parts of the overall marketing pie. Here's a brief look at how much the fifteen largest brands spend annually for advertising.

| Brand | Media $ (Mil.) |
|---|---|
| McDonald's | 776 |
| Kellogg | 367 |
| Subway | 361 |
| Wendy's | 360 |
| Coca-Cola | 334 |
| Burger King | 285 |
| Taco Bell | 260 |
| KFC | 251 |
| General Mills | 221 |
| Campbell's | 218 |
| Nabisco | 212 |
| Pizza Hut | 206 |
| Pepsi | 192 |
| Gatorade | 183 |
| Quaker | 183 |

So here's a proposal that could raise the profile of every participant: What if every food and restaurant company contributes a portion (say one-half of 1 percent, or .005) of their advertising budget to a special "Food Superfund." It's not unlike the theory behind any revenue-sharing arrangement you see in other industries. It's a commitment that everyone is contributing to the solution of a large problem that affects all of their customers. The purpose of the Food Superfund would be to attack the most intractable problems involving our nation's collective health. The money could go—in a general way—to fighting the things that make us fat. It could also function to bring down the cost of healthier foods, or if not reduce these prices, at least make them more affordable.

Key uses of the fund would include doing basic research, such as finally answering the difficult health and nutrition questions that science hasn't yet answered. What's more harmful for our long-term well-being, a sugared beverage or one with artificial sweeteners? (Or, to put it in parental terms: Do I feed my kids regular

Pepsi or artificially sweetened Diet Pepsi?) Some of the monies could be used to get the calories out of foods in ways that went beyond simply extracting sugar and fats. A central lab could be engaged to do research into making foods healthier without compromising taste. Or, at the very least, we could have a clearinghouse that kept track of the important studies, highlighted the consistent findings, and provided guidance to consumers on what's important and what needs more work. In short, why not a reliable, independent organization that sifts through the data so we don't have to decide whether Rick Berman or Michael Jacobson is selling us biased goods?

Monies could be invested to fund megastudies to find out—perhaps definitively—whether it is carbohydrates or fats that make us fat. We could also subsidize a public relations effort that educates Americans on a very important topic: Let's demythologize the conventional thinking that has led most of us to believe that all saturated fats are bad. This is not true. Some are neutral and could lead to better frying oils that are less absorbed into fried foods (for less grease and fewer calories). This could have a huge positive impact on the obesity problem.

The superfund could help us discover and commercialize ingredients that make us feel full faster—the satiety problem—so we don't consume as many calories. We could learn how to make fried items like french fries and doughnuts healthier, and we could fund processes of all kinds that make foods intrinsically better for us. We could forge a deal that allows participating companies to use the research in a responsible manner in future advertising and marketing efforts, enabling them to think of this more as an investment than as a tax.

If all soft drink, packaged goods, restaurant, meat, dairy, and confection corporations contributed only a half percent of their marketing budgets, the fund would have *$37.5 million* to begin its work. This is based on the recorded advertising figure of $7.5 billion annually for food, beverages, and candy (excluding retail). I would remind all that the annual amount of advertising dollars spent is among the most "inefficient" outlays that a corporation makes. There are huge amounts of waste in this spending, and it's almost impossible to quantify how much return on investment there is. Companies know they have to spend on marketing, advertising, promotion, and media, but they are never certain what extent of it works. Imagine the publicity they could gain if they committed a small amount of it *pro bono publico,* namely to public health. It would help the marketing execs sharpen their pencils come budget time, and they'd think twice about some of the marginal expenses they incur. (Think of BP's relentless "green" campaign: It's all about image change.)

Where would I start to launch such a plan? I would call on the officers of the Grocery Manufacturers Association and the National Restaurant Association to work in tandem to provide leadership on this initiative. We could prevail on these powerful trade groups to convince their member corporations that this is a serious matter affecting the industry at large. Perhaps a combined lobby could cajole our government leaders to provide appropriations to match funds contributed by the industry. It could be a joint private sector–public sector project.

By using a joint industry-government initiative, an independent scientific panel would be set up to oversee studies and ensure that they're conducted properly so that the results are not second-guessed. Knowing that some companies would not contribute, those who did would have free access to use any and all outcomes and patents derived from the effort. Noncontributors would be excluded or be compelled to pay patent licensing fees to use new food technology, and also face exposure to government intervention and sanctions.

The half-percent levy on the industry would not preclude their propensity to market products in their own way and retain proprietary research by individual companies. This idea provides a supplement to the status quo. The superfund would have as its fundamental mandate to tackle the common problems that virtually all companies are facing.

It's very possible that the addition of marketing muscle and ad dollars alone could be a link to help healthier products catch on and gain greater, constant visibility. If a healthy product's paltry advertising and marketing budget ensures that it will remain a niche-market item, there's little hope that it will ever become a staple in American homes. However, if food and beverage companies invest a bit more to make these healthy products a success, they'll be rewarded on the back end. The more consumers adopt healthy products for their own sake, the more their prices and built-in costs will come down.

Something like the Food Superfund could offer a new way for food companies to connect with consumers on issues of health. Everyone can benefit from it. Failing to provide healthy food is no longer an option. We've demonstrated throughout this chapter that food companies and restaurants can do this profitably. And they can do this without asking the consumer to change any of his eating habits—a change that never worked in the past.

# 11

# stealth health

Steve Carley is one of those rare restaurant CEOs who not only proudly eats his own cooking, but can also boast that he's lost twenty-five pounds doing it. Carley still looks fit and athletic, despite carrying a bit of middle-aged heft. His build suggests he was a pretty serious jock in his youth. Today, he runs El Pollo Loco, a regional fast-food outlet based in Sherman Oaks, California. El Pollo Loco's core offering is chicken prepared with Tex-Mex flavors. There are 400 restaurants, and the chain is in the process of rolling out new ones on a nationwide basis, including the South.

Carley is also civic-minded. He's on the boards of the California Restaurant Association and the California Chamber of Commerce. More important, he's one of the few executives I know who is deeply immersed in the complicated debates surrounding the health issues in QSRs and other food providers. Carley is one of the more progressive food purveyors in the QSR business because he understands that eating healthier dishes is a shared responsibility—consumer, seller, parents in command of the household, and, *only* when appropriate, the government.

Of course, as someone who is an industry advocate, he's leery of the bureaucrats, and it's no surprise. There are some beaches in California that have banned smoking, and when a local government official saw a food wrapper on the sidewalk, he put the blame on the fast-food restaurant—not the unthinking, selfish consumer who littered. "If you talk to certain elements of the political spectrum, all the litter in the United States is caused by restaurants," Carley said, shaking his head. His brain is just boggled when he notes how his industry is under attack for the wrong reasons.

Because Carley is a reasonably astute man, he senses the future with the same tinted glasses that I do. He believes that it's up to the food companies to accommodate consumer demands *before* they're forced to do so by regulation, as with the move toward providing nonharmful cooking oils. He said, "I'm one of the few guys for whom this is a nonissue. We did it and we didn't even tell anybody. We said, 'This is just silly. Let's just get rid of the trans fats.' We made some operational enhancements so we could pay for more expensive oil that was trans fat–free, and it gave us a better product. We just did it."

Almost more important, though, *he did it quietly*. To his credit, he didn't ballyhoo the move with a massive press initiative just to prove how responsible El Pollo Loco is. He frequently cites the fact that consumers need to be continually informed about nutrition, and they should be allowed a wide variety of choice—low-fat and low-calorie foods as well as the sour cream and guacamole add-ons. He's maniacal about a customer's right to order what he or she wants. But he'll be the first one to tell you that the Caesar salad at his restaurant is much healthier without the dressing, which adds costly calories in any recipe.

Carley understands that fast food is about loyalty and repeat business. He would like his customers to be customers for life. So he encourages healthy eating habits, but he also recognizes the human propensity for indulgence in tasty items that might be frowned on by the dieticians and nutritionists. His menus have extensive nutritional breakdowns. Here's the nutritional information about his Caesar salad, available on his Web site to anybody who wants to know:

| | |
|---|---|
| Serving size: | 225 grams |
| Calories: | 230 |
| Calories from fat: | 110 |
| Total fat: | 12 grams |
| Saturated fat: | 6 grams |
| Cholesterol: | 20 milligrams |
| Sodium: | 500 milligrams |
| Carbohydrates: | 14 grams |
| Fiber: | 3 grams |
| Sugars: | 4 grams |
| Protein: | 16 grams |

Carley is a food executive who sees the health issue from many angles and so believes that it will take several steps to change what we eat and how much we eat. By shared responsibility, Carley also believes that food purveyors need to play a huge role in getting healthier food on our plates.

To that end, he related the saga of El Pollo Loco's Smokey Black Bean side dish, which has been a favorite of his clientele. A single supplier from New Orleans produced the black beans, which was a risky proposition to begin with. Carley recalled, "After Hurricane Katrina, their entire plant was destroyed. We had no other backup, so we had no more black beans. We were forced to take it off the menu. The consumer response was unbelievable. They inundated us with requests for black beans.

"We sat down with the manufacturer and looked at our black bean recipe, which was popular in a couple of regions. The recipe included ham, ham fat, molasses, and lard. None of this stuff is particularly good for you. I said, 'If we're going to bring this product back, let's seamlessly introduce a product that deals with all of the health issues.' We had our nutritionist completely formulate a new recipe to prepare the black beans. We knew there were these issues to start with, and we had a chance to take a look at it and say, 'Let's do it.' So we eliminated the trans fat, the molasses, the ham, and the lard.

"We actually tested the new dish in the marketplace and had everyone taste it and give their response if there were any issues in how we prepared it. People were ecstatic. The vast majority of our customers could not tell the difference between the old black bean recipe and the new one we developed."

Still, there was one more crucial thing about this reintroduction, he said. "We didn't make a big deal out of the change. We didn't do any marketing campaign, or any publicity. We took that opportunity to say privately, 'This would be a good thing to do.' "

Serendipity took a strange turn in the Smokey Black Beans story of El Pollo Loco. Had it not been for a devastating hurricane, it's likely that none of this would have happened, at least not when it did. It took a year to get the beans back on the menu in part because Carley was loyal to the manufacturer. "We felt a little bit of social responsibility," he said. "Those guys got slammed down there. We said, 'As soon as you're back up and rebuild the plant, we'll be there when you get back on line.' "

Carley was adamant about keeping a low profile. And that's why you didn't read about this in the newspapers. If my optimism is well founded, then we'll begin to see a trend among the small- and medium-size QSRs to quietly make moves toward healthier ingredients. I'm hoping that fast-food purveyors will understand that this silent approach can benefit both the customer and the restaurants.

The other upside of this story is that not only were there health benefits with the new recipe, but there was an economic plus, as well. The manufacturing cost of this dish is *less* than the original. Mutual benefit for the customer *and* the food seller—foodonomics in action. And the whole thing was possible because this food executive was willing to rethink the tried-and-true rules of the trade, because he was willing to think that perhaps health and profits were not mutually exclusive. I've often thought, "What if El Pollo Loco had had a CEO without Steve Carley's imagination? What would he have done?" The obvious solution would have been to respond immediately to customer complaints by finding a new source and not changing the menu, except perhaps to accommodate the new supplier. This would have been the common reaction from executives who begin and end with the simple idea that they need to keep their customers happy. Carley realizes he needs to keep them healthy, as well.

The restaurant business is competitive and even cutthroat, but guys like Carley demonstrate that you need not be greedy, and you need not be timid, and you need not be a saint to be financially successful and do the right thing. (I'm hoping that other CEOs with Carley's insight can take the lead and repeat this kind of change without waiting for some natural catastrophe to accidentally motivate them.)

Tom Ryan has similar practical views when it comes to running large restaurant concerns. When he was an executive with McDonald's, he was largely responsible for introducing the famous Dollar Menu to his patrons, as well as the salads. The salad, of course, was a major step forward, especially since Ryan put an item on the menu that was healthy (if you go easy on the dressing) and also profitable. But let's recognize that the salad is not a solution to reducing waistlines. Someone who wants the dollar menu is not going to be diverted to the salad bar. It just makes good business sense.

When he worked for Quiznos, a submarine-sandwich chain with 5,000-plus restaurants in fifteen countries, Ryan had a chance to make a huge impact, and he did. While he was growing the business, Ryan did what Steve Carley did. He sold healthier goods and didn't tell anybody.

"Do the best job you can giving people what they really want, and get caught doing the right thing," Ryan told me. "That means don't go out and talk about it unless you absolutely have to. What I loved about Quiznos is when anybody cared [to ask], we could say, 'Our whole menu is zero trans fat.' It's never been said out loud in any kind of public communication. It's never been put in print. It just happens when someone says, 'What about you guys?' 'Well, we've been zero trans fat for five years now, or six years now.' That's cool; we got caught doing something right."

Quiznos is doing other things the right way. They introduced a new line of flatbread sandwiches called Sammies in November 2007. Sammies are limited to approximately 200 calories and sell for $2. They include flavors such as Black Angus steak and premium chicken breast. It's a good example of moving lower-calorie versions of popular items.

Ryan thinks that today's food executives have a reluctance to try something new and daring because it's not compatible with their vision of where they want to take their company. He also thinks the decision makers are using a poor argument or making lame excuses. Making healthy changes on a large scale is not too difficult for some restaurants with thousands of outlets. Is it really more of an issue for McDonald's, Wendy's, or Burger King than it is for the lesser-known QSRs? We happened to be talking about the frying oil controversy. He thinks the powers that make these decisions are overcomplicating the issue.

"Replacing an oil is easy," Ryan said. "The next time you empty that, throw it away and put this in instead." It's simply about swapping one product for another.

Ryan believes right-thinking executives want to provide healthy options, but they're still understandably nervous about it. "Any good guy that sits on top of the brand, like a chief marketing officer or a consumer relevant CEO, is going to say, 'Do I really want to do this?' The problem with trying to extend a line or flank yourself is you cast a shadow on your own core business. I think you need to find a solution where it has some dimension of upside for the consumer, and that it's easy for the operator to do it."

The concern many executives have is that, like Outback Steakhouse, for example, execs think that highlighting a newer healthy option implies that the rest of their products are unhealthy. Ryan is simply saying that if you offer a product that provides a benefit the consumer wants, just do it. It's smart. It won't hurt the rest of your lineup (witness Diet Coke, or Honey Nut Cheerios).

What do Ryan and Carley have in common besides the fact that they have both put their personal commitment to health into practice? When taking these strides, neither felt the need to call attention to them. On a large scale, corporate level they introduced change slyly—without fanfare and a press release about corporate responsibility. These were prescient and forward-thinking moves that outlined one possible roadmap for how food companies are going to help undo the damage from the last thirty years.

I call it Stealth Health. When used correctly, this concept could be one of the food industry's most effective weapons for making people healthier. After all, one of the only ways to really attack the problem is to fix the foods that people eat the most and don't tell them they're eating something different. We learned in chapter nine that to eradicate rampant obesity, we must not advance initiatives that require wholesale changes by the consumer. So if we can't change the way we eat, we must—and can—change the makeup of what we eat.

In the last year, discussion of these hidden health issues came front and center with cookbooks like *Deceptively Delicious* and *The Sneaky Chef.* While those books were good about introducing these ideas into recipes at home, they aimed to bring change into the kitchen. As a result, their popularity did not influence the food companies to take action on their end before food even gets to the home. Those recipes were designed to fool children into eating right, but why not take that a step further and apply it to everyone? After all, this is a problem that we all suffer from.

Consider the noble efforts of a cardiologist named Dr. Arthur Agatston. If you've heard of him it's likely because you've been on his popular South Beach Diet or know someone who has been on it. In 2004, Agatston took some of the profits from his best-selling book and put them to work in a research foundation dedicated to understanding and helping to improve the dietary habits of children. In a bold move he decided to fund pilot programs in Florida for school lunches with special menus that included healthy food alternatives. His idea was to see if changing the menus to healthier fare could make a difference. Along with a public administrator and Maria Almon, a dietician who developed most of the recipes for his book, Agatston identified a Florida school district that had a high rate of elementary school children who were in federally subsidized lunch and breakfast programs.

In 2006, some of the results of Agatston's early experiment—called HOPS, for Healthier Options for Public Schoolchildren—were documented in the *New York Times Magazine*. The initial findings were not encouraging. According to the article, "The first step was to ban white bread and Tater Tots, replacing them with whole-wheat bread and sweet potato fries. Other favorites, like turkey with gravy or pork with gravy, went too. There was 'almost a mutiny,' Almon says, when she took away Lucky Charms and Fruit Loops at breakfast, replacing them with Total and Raisin Bran." Many children had no clue what a sweet potato was, and they were unhappy when breaded foods went unbreaded and the ketchup packets disappeared.

Laudable as it is, the jury is out on this approach. The kids are resisting and opting instead for junk food. Sweet potatoes just don't have the appeal that french fries have.

Agatston's effort mirrored several such programs implemented across the nation, many funded by various groups including the Kellogg Foundation. The prevention studies have had "mixed findings," meaning some showed promise and others failed. "There just isn't definitive proof," said Benjamin Caballero in an interview with the *New York Times* (August 20, 2006). Caballero should know; he headed a large-scale study of this in the 1990s. In that program $20 million was spent changing menus and exercise protocols, and educating kids about nutrition. The body mass index of those children in the study showed no appreciable change. (I'm not very optimistic that we can force-feed the right foods to kids. In a recent study in Mississippi—the nation's number one "fattest" state—fruits and vegetables were made available to fifth graders at *no cost* and it made absolutely no difference in what they chose to eat.)

There is no doubt that Agatston's efforts to get kids to eat fruits and vegetables are rowing against the tide. I'd rather we adapt those popular foods that kids and adults really want to eat and provide the proper (or at least better) nutrition. We know that people haven't changed. This is why education and awareness haven't gotten the job done. Why do we expect people to change now? We shouldn't, and that's why we have to use sneaky tactics to get everyone on an acceptable diet.

What is my concept of Stealth Health? Simple. Making a food or beverage more nutritious without bragging about it to the consumer. In fact, keeping consumers in the dark about these improvements might be an even bigger advantage. "Honey, does this taste different? I knew it" is not likely to be a question and comment often heard at restaurant tables.

Virtually every piece of research I have encountered in thirty years confirms that, for foods that are typically more indulgent or junk food, the consumer believes that making these foods more healthy results in poorer taste. It's a perception perhaps born in the early days of health food, the "nuts and berries" phase. Eating cereals that tasted like cardboard or trying the first soy hot dogs left a bad taste (literally) in everyone's mouths. And low expectations about healthier food tasting good have survived. Thus, one must sneak in nutrition without letting anyone know, to preserve the all-important taste perception.

Would this approach be useful in packaged goods or restaurants? Actually both. Products that are already perceived as intrinsically healthy (for example, yogurt, oatmeal, and orange juice) can tout all the good-for-you ingredients they want. The consumer buys them (at least partially) for their health benefits. It's the most popular Darth Vader–esque products where you need to be sneaky regardless of whether they're sold in supermarkets or restaurants. Again, look for the worst offenders, like Lunchables. The whole notion of the idea behind Sprouts was to market a Stealth Health version of Lunchables without ever telling the kids it was better for them. The Sprout character made it fun and the products would be more nutritious. Next up—a healthier Kid Cuisine?

On the restaurant side, we've already seen how operators like Steve Carley successfully restructured his beans. We've also reported how fries cooked in less-absorbed oil can result in fewer calories and basically taste just as good as, if not better than, the original recipes. Can we do the same with Big Macs and other foods? Why not?

So how do we put Stealth Health into action? Here are some steps that the industry could adopt:

1. Reformulate recipes with healthier or less-harmful ingredients, and do it with a nominal price hike (or, better yet, none at all). For years, corporations have rejiggered their products to effect cost savings without ever telling the consumer. Do you think Nabisco cookies are the same as they were twenty years ago? How about when the soft drink companies switched from sugar to high fructose corn syrup to lower their costs? So why can't the food companies change their products to make them healthier (and also improve the cost)?

2. The healthier alternatives must pass the taste test. The new taste must be just as good if not better (already proven to be doable). If the customer notices that it's not the same, then it doesn't work. We also know that the word "health" implies worse taste when applied to the more popular products. Any improvement to the health profile of a product must be within range of what the consumer expects the product to taste like.
3. If you can innovate and come up with a completely new product, focus on the taste and hide the fact that it might be healthier or help you lose calories. Coca-Cola Zero is an excellent example of this. There's no focus on diet; it's just likened to delivering the real taste of Coca-Cola in a zero-calorie version. Capri Sun Roarin' Waters, a low-calorie version, also does this well for kids. The emphasis is on taste and fun, and not the fact that it's only 35 calories per pouch.
4. If you're concerned that customers might *perceive* poorer taste due to the health components, fly below the radar. Don't call up the PR department. Don't even think about boasting to your customers that it's "new and improved." Get caught doing the right thing.

Let's see how this might work for the restaurant business. Fast-food chains are worried about moving french fries and soda quickly, while sit-down restaurants stress about the number of "turns" a table has on their busiest evenings. They focus mostly on operating their businesses and live in the present, relative to their packaged goods brethren, and don't anticipate the future as much. Even though the restaurant guys have the most opportunity to implement Stealth Health solutions, they are also more likely to stick with tried-and-true beliefs about health conflicting with taste and what their heavy user (currently) wants.

The analogy I like to give is that the restaurant industry (and not quite as often, the packaged food goods industry) is the antithesis in philosophy to Silicon Valley companies—where innovation in technology dominates thinking, from the boardroom down to the cubicles. In Silicon Valley, if you do not constantly improve what you're selling, your competitor will, and your business will die. The saying there is, "If you stop for lunch, you become lunch." The restaurant guys generally don't look far ahead. Long-term planning *is lunch*. Though adopting a new strategy of innovation might take some time, I'm confident that it is possible to cajole them to adopt a different, far-reaching strategy, one that will formulate a different way of thinking—where they not only make money, but make money in a way that's responsible to their customers.

Go back to the South Beach Diet doctor's Florida school experiment. The kids don't want sweet potatoes. They want french fries. Forget the sweet potatoes then; let's give them a healthier fry.

We can begin with the most popular items in restaurants. In the last ten years, nine of the ten most popular food products sold (fries, soft drinks, fried chicken, burgers among them) are still the same. Let's not hold our breaths and hope that salads will supplant the Whopper. They're just an alternative for customers who don't eat burgers in the first place. They're a smart marketing strategy, but it's not changing anyone's eating habits. (When the salads taste like a Monster Thickburger, maybe then they'll outsell burgers.)

How about a healthier hamburger that also tastes great? Here's an example of how to reformulate a hamburger with omega-3 fatty acids. You could swap out some of the saturated fats in the burger with heart-healthy omega-3 fatty acids. This process will keep the burger juicy. With the proper selection of the right omega-3 oils (odorless, and purified to be stable), you can maintain an excellent taste profile. You now have a burger that is better for your heart.

Now, I didn't call it a "healthy" burger, but for someone who eats fast food five to seven times a week—those most prone to heart problems and diabetes—this will go a long way toward improving their condition.

. . .

While the restaurant industry has a winding road to travel if it's going to keep its core base of customers coming back without lowering their life expectancy, at least some packaged goods marketers have seen the light and are making strides to improve their products. In an article in *Newsweek* about Frito-Lay's initiative to make less harmful snacks, the writer called the company's Eden Project an attempt to produce the "ultimate oxymoron: healthy junk food."

The challenge (and risk) of this project was to address the trend to healthier food without alienating so-called taste junkies—heavy users of Doritos, Fritos, Cheetos, Tostitos, and Lays potato chips. Frito-Lay was one of the first companies to remove trans fats from their chips. They have replaced their oils with sunflower oil, about which Bob Brown, Frito-Lay's director of nutrition and regulatory affairs, told *Newsweek* magazine: "We're telling customers that it may seem counterintuitive, but there are good fats, and the fat you are going to get in our products is going to be beneficial."

Frito-Lay's conversion to sunflower oil, however, demonstrates the complexity of addressing consumer awareness about nutrition on such a large scale. When the company first eliminated trans fats, it switched to cottonseed oil, which, although healthier in some respects, was still high in saturated fat. Amid mounting evidence of a link between saturated fat and heart disease, Brown said the company knew it would need to evolve further, but its choices were limited: soybean oil, which spoils easily, or sunflower oil, of which there was little supply. It took several years and millions of dollars for Frito-Lay, oilmakers, and farmers to develop a sustainable sunflower crop. It was only last year that the supply was steady enough to make the switch—"eliminating 60 million pounds of saturated fat from the U.S. diet," as the company crowed.

My take on this initiative: This is a packaged goods company that saw the trend to healthier eating and got ahead of the curve. They got rid of trans fats in the right way: by substituting a healthier (if more expensive) oil—though their PR department didn't exactly keep quiet on the issue. While some of their claims implying that the consumer will be healthier are a stretch—the new oil still brings the same amount of calories as the old trans fat oil—this is a step in the right direction. Their customer still gets to enjoy their chips, but they are more heart-healthy.

I strongly disagree with the skeptics and nutrition purists on this one. People love their chips—we just need to make them less harmful. My wish is for Frito-Lay to take the next step and make changes to their processing techniques, ingredients, and marketing practices to cut out more of the calories consumed by their loyal customers. In that way they will make a serious dent in the obesity crisis.

An industry associate, Steve Allen, the vice president for new ventures, Nestlé USA, is in a position to move the needle forward on the health issue. English-born, he has been in the food industry for more than twenty-five years and has experience working in Africa, the Middle East, the Far East, and Switzerland. This wide swath of experience has made him a brainstormer, and part of his job is to forecast consumer demand and suggest new products. He is steeped in the history and language of nutrition, comfortable with exotic New Age nutrients like phytosterols and probiotics. He's been working in and watching the health food movement from his perch in a California office for some years, and he was impressed that the 2007 Natural Products Expo he attended attracted 42,000 visitors. About 10 percent of the booths he saw mentioned the word "obesity" and were devoted to healthier products. It's certainly on his mind.

I stopped in to see Allen at Nestlé headquarters in Glendale, California. It's difficult not to think of the less-than-delicious irony surrounding the world's largest food company (with $80 billion in annual revenues). On the street level below one of the tallest buildings in this Los Angeles suburb is a small retail store selling a wide range of Nestlé products. You can scan the frozen food cabinets and buy their Lean Cuisine products, or opt for the wide array of indulgent foods in the form of candy bars. The Nestlé Crunch bar packaging hasn't changed since I was a boy. And why should it? It's an iconic brand.

But I wondered when I talked with Allen why Nestlé couldn't concoct a healthier version of this milk chocolate and rice treat? Allen's response embodied the problem at work in the food industry. He said that they could make a healthier version of this classic candy bar, and it wouldn't necessarily cut into the real Crunch bar's sales. But it would have to be marketed as a healthy alternative, thereby limiting its marketing appeal. And almost more important, he felt that to make it healthier the cost would have to go up substantially.

"In order to do it, we'd have to double the price of the candy bar," Allen said.

I fully understand Allen's point of view, but I'm not sure that I totally agree with him. Nestlé's Crunch bar may be an icon like Coca-Cola that "is what it is." However, there are several roads Nestlé could consider going down: First, it could use marketing tactics to deliver less calories per serving, such as 100-calorie packs of Nestlé Crunchies. Second, it could take a page out of Coca-Cola's playbook and extend the line, just like Coca-Cola Zero. One can take the core Crunch brand and introduce it to new users who care more about their health but still want the real chocolate taste. I cannot believe there isn't room for a healthier, great-tasting line of Nestlé Crunch "Lovables" (notice we don't call it a diet version) that would eat like a Crunch bar but deliver fewer calories and less saturated fat. This solution at least shifts some consumption to a lower-calorie item (plus Nestlé might make a larger margin). It's hard to hear pronouncements like that even from someone as nutrition-minded as Allen and not wonder if this is simply a food executive protecting his brand. It seems hard to believe that the situation is really that bleak. Or maybe I'm too optimistic.

Allen's point about how changing the marketing of a product will enhance the effectiveness of Stealth Health is already at work in some companies. Land O'Lakes has quietly introduced a buttery spread with canola oil, meaning more monosaturated fat instead of saturated fat. Chris Policinski, the company CEO, told me that his communications strategy for their new Spreadable Butter with Canola Oil focused on the spreadability of the product and not the health advantages of canola. He said his challenge was that butter is an icon, and it takes time to change consumer expectations. Policinski ultimately believes that taste and performance are the keys to a successful product. (If it doesn't look like butter and have butter's texture, then the marketer is in trouble. All marketers of icon brands like Coke and Campbell's face this issue.) Land O'Lakes did this with little fanfare, even though this spread is far better for your heart than their conventional butter. This was a heart-healthy move that was not trumpeted through a sheaf of press releases.

It was the epitome of Stealth Health. This wasn't about trying to convince the consumers to choose healthy over unhealthy; it was about introducing a new product with new benefits that *happened* to be healthier. This was precisely Allen's point about a healthy Nestlé Crunch. The Land O'Lakes effort demonstrates that for Stealth Health to be effective, it's not just about being quiet, it's also about marketplace perception.

But what works for butter won't necessarily work for chocolate. I don't expect the Nestlé Crunch bar to change its formula, or for a diet Crunch bar to be introduced any time soon. In fact, chocolate may remain an untouchable, a food that even some nutrition activists feel should be a reward in modest amounts. Still, there are diet chocolates, and I've tasted some of them; while at this point they're noticeably different, that probably won't be the case forever.

The chocolate issue has been simmering for some time now, and I expect that it will become more important in the nutrition debate very shortly. The average American eats almost twelve pounds per year. That's 27,000 calories, 1,530 grams of fat, 1,130 milligrams of cholesterol, and 4,400 milligrams of sodium. Nearly four out of ten Americans (38 percent) eat chocolate at least a few times per week. We could certainly use some Stealth Health here. The debate can be distilled into this: Can we call a product chocolate if it doesn't contain cocoa butter? Federal regulators are now considering a proposal from several food industry groups that would allow the substitution of vegetable oil for cocoa butter in products that could still be called chocolate. These new concoctions would be cheaper and perhaps a lot healthier than real chocolate.

Cocoa butter is a saturated fat, though when used in chocolate it may not be as bad for you as other similar cooking oils. Studies suggest that flavonols, which are found in dark chocolate, maintain a healthy vascular system, lower blood pressure, and increase blood flow to the brain. In short, eating dark chocolate in correct and modest amounts could stave off strokes. (The chocolate makers would love to make more of this in their marketing efforts, but they're understandably cautious because the FDA might not buy into their claims.)

There's already been a groundswell of protest coming from companies like Mars and a number of purists who complain that the chocolate bar just won't taste the same. They claim the texture will be different and it just won't melt in your mouth the way the real thing does.

There will be pure chocolate, and vegetable oil "chocolate" (it's already here and is popular in baking recipes, where it's difficult for the eater to taste the difference), but I think we have to get over the labeling debate about it very quickly. Purists already have flooded the blogs with "Don't Mess With My Chocolate" postings, and that's fine with me. Consumer choice will rule. Those who want the modified versions and can't tell the difference—Stealth Health at work here—should be allowed to be happily fooled.

Stealth Health won't necessarily work for every product. To really be effective, it needs to be a combination of the right product and the right positioning. For some specific products, like yogurt, companies will want to play up the health benefits. For others, like fast food, stealth is a better option. For others still, like chocolate, there may not really be a way to make a deceptive alternative that's convincing. So Stealth Health is just a tool in the arsenal, but a tool that must be used to make some serious progress in the fight against obesity.

While all these various food company initiatives are ambitious, General Mills has put into motion a set of Stealth Health ideas that could overhaul companies' relationships between their bottom line and their customer. General Mills is a brand you know from the supermarket aisles. They market everything from Cheerios, Total, Kix, Wheaties, and Cinnamon Toast Crunch cereals to Hamburger Helper, Progresso soups, Green Giant vegetables, and Yoplait yogurt, not to forget Betty Crocker mixes (which always remind me of my early years of pushing cake). Their goal is to make their customers' lives "healthier, easier, and richer." Okay, nothing wrong with that. The phrase cleverly blankets their entire product line, and many other companies make similar claims.

But what they're doing internally is startlingly progressive, and there's no reason for the company to trumpet this to consumers because it's all about the workings of their inner gears. Brand managers and executives now have their bonuses connected with building health into the food they sell. The company has a "health matrix" that measures the number of "limiters" (bad stuff in food) against "positives" (healthy ingredients). Limiters include items like trans fats, other fats, calories, sodium, and sugar. Positives are whole grains, fibers, calcium, certain vitamins, and fruit. Begun in 2005, the idea is to improve every product by 10 percent total, in limiters down and positives up, every year. Though the program has been in place for a few years, they did not go public with it until 2008. It's an effective way to improve the nutrition of some products in a totally behind-the-scenes way. I first discovered their plan by accident—at an industry conference.

During the first three years of the program, General Mills lowered the limiters by 43 percent and increased the positives by 57 percent. The companywide goal is to get to a 40 percent improvement level on all their products by 2010. What's unique is that they've built health into their bottom line. They are planning and projecting goals in the same way that they would with money. It's not about having the two forces of nutrition and profit in opposition to each other; it's about making them work together, and making that a fundamental part of the corporate philosophy. The workforce is now faced with an incentive that is not just about sales growth. When they get to work in the morning, they have to think about their customers' health as much as they do about selling them more goods. In short, it pays to think healthy.

And it's not just food companies in the United States that are catching on to Stealth Health. All over the globe, a small sampling of companies has begun to rely on these principles to change the way that they create and market their products. Unilever, a multinational conglomerate that derives 57 percent of its revenues from food products, sells its wares in 150 countries. And while executives there do not lose sight of the notion that taste is the most important demand made by consumers, they've been responding to the enemy of health officials everywhere: sugar. In 2005 and 2006, Unilever has removed 17,416 tons of sugar from its food portfolio, and *they made a point to not make it a point.*

Danone, one of the world's largest beverage companies, has begun modifying its portfolio of drinks. In the United States they're primarily known for its Evian water. But they're ubiquitous in France and throughout Europe. The company is committed to improving the health of its products. In 2005 and 2006, it started an initiative to remove sugar from their offerings in Spain, Mexico, the UK, France, and Germany. They're now steadily working toward eliminating thousands more tons of sugar across the board by 2009. According to a company source, Danone believes these goals are "conservative" because "we have projects to help formulation teams develop better products with less sugar."

It's readily apparent that Danone has a head start on many of its American competitors on this critical health issue. My prediction is that because sugared beverages are such contributors of calories in the obesity issue, we'll see levels of fatness drop in western Europe well before they do in the United States. Most important of all, Danone is a very profitable outfit. If you check the company's financials, you'll see that it has been enjoying very steady growth. Once they've established a market for a product, they're able to reduce the calorie content and still be successful. Danone is flying under the radar on the sugar issue simply because they're doing the right thing and barely anyone has noticed.

Case studies like this have convinced me that health/wellness and profits are not mutually exclusive on a large-scale basis. The bottom line of Stealth Health is to get companies—whether they're selling burgers at lunch or launching their next big Halloween sales initiative in chocolates—to start thinking about the long term. Each day that they avoid starting the process, the harder it will be to surface long-term solutions. While some companies have begun to get on board, there is still a great deal of work to be done. It's in their best interests and it is possible to make healthier foods. I know the large conglomerates can do this without sacrificing taste or profits or risking the reputation of a single cash cow brand. It can be done now. And it can be done without a shareholder (or consumer) revolt.

And if it works for the corporation's bottom line, it certainly will benefit the consumer. Applying Stealth Health to the most popular foods and beverages will go a long way to helping consumers in their fight to maintain their health. Knowing that it is so difficult for consumers to change the way they eat, Stealth Health comes to the rescue. When the foods and beverages you consume on a daily basis automatically come with lower calories or better fats, it's a huge boost in your ability to recapture some control.

Stealth Health offers all the ingredients for a win-win solution. Mass-market products like burgers and fries must undergo secretive nutritional surgery in order for there to be a significant impact on the nation's collective stomach size. This way, companies are not pressured to eliminate their best sellers; they just quietly go about modifying their nutrition or putting their marketing behind healthier items. All at an acceptable profit. And the consumer is not asked (again) to change what or how they eat. The heavy lifting is already done for them.

# 12

# future foods

George: *Yum, it's been light years since you programmed synthetic brownies.*

Jane: *Our home food dispenser broke and I had to wait 20 seconds at the checkout counter, such inefficiency.*

—*The Jetsons*

McYum's, circa 2040, anywhere on the planet. The sign below the Golden Arches reads: "Trillions of servings sold." (McDonald's acquired Yum Brands—KFC, Taco Bell, and Pizza Hut—as part of the food merger mania of the twenty-first century.) When you enter the restaurant, your handprint is scanned at the screen on the kiosk near the entrance as you check in, a valued customer, eligible for a variety of discounts depending on the frequency of your visits. There are now robo-servers in all fast-food outlets, kiosks where customers order and pay for meals. You can plug in your portable data manager into a robo-port and it instantly coughs up the information you need. This results in your usual order and the food combos specific to your genetic and metabolic makeup, as designed by your doctor and nutritionist.

You're completely comfortable with this process. The information in their files has been compiled and approved periodically by you and you alone, and it may contain your allergies, your favorite foods, your total calorie consumption, fat consumption, carbohydrate intake, vitamin deficiencies, metabolism rate, cholesterol levels, medications you're taking, and so on. It will update the average intake of all the ingredients of your typical meal, collated from past visits. McYum's will have the usual data-mining marketing information as well; the date and time of your last visit, how much you spent, what you ordered, whether you complained about the food or service, or complimented anyone on the staff.

With a discrete code, like the transponders used in aircraft, the restaurant can track your arrival via GPS and have your order waiting when you arrive, even accommodating for traffic delays or a stop at grandma's house to pick up another customer.

The plastic seats are gone; soft cushions with stain-resistant material that encourage longer stays have replaced them. The high ceilings have skylights, and there are solar panels on the roof.

And then there is the big change: the food preparation. The nanofryer uses heart-safe oil that lasts five times longer than the oil used a generation before, maintaining quality and helping to keep costs down. The spent oil is recycled for automobile fuel. You marvel at the notion that the gas you used to drive here could have begun in the deep-fat fryer. All meat, beef, and chicken is antibiotic-free. In fact, no restaurant food comes with antibiotics anymore.

The science of nutragenomics—nutritional products keyed into an individual's mapped genome—has been fairly advanced by this date, so customers can have their meals personally tailored to match their profile. This may especially appeal to the elderly, who by this time will by far be the largest age group in marketing demographics. Good thing you stopped to pick up grandma.

If you are such a customer, you can ask your robo-server to call up any special dishes that accommodate your diet or whatever it is your eating profile specifically demands. This will include alternatives so you're never bored, and the portions will be allotted based on what your profile says is best for you—especially if you're on a training regiment for a certain weight target or body type. You'll pay for many such servings by the ounce. You can charge your special McYum's account, or your debit or credit card. And the company will gladly keep track of all the data.

It's the Jetsons' answer to the Happy Meal. And trust me, this is all way beyond freeze-dried ice cream for astronauts.

Not everyone, of course, will prefer such a regimented meal. You can order conventional fast food as well. The overhead menu is different from what it was a half century earlier. People no longer eat appetizers, entrées, or desserts. They now eat single portions of everything in the same size, dim sum–style.

When you leave, all the waste—wrappers, containers, cups, and bottles—is automatically recycled. It's all biodegradable. You just dump everything off your tray into the bin.

If we can dream it, it can happen.

Okay, so maybe all this is a bit too "pie in the sky," but it's safe to say that food in thirty years is going to look pretty different. In fact, food in ten years might look pretty different, but the real change will be what's on the inside.

I want to show you what's coming down the pike, what you can expect to see in your food and drink in a few years, and how it might be able to help Americans lead healthier lives. The technological advancement of food design and production is here now; it's practical and becoming more affordable; and it holds the promise of delivering tasty *and* healthy food for tomorrow. Think of it as the ultimate in Stealth Health. No longer will a food that's good for us automatically imply that it might not taste great. Or that it will be loaded with fats, sugars, and calories. We will be able to have our cake and eat it, too.

New healthy ingredients are starting to show up in foods and beverages already. These modern products are usually referred to within the industry as "functional foods," so far populated mostly by "nutraceuticals"—a portmanteau of nutrition and pharmaceutical. The most common functional foods on the market right now are energy bars, yogurts, dairy products, and beverages. Items containing branded "active ingredients" already account for more than $1 billion in annual sales for Nestlé. This segment of its business has finally achieved some significant critical mass (though it's a mere 2 percent of annual business), and it represents a growing market for its competitors.

These emerging advances look quite promising. Consumers can expect to benefit from a whole host of novel ingredients, from those that can significantly lower your risk for heart disease to others that help you gain control of your weight. All without sacrificing the enjoyment of eating or drinking.

Now, some may raise arguments against *any* new technology or the production of modified foods (I'm thinking about the controversy over genetically modified foods). The kinds of ingredients I'm talking about here derive from natural sources and can be processed in totally familiar ways. Given the vast benefits that will accrue from these breakthroughs, I wholeheartedly endorse their study and application into foods and beverages. There's much that still has to be learned, but there's a lot that we already do know. Already we've begun to see future food trends that will no doubt continue for years to come.

Today, omega-3s are starting to pop up in a select number of products. Derived mostly from fish or algae, omega-3s have been shown to be beneficial in helping to improve heart health and mental acuity, with potentially many other positive benefits that may include relief of joint pain and arthritis, high blood pressure, Alzheimer's, and cancer. While the most common advice given by cardiologists is to "eat more fish," this is impractical for too many people. Many eaters don't like fish, and those who often do live in areas where fresh fish is at a premium.

The use of omega-3s in the United States was initially confined to infant formulas when studies showed a modest increase in a cognitive measure. Every major infant formula brand now incorporates an omega-3 component known as DHA. In 2004, the FDA gave qualified health claim status to some omega-3s, saying that they may reduce the risk of coronary heart disease. People with certain circulatory problems could benefit from fish oil, a major natural source of omega-3s. There is strong evidence that omega-3s reduce blood triglyceride levels, and regular intake reduces the risk of heart attacks.

Following these health claims, interest in these fatty acids increased. Today, omega-3s have been incorporated into an increasing number of foods and beverages. Nestlé has been selling children a strawberry-flavored drink with omega-3s added; Tropicana and Minute Maid have been marketing juices containing omega-3s; and Breyers has touted its Smart! yogurt's brain-boosting benefits. They're even showing up in sliced meats on delicatessen shelves in Portugal and in olives now found in Spanish pantries. Food pundits expect to see them soon in baked goods, cookies, ice cream, and other desserts. Imagine the potential for children who can't stand the sight of a piece of salmon or flounder—but ice cream?

But my real excitement for omega-3s and the new technologies that have surfaced is in restaurant food. Let's imagine you walk into a McDonald's, perhaps sometime between 2010 and 2015. You check the familiar menu above the ordering counter, and you see next to the usual fare the "Omega Mac." It costs about the same as the Big Mac used to, and it looks and smells exactly like the Big Mac of your youth, but it now comes with an important additive—omega-3 fatty acids. And surprise! It tastes superb. The taste is in the fat, and it's still in the burger, but now it's mostly good fat.

This is a giant step beyond the vegetable burgers and turkey burgers we're accustomed to eating today to avoid a diet heavy in beef. Who would have thought we could engineer heart-healthy red meat? Actually, I don't believe such an offering is that far off if the restaurants kick it into gear. Studies conducted at the University of Minnesota using a proprietary patent have demonstrated that a full day's supply of omega-3s can be added to hot dogs without any off-taste being detected. I have personally tasted these and they are quite good. All that was done was to replace one-third of the existing "bad" fats with specially purified omega-3s. I have also tried some prototype hamburgers and did not detect any impact on taste or smell.

Consumers will not taste the difference, and they don't have to give up their fast-food fixes. The integration of healthy ingredients into commonly consumed foods could revolutionize eating and improve nutrition across every demographic segment. What a boon to both the consumer and the fast-food business when products like these show up on the menus!

Another nutraceutical that's starting to break through is phytosterols, or plant sterols, which are increasingly popular additives that have been proven to lower LDL ("bad") cholesterol and are being touted as a possible cancer-fighting agent. Phytosterols are found in all plant foods, but the highest concentrations are in unrefined plant oils including vegetable, nut, and olive oils. Soy-based products have the largest amounts (Cargill and Archer Daniels Midland are the biggest producers of both soy-based products and phytosterols). Nuts, seeds, whole grains, and legumes are also good dietary sources of phytosterols. Vegetarians, of course, swear by phytosterols, and they may be on to something.

Plant sterols are showing up in products like Minute Maid Heart Wise orange juice, Nature Valley Healthy Heart Chewy Granola Bars, and Rice Dream Heartwise, a rice drink substitute for milk. They're also available in butter and margarine substitutes such as Take Control and Benecol.

What I like most about sterols is that they reduce cholesterol naturally. In October 2005, I gave a speech at WorldNutra in Anaheim, California, and highlighted the benefits of phytosterols as a preferred means to lower cholesterol over the conventional pharmaceutical approach. Here, take a pill and make the problem disappear. While sterols do not lower cholesterol as dramatically as drugs like Lipitor, they certainly help avoid such nasty (and often unspoken) side effects as liver problems and muscle myopathy.

Clearly, the addition of sterols to more foods and beverages would go a long way to improving America's heart health, but a bigger benefit would accrue if we started incorporating them into restaurant food. I know of one patent for sterol-infused frying oils that claims that no cholesterol would be absorbed by the consumer after eating fried food. Think about it: One of the biggest concerns about frying oils is that they add calories and bring a lot of, well, fat. If you could now go to KFC and know that you won't be picking up any added cholesterol from your food, wouldn't you consider it? That *is* "finger lick'n good." All the taste, and none of the cholesterol. And while we're at it, what if sterols were added to ketchup? You could be eating your burger with ketchup and you don't have to worry about all the cholesterol that comes with the beef.

Phytosterols, as well as other well-being nutrients, is a topic of great interest to Glenn Armstrong, PhD, who has served as the senior director of Wrigley's new ventures group. He did a stint with Gatorade, which, in my view, was the first functional beverage. When I was in Chicago for the National Restaurant Show in the spring of 2007, I ventured out to the industrial district where his office in the huge chewing gum company is located. His group is in charge of innovation, and his headquarters is a symbol of the company's commitment to research. It's a modern facility with an atrium and courtyard, a welcome surprise among dull industrial buildings. Armstrong is middle-aged, but he looks young and extremely fit due to an extensive regimen of cycling roadwork. This is a guy who stays in shape.

To understand the role phytosterols could play for various food products, Armstrong talked about how the Mars chocolate company came out with a candy bar called Coco Via that had phytosterols in it. He said, "They tried to go down an antioxidant path because dark chocolate has a lot of antioxidants, but they couldn't justify their claims. [The benefits are] so tough to prove. With phytosterols, you just put it in there and say, 'Dark chocolate is good for the heart.' There's no need to back up the claims solely on the basis of the dark chocolate. The sterols carry the day."

Armstrong also noted another ingredient that he was particularly high on: probiotics. Probiotics are live organisms—"good" bacteria, to summarize them—that can provide health benefits to your gastrointestinal system. There are indications that they may lower cholesterol and blood pressure, and also bolster the immune system against potentially dangerous diseases such as colon cancer. Most probiotic cultures are found in yogurt products, but they're beginning to appear in other drinks and supplements in the health food sections of grocery stores. Brands include Yakult, Multibionta, and Dannon's Actimel—all drinkable yogurts.

New research announced in January of 2008 from Nestlé shows that probiotics may affect metabolism in a way that holds promise for weight management. They learned that the amount of fat absorbed by the body when consuming yogurt drinks could be controlled by the probiotics. If proven, this would have big implications for a multitude of products ranging from dairy drinks to juices to restaurant shakes. Armstrong confirms the lure of dairy as a carrier for health benefits. With conviction, he said, "If I were going to give other food companies advice on what to do with wellness, I'd concentrate on dairy. Dairy is going to be huge. That's the first thing. Probiotics."

Probiotics aren't the only ingredients of the future that may hold weight-loss potential. There are several promising ingredients that provide a range of benefits, from enhancing metabolism to preserving lean muscle to making you feel full sooner.

Let's start with green tea. It's a product that has been around a long time. According to ancient Chinese legend, tea was discovered by the Chinese emperor Shen-Nung in 2737 B.C.E. Green tea contains a powerful antioxidant called epigallocatechin gallate (ECGC). The purported benefits are numerous, but some recent studies have indicated that green tea may aid in managing weight. The *American Journal of Clinical Nutrition* reported a study in 2005 in which thirty-five Japanese men who drank a daily bottle of tea fortified with this green tea extract experienced significant reductions in body weight—more so than their counterparts who drank a regular bottle of tea daily. Preliminary studies on animals reported in January 2008 that green tea might promote fat loss and keep extra weight off. In 2006, Coca-Cola and Nestlé introduced Enviga, a green tea beverage with added caffeine. The studies, conducted in conjunction with the University of Lausanne in Switzerland, indicated that this combination of ingredients increased calorie burning. As we discussed earlier, Coke was chided for making claims suggesting that consuming Enviga would result in actual weight loss, but the basic research appears sound and looks promising. Should the evidence prove out under more rigorous testing, green tea or green tea beverage blends could prove to be serious weight-management tools.

CLA (conjugated lineoleic acid) is another promising ingredient. Basically, CLA is a fatty acid found primarily in meat and dairy products. Most manufacturers convert it from safflower oils. CLA inhibits lipoprotein lipase, an enzyme that breaks down fat from our diets. By suppressing this stored-fat enzyme, CLA helps reduce the amount of fat broken down and, ultimately, the amount of fat deposited and stored in the body. CLA has been the subject of dozens of lab studies, and the results and claims have varied widely.

Put simply, it has been shown that this compound can reduce body fat and increase or preserve muscle mass. Perhaps its most significant benefit will be attractive to those people who have been victims of the so-called yo-yo diet syndrome, where they're constantly losing and gaining weight in predictable cycles. Oprah Winfrey, a celebrity with considerable resolve, is probably the poster person for this syndrome. If dieting is difficult for her, how hard is it for those without her sense of commitment? Researchers have indicated that those who have used CLA supplements—the most notable is Tonalin from Cognis, found in health food stores—have been resistant to the weight gain experienced by those who haven't used it.

Tonalin is sold as a supplement because it is difficult to mix into foods and beverages. The advent of nanotechnology, however, might make a difference in recasting it as an additive. Nanotechnology is the science of using very small molecules—in increments as small as a billionth of a meter—to develop products. Initial applications have gravitated toward metallurgy and materials. But there is enormous potential in food. Imagine getting all kinds of good things into foods you love without altering the taste. Why would one care about a CLA in a Diet Coke, you might ask? The answer is that studies show that people who consume diet drinks often have as much trouble controlling their weight as those who don't. It's the old syndrome of ordering the whole pizza and using the diet drink as an excuse to consume too many other calories.

Kraft took the industry lead in nanotechnogy in 2000 when it established the Nanotek Consortium, a collaboration of fifteen universities and national research labs. Kraft's focus is on interactive foods and beverages, hoping to invent products that can be customized to fit the tastes and needs of consumers at the individual level of personalized nutrition (I speculated about this at the beginning of this chapter). Possible products include foods and drinks that can recognize and adjust to a consumer's specific nutritional needs, including the oversight of their weight.

While nanofoods will take some time to develop, there are already some minor applications. In Australia, for example, nanocapsules are used to add heart-healthy omega-3 fatty acids to one of the country's most popular brands of white bread: Tuna fish oil has been added to Tip Top Bread, and the encapsulation process actually keeps the bread from tasting fishy.

One of the biggest problems with obesity and weight control stems from the fact that even the most disciplined dieters find themselves continually hungry. As some of the latest research is showing, in the future, foods will not only be able to help make what we eat healthier, they will be able to help us eat less. Tackling the satiety issue—the feeling of fullness after eating—is a vexing problem that scientists and researchers have been looking at for several years.

The resurgence of protein as a weight-management tool, for example, leads me to expect to see new beverages that can finally taste good with high levels of protein. High-protein foods satisfy hunger by allowing the body to release an antiobesity hormone known as PPY. We can incorporate protein into beverages and foods through new technologies without impairing taste. Kellogg's, for example, is already launching its Special K20 Protein Water Mix as a weight-control product. Today this stuff doesn't taste very good, but new technologies can improve on this problem.

Clinical trials of Fabuless have shown promising results. Fabuless is a novel combination of palm and oat oils. Four independent studies conducted at the University of Ulster in Northern Ireland substantiated the product's ability to reduce caloric intake by 12 to 29 percent at subsequent meals. Participants who used Fabuless were less hungry than the placebo group after four hours. The reason: The palm and oat oil combination causes digestion to be delayed, sending a message of fullness to the brain. Fabuless is made by DSM (a multibillion-dollar life science and materials science corporation based in the Netherlands), and it is used primarily in dairy products, most notably yogurt, throughout Europe. The specific oat portion is digested very slowly, allowing Fabuless to be absorbed into the intestinal system. By slowing down your digestion cycle, you're less likely to immediately crave something to eat.

Fabuless is not merely a European phenomenon. On April 29, 2008, the *Wall Street Journal* reported on a new appetite-suppressant product called SlimShots that started appearing on store shelves in the United States. It contains Fabuless and comes in a small coffee creamer–like container. It's intended to be taken at breakfast: $39.95 for thirty shots, $1.33 per day.

I am particularly keen on satiety ingredients because feeling fuller faster means we will still be able to enjoy our favorite foods without pounding down as many calories. It's artificially induced portion control. It represents the ultimate win-win solution. Consumers can enjoy their favorite foods and feel pleasantly full without having taken in as many calories. Restaurateurs and packaged goods makers will be able to use less ingredient, since the portion sizes would be smaller, thus charge slightly less. They could actually make more money—it's like a reverse supersize. I save some money on ingredients but I don't discount the meal proportionately. This type of scenario would motivate business to support this kind of satiety food, yet do right by their customers' health.

Not to be overlooked in the quest to curtail people's appetites, Armstrong pointed to Wrigley's industry-leading efforts in nutrient delivery through chewing gum. To date, one of the most popular vehicles for functional ingredients is gum, which is being used not only for its appeal as a unique and inexpensive delivery means, but also as a way to improve the delivery of a specific ingredient.

Research studies have shown that chewing gum can get certain ingredients into the bloodstream faster than other delivery systems such as nutritional bars or beverages. One industry executive noted that "energy" is being touted in chewing gum launches, with most products including caffeine or ginseng. Green tea also is being highlighted in new chewing gums. I'm hoping the gum makers—or perhaps other food companies—will start to think about producing "chewable" snacks with healthy ingredients that have a texture like gum but make you feel like you're eating without consuming the calories. It could be like a space-age taffy that's easy on your teeth and either consumable or disposable.

In 2006 alone, Wrigley supported ten groundbreaking studies in the United States and the UK to investigate the potential role of chewing gum in appetite control and weight management. Wrigley's R&D management has signified that at just five to ten calories a serving, chewing gum instead of eating a high-calorie snack can help reduce calorie intake. Or it may be simply a diversion to prevent "mindless munching."

Wrigley announced the formation of its Wrigley Science Institute to study whether chewing gum may help consumers as a tool in weight management, stress relief, and increasing alertness and concentration. Wrigley claims chewing gum is the number one snack choice among U.S. adults aged eighteen to fifty-four. They're hoping that new research might provide even more motivation to chew gum. (One idea could be highly caffeinated gum for soldiers on the battlefield—much easier to consume than, say, a Red Bull drink.) In 2006, Wrigley planned to support at least ten studies investigating the health benefits of chewing gum.

Armstrong points to one very important aspect that chewing gum provides: Consumed for just a few minutes after a meal, it deters diners from going back to the kitchen or buffet table. It retards the desire to overstuff.

Can we make it taste like fried chicken?

An initiative that could outdo satiety ingredients in terms of impact is a project currently under way involving commodity trader Cargill and the Coca-Cola Company. These two giants have joined in a partnership to develop and introduce the industry's first natural, zero-calorie sweetener. The sweetener, called Rebiana, is derived from stevia, a shrub first discovered by the Guarani natives of Paraguay who used the plant's leaves to sweeten drinks. Plans call for Rebiana first to be introduced by The Coca-Cola Company in its family of beverages and as a food ingredient by Cargill. Rebiana's breakthrough is that it has all the sweetness of stevia but none of the lingering aftertaste like current artificial sweeteners in the marketplace.

Rebiana has not yet received FDA approval, but if and when it does, it could prove to be a revolutionary product in targeting weight control, and could assuage the fears of those who balk at consuming products with anything "artificial" in them. Cargill just submitted data to the FDA that claimed Rebiana was safe for consumption, and it is under review at the time of this writing.

I cannot stress how monumental it will be if this natural sweetener is approved as an additive for foods and beverages. The natural aspect addresses one of the key anguishes for consumers: Is it okay for me to feed my child a "diet" soda? Second, presuming the taste is as advertised, the door opens for an armada of products to be reformulated and marketed to consumers awaiting low-calorie options that taste wonderful. A true win for everybody—assuming the price isn't through the roof.

Ultimately, the quintessential psychological breakthrough might just be the "healthy doughnut." This is the ultimate oxymoron. But things are actually looking up. As reported in the *Journal of Food Science*, researchers evaluated doughnuts that contain small amounts of soybean hulls. Fat content of the doughnuts was reduced by 36 percent with no detrimental impacts on flavor, taste, crispiness, and general liking. This is huge if the findings hold up under more rigorous testing. Basically we have a lower-calorie doughnut. It's a great example of Stealth Health in action. The consumer never really sees the frying oil or any soybean hulls, just the resulting healthier doughnut.

As we move toward future foods, my most optimistic dreams begin with nutragenomics, which will lead to the ability of food makers to customize diets to individual needs. Some have referred to the field as "nutraproteomics," since many diseases are the result of the abnormal functioning of genes and their protein products. Whatever it is called, it deals with the effect of nutraceuticals and how they interact with genes and proteins in fostering health benefits, and is a major factor in the development of future foods. Summed up, nutragenomics is the study of how an individual's genetic makeup predisposes him or her to certain food and health issues. I believe there will be a time when healthier foods will be engineered to stave off many kinds of illnesses and infirmities. As people come to have a better understanding of their genetic relationship to food, they will know what to eat. Tailor-made foods will be here for the next generation. It's already under way. Companies like Genelex out of Washington state take your blood sample and examine it for nineteen genes, then combine that with your responses to a lifestyle questionnaire, and generate personalized diet recommendations. It's early-stage stuff, but on its way.

This is an exciting time to be involved in the food arena. "We're on the brink of a revolution that will change the way many foods will be formulated," stated Nestlé's Allen. Despite the historical "status quo" industry mentality that has prevailed, the future—even in the near term—will be explosive. Though there are a lot of uncertainties here, the one thing we do know—and must continually be aware of—is that nutrition science is a complex, multifaceted discipline where every action causes yet another action.

But we are gaining more knowledge in many areas, and it's going to take public pressure throughout the marketplace to demand healthier foods that are both alternatives and substitutes for what we're accustomed to consuming.

I'm willing to bet that the packaged goods makers will take the lead in future foods well before the restaurant industry, as they've done in other areas involving food and health. It's been a predictable pattern. We see trendsetters first in other countries, and when American corporations catch on to the market potential, they finally take a new-product risk. As we've seen, restaurateurs shun anything "healthy" because they think it's anathema to their customers. Only a few will have the insight to take any initiative, and the great majority will wait until government mandates force them to change, as we've already seen with the trans fat issue. There are board members of quick-service restaurants who should be prodding their executives to think about this right now. If I were a McDonald's director, I'd be asking what tomorrow's Happy Meal should look like. Should it include a 10-calorie, nutrient-fused alert-sustained energy beverage? A great tasting, low-calorie burger? Healthier fries (fried using soybean hulls in the potatoes)?

Conversely, I'd continue to put the packaged goods companies' creative feet to the fire. I firmly believe in the notion of "healthy junk food"—that some day will not be a laughable oxymoron. Lunchables, my favorite topic, can be reformulated in a healthy way. In fact, we can come up with several items that are made with vegetable-infused ingredients that taste like other indulgent snacks. And if we can happily fool the kids during recess or lunch, we can also happily fool ourselves.

General Mills is starting to think in this direction. So is Pepsi. Their Frito-Lay subsidiary has started an entire division to develop healthier alternatives. In fact, Frito-Lay hired a former USDA executive who is knowledgeable in fruits, and also asked a pair of experts in vegetables to be on this development team. Here is a company known for its corn chips (some of you may remember the jingle, "Munch a bunch of Fritos"), and now they're looking toward fruits, vegetables, and dairy. Frito-Lay made a substantial investment in this because they're concerned about their core business. They know their future isn't in corn chips *as they are* because they're filled with salt and calories and inherently are not good for their customers in great quantities. Can this be the start of a megatrend? If Frito-Lay does it, maybe other firms will see a similar value in doing it.

There's a lot to consider in the future of producing and selling the food we'll be eating many years from today. I think there are a lot of advances in food production we can aspire to, especially if we're still hooked on hamburgers, fries, and soft drinks, and we continue to spend our food dollars at places like McDonald's, Wendy's, and Burger King. If everything is done right and the industry works with science to do its job, the real winner here is the consumer.

My idea of future foods means that we won't have to figure out what's good for us. The whole process would be automated, just as I mentioned at the beginning of this chapter. No more fretting about how many calories or fat grams we're consuming. The Food Pyramid is finally retired. Diet plans are a thing of the past. The South Beach Diet was a passing fad and Jenny Craig went out of business long ago. Since nobody stuck to those plans anyway, they don't have to worry about it any longer. With advances in nutragenomics, we can arrive at a place where the consumer no longer has to even think about whether they are doing their bodies harm when they eat. It's now out of their hands. No matter where or what they eat, foods and beverages will be right for them.

I probably won't live long enough to visit McYum's, but my grandchildren will. The restaurants will be energy efficient and your favorite foods will taste even better than you remember. Yet I'm looking forward to the day when I scan my hand and I'm told that I'm getting that 50-cents-off omega-3 reduced-fat, low-calorie quad burger—and I don't have to worry that it's leaving any deadly plaque in my arteries.

The future of food can be a rosy one, if the powerful companies that produce these goods have the foresight to understand that they can help us live longer and healthier lives. We will be able to buy their products and enhance their revenues and profits for a longer period. Once they recognize that technology can be safe and useful in everything from condiments to meats to beverages, the public will line up at their windows.

# 13

# how big brother can (really) help

One single steer nearly ruined me.

Back in May 2003, the first incidence of mad cow disease in North America was discovered in Alberta, Canada. I had a potential hit product: a safer cooking oil—no trans fats, and all the cholesterol removed—but it contained beef. The company that was processing it was located in Canada. Because of the health scare, the borders were sealed indefinitely, and we couldn't deliver any orders. Customers canceled in droves. We had violated one of the purchasing agent's cardinal rules: Thou shalt not mess up supply. We were stuck until a new U.S. facility went on line in October. In just six months, we lost millions of dollars in business; Canadian beef producers lost billions.

Clearly, in this situation it was appropriate for the government (the USDA) to intervene. After all, the safety of the meat supply was in question. Still, some food-industry critics argued that the government went too far in their ban, and they did make a good case for themselves. Frying oil, even one that contains beef, is highly refined at temperatures sometimes over 500 degrees Fahrenheit. The World Health Organization had concluded that all food, cosmetic, and pharmaceutical products containing gelatin or beef tallow were safe and could be used with confidence.

Despite the controversy that this case caused and the personal hardships that it generated for my company, I am the first to acknowledge that this type of intervention is what the primary role of the government should be in our food. When the safety of the American public is in question, the government needs to act, even if their actions leave some of us in the food industry up a creek without a paddle. While some might argue that their methods were too extreme, no one can doubt the importance of the government when it comes to oversight of this kind.

Though outbreaks of mad cow disease or *E. coli* give ample demonstration of why it's so important to have the government monitoring the immediate safety of our food, where the water becomes a bit muddier is what the government's role should be when it comes to our nutritional health. It's one thing to protect us and to ensure our safety; it's quite another to decide that certain foods are in our "best interest" while others are not.

Despite the good intentions that the public sector might have when it comes to promoting our nutritional health, we have seen that the government does not have a stellar track record in achieving its stated goal of reducing obesity.

This is not their strength. They are not good implementers. Banning particular foods (like cupcakes) or ingredients (like oils) does not guarantee a healthier public. These are well-intentioned suggestions, but serve only as Band-Aids on the patient who needs surgery.

Earlier we talked about the movement to ban trans fats from fried and baked foods. A noble idea. After all, they have been proven to be bad for your heart. But what happens in reality? Consumers believe that the authorities are doing something good for their health. In many cases, however, oils with higher levels of saturated fats, also linked to heart disease, are substituted so that pie crusts and biscuits can deliver the same texture and mouthfeel. So while we're eradicating trans fats, we're bringing back saturated fats.

Are we effectively addressing heart health? I think not. We've just swapped out one problem for another, just like what happened the last time there was a major overhaul in the frying oils restaurants were using (when they converted from beef fat or lard to high–trans fat vegetable oils). The cost of these failures to the consumer, health-wise, is high.

A more prudent approach is for government, in its role as guardian and protector, to determine what the priority public health issues are, then set general guidelines it wishes to achieve. Then it's time to back off. Let the guidelines push the industry to solve the problem rather than advancing legislation that results in unintended consequences. After all, they are good at getting things done. The government should only care that the problem is going to get solved. Once timetables and guidelines are agreed to, it's up to industry to deliver. If not, then government would have the right to intervene and impose stern penalties if it deems necessary.

Rather than banning specific ingredients or micromanaging the implementation of new health initiatives, the public sector must stay true to setting the overall agenda. The goal is to reduce people's risk of becoming obese and more susceptible to diabetes and heart disease. By focusing actions and regulations on individual components such as trans fats, saturated fats, and cholesterol, we lose sight of that ultimate objective. This is "line item" regulation. It misses the big picture.

If anything, policies should require the food companies to modify their product portfolios so that the consumer is automatically exposed to better eating options over a longer period of time. In the case of obesity, lowering calories is a huge factor, probably the most important one. I would rather see government advance a proposal to declare that total calories in marketed food products must be reduced by 25 percent in five or seven years. Then the corporations could play to their strengths and figure out how to achieve this. If they don't deliver, the government could set the penalty.

In short, let's give businesses the opportunity to take the high road. Lower the calories overall; don't ban the individual products. The more government provides workable guidelines that stimulate industry to do the right thing—and still be able to make money—the quicker we will arrive at a solution.

I've already explained in detail my problem with one guideline that doesn't work at all—the Food Pyramid. While a new pyramid under construction might be more comprehensive from a lifestyle standpoint, it's likely to be so much more complicated. Some will benefit from the new Food Pyramid, but I maintain that the overall health of our populace will not be affected measurably.

Simply labeling certain foods and beverages themselves as "bad" for us is also convoluted thinking. Everyone knows they're not going to drop dead when they consume a sugared soft drink and french fries. The issue is *how much and how often*, isn't it? These items only become problems when they are consumed in large quantities on a regular basis, when they become Weapons of Mass Consumption. Instead of attempting to eradicate certain enjoyable foods, we should attack the marketing practices that make them harmful. Government would better serve us by providing tangible situational examples of what not to consume and when not to consume it.

Rather than just demonizing "fat," wouldn't it be more helpful to depict a supercombo meal like a 1,420-calorie Monster Thickburger with large fries and a 44-ounce sugared soft drink as being problematic? Or an overstuffed 500-calorie muffin? Or a giant-size popcorn with butter—you know those humongous bathtubs I'm talking about—in a movie theater? Or suggesting that half a dinner portion piled five inches high be packed off in a doggie bag? This presents things in a more tangible and understandable way. It's the way most people think about what and how they eat. They don't order ingredients like fats and oils; they order hamburgers and fries.

Despite its good intentions, let's just scrap the idea of the Food Pyramid as it exists today. It should be mothballed forever. Better to depict which real-life eating situations to limit, so it's clear what "real food" is being recommended. Better to send out monthly e-blasts to the nation's e-mail addresses in the form of what occasions and sizes of certain foods the public must pay attention to. Consumers must be appealed to on terms that they are familiar with. That would be a lot more meaningful, and most likely more effective.

Offering guidelines and eliminating the Food Pyramid are steps in the right direction, but do little to curb the swelling problem of childhood obesity. Federal, state, and local governments have failed miserably in their regulation of food in the nation's schools, but with jurisdiction over public schools, here's where the government can have the biggest role.

Vending machines are already there. Do we remove them? Do we just change what's in them? Can we finally implement healthier lunches in the cafeterias? We should understand that the school corridors are like movie theaters—your children are the victims of the "captive audience" syndrome. Knowing that diet affects the quality of life and longevity, what are we thinking when we cocoon kids with high-calorie foods all day?

Let's look at the school vending situation a bit differently, perhaps along the lines of satisfying all the parties' needs. Schools need money. Corporations have money. Schools have something corporations want: a built-in consumer base for their products, and a market-hungry core (preteens and teenagers) to build long-term brand loyalty.

I am not convinced that schools' total withdrawal from the corporate juggernaut is in the best interests of either party. And I'm okay with corporations beginning to build brand loyalty at an early stage in a consumer's life, but they have to do it more responsibly. Keep your vending machines in schools, but follow the School Beverage Guidelines brokered by the William J. Clinton Foundation. Adopt some programs like the Minneapolis school example, where more machines with lower-priced healthier products resulted in all sides winning. Add healthier snacks in smaller package sizes that provide balanced and sustained energy, not the "peak and crash" type that comes with a Snickers bar. And, by the way, how about limiting the time the vendors are usable to once each midmorning, at lunch, and midafternoon?

At this late stage in the game, breaking the pattern of subsidizing budgets by consumer products companies would be incredibly difficult and unwieldy for both sides. Rather than go to that extreme, let the companies look at it as a marketing expense to build trial and repeat loyalty for their products. Now we have a win-win situation. The school gets its needed added revenues (no longer the threatened tax burden for homeowners), the food guys sell their (better) products, and our children finally get to eat healthier.

School lunches are another matter, and this is a complex problem that continues to confound even the smartest nutritionists and well-meaning experts. While we are starting to see signs of change, why, after years of the expanding obesity crisis, are schools just finally acknowledging the problem? It's as if school authorities just discovered that they're feeding high-calorie meals to an ever-expanding (in pounds) student body. Why is the lunch menu not consistent with current federal thinking about managing childhood obesity?

Many school lunch programs are not even remotely compatible with the government's own suggestions. This is yet another example of government not walking the talk. After parents, the schools are our second lines of defense in steering our children toward healthier eating habits.

The USDA's own School Nutrition Dietary Assessment released in November 2007 confirmed the predicament of in-school eating. It noted that fewer than one-third of public schools served lunches that met USDA standards for total fat and saturated fat. It also noted that consumption of permitted "competitive" foods—those foods and beverages sold on an à la carte basis in cafeterias, vending machines, and snack bars—was concentrated in high-calorie, low-nutrition products. The three product groups consumed the most were candy; cookies, cakes, and brownies; and carbonated soft drinks. Definitely an Axis of (Food) Evil.

But perhaps most damning was the fact that students participating in the National School Lunch Program consumed significantly more calories (733 versus 661) and higher total fats and saturated fats than those students who did not take advantage of the government's program.

Clearly something is amiss when the government's meal plan doesn't meet its own standards. This is yet another example of a well-intentioned program that has not been well implemented. Great idea to feed our kids; bad execution.

I truly believe that to shift consumption to healthier foods in our schools, Stealth Health is called for. If our youngsters prefer to eat chicken nuggets and french fries, change the frying oil so the food's less greasy and less caloric. And all those cakes and cookies don't have to be 270-calorie Little Debbie Brownies. Schools can switch to 100-calorie versions only, like the Little Debbie Nutty Bar Singles.

Kids and teens expect to enjoy the tasty foods they are used to. Let's give it to them, but not in a format that encourages them to take in too many calories. Let's insist that school administrators ban Weapons of Mass Consumption in our schools. In short, let's mandate the possible, not the impossible.

Which takes us back to the noble cupcake.

I've devoted a long discussion toward the Great American Cupcake. It's a hot-button issue that drags the bloggers out in droves. Everyone has an opinion on this tasty little—all right, and sometimes big—treat. So let's look at the cupcake rationally and make an attempt to reinvent it. It's the ultimate single-serve snack; it has its own holder; it can be right-sized to achieve satiety without too many calories; it encourages the consumption of just one as a treat, not a pig-out.

I believe the cupcake can be designed for optimal healthy eating and still be a satisfying and enjoyable snack experience. It's not that difficult, and I would encourage cake mix manufacturers—and home bakers, as well—to take a stab at making a healthier cupcake. Frosting can be made with no-calorie sweetener. And it's certainly possible to use less oil, butter, and other such ingredients in the formula. I see no reason why vitamins and nutrients couldn't be added (in the same way it's done in vitamin waters). In short, the cupcake is the perfect food to illustrate how the real solution is to make the most popular foods better. Let's not ban them, let's not excoriate them, let's just improve them.

"I think one of the good things about the cupcakes is that they are so variable," Rachel Kramer Bussel, the blogger I introduced you to earlier, so aptly put it. "They can choose from all these different flavors, and they can make them smaller and healthier and use less frosting. A lot of bakeries use too much frosting. People don't want that much frosting."

And here's my take on how to sell a healthy cupcake to school boards, parents, and educators. For schools, I would not announce that the cupcakes are healthier (except perhaps to the parents). Make an example of them as symbols of Stealth Health, and be especially silent or low-key with the kids. I would start with the Hostess 100-calorie cupcake (with 25 percent of calories from fat) and step up its nutritional profile. I don't think it's much of a stretch to market a 100-calorie cupcake as an industry standard. This is the acceptable size for a decent, hunger-satisfying snack.

Let's go a step further and rename the new cupcakes as well, and position them as reward snacks. "One Hundred," "A-Plus," "Ace," "Gold Star," and "High Score" are all possibilities that can give teachers and educators a chance to use them as an incentive for academic performance. In this way, they can also limit the number of cupcakes given out in a given time period. (And yes, put a cap on the precocious overachievers in the classroom.)

The key is not to stress the lower calories or fat content. If they taste good, and if the kids aren't complaining, we'll have nothing to worry about. It's much like the strategy we used when we introduced Diet Coke ("Just for the taste of it"). I know plenty of consumers who once drank nothing but regular Coke, and when they weaned themselves away from them and onto the diet version, they quickly adapted. Now many converts tell me if they try a sugared beverage, it's so sweet it's almost impossible to drink. They've reconditioned their taste buds. The same thing can occur with a dessert, especially if we begin the process with young children.

I'm not dreaming when I say we can have healthy cupcakes. "One thing we're seeing is cupcake innovation," Bussel told me. "There's an organic cupcake being made in L.A., and there's a vegan and gluten-free cupcake, and we're seeing a lot more of this, and they're taking off."

If the reconfigured cupcakes pass a minimum safe nutrition threshold, I would have no problem with putting them into high school vending machines. I would, however, place stricter limits in elementary and junior high schools. There it should remain a *teacher-controlled* product.

Bussel, again, has a sound rationale: "For kids it's about the frosting and the tactile nature, and because they're already small, you can decorate them so kids can enjoy them. For kids' birthday parties, you can do Dora the Explorer, and smiley faces, and Spider-Man, in ways that enhance the look of it that don't add too much in terms of sugar."

So can we lower the debate volume a bit, cool the hot tempers, and bring about a solution that satisfies almost everyone? It takes but four easy steps:

1. Don't even think about banning them. It's comfort food, and we all need comforting now and then.

2. Make a healthier, nutritious cupcake that tastes good. They have to be lower in calories and smaller in size, but still taste good.

3. Use a reasonable approach in schools to limit their consumption. Cupcakes are an occasional treat, not part of an everyday diet, and they should be treated as such.

4. Don't tell the kids about step number two.

Here's a final thought about the cupcake, directed squarely to three of the top commercial baked goods suppliers in the nation—Interstate Bakeries (Hostess), McKee Foods (Little Debbie), and Entenmann's. Why doesn't a large company develop a recipe for a "National School Cupcake," one that fits in the mold of today's model? Tastes so good the kids don't know that it's nutrition-friendly (or at least not as bad as a traditional cupcake), "normal" size, perhaps frosting regionally aimed at school colors, and so on.

Better still, perhaps some of the cake mix companies could sponsor a bake-off aimed at kids who like being in the kitchen—just like the Pillsbury contest. Challenge our children to come up with a great cupcake that nobody will have any arguments over. Are you marketing executives listening? Think of the terrific publicity you'll get; it could be a jump-start to a national rollout.

I see the cupcake as a classic example of how we can take the most popular foods and drinks, secretly improve their nutrition profile without compromising on taste, control their portion size, and still make them desirable to eat. My view is that a healthier cupcake could end the debate and ultimately make a small contribution to slimming down many of our overweight schoolchildren. We can have our cake and eat it, too.

My last word on the government: Do what you do well and avoid trying to accomplish the improbable. Regulate for safety, and do so with vigilance, but don't regulate specific products. Put the responsibility on the food companies. Set caloric reduction goals, but then give the industry some sway. Don't tell them how to do it. Let them find their own way. I can draw an analogy with the auto industry. The government sets emission standards, and the car companies must achieve them, but Uncle Sam doesn't design catalytic converters.

# 14

# the quest for healthier food

*Chapel Hill, NC, October 2007*

There was a photo of a 60-pound block of hydrogenated fat up on the projection screen. It's the kind of stuff that goes into food, and eventually the human body, and when you think about this fact it's suddenly a bit scary. I was watching Dr. Walter Willett's slide presentation. Willett, a white-mustachioed, soft-spoken scientist in his early sixties, was cleverly engaging his audience. As a professor of epidemiology and the chair of the nutrition department at the Harvard School of Public Health, he is a pioneer researcher and international authority. Willett is the guru of trans fats and the most-quoted nutritionist in the world. Everyone in the audience was engrossed. There had been some discussion, almost a disclaimer, if you will, about how trans fats are not the reason why everyone has become fat. It's because of too many calories. Still, Willett said, "Diabetes and heart disease on a worldwide basis; this is going to be the public health epidemic of the century." Nobody disputed this.

We were in a hotel ballroom, and I had just welcomed some forty-odd experts from science and industry. This was the first meeting of the Global Obesity Business Forum, what I hope people will look back on as a historic occasion. Barry Popkin, who heads the Interdisciplinary Obesity Center at the University of North Carolina, Chapel Hill, and I decided that nothing was ever going to get done on this issue until we got the leading PhDs, nutritionists, and the larger food companies sitting together in the same room. We were hoping that a gathering of massive brainpower could find some common ground amid the clutter of the daily rhetoric. We were also hoping that we could jump-start the notion that everyone working together could get healthier foods in restaurants and on the dinner table. This was our notion of a global food peace summit.

Executives from Coca-Cola, Kraft, Unilever, Kellogg's, General Mills, McDonald's, and Cadbury Schweppes were there, and at the outset there was a wariness wafting within the room. It was somewhat expected. The science folks know what actually goes into what the food-and-beverage folks are selling. I hoped that over the course of the two-day event this wariness would abate and some trust and creativity would eventually take over. At the very least, more than one attendee marveled at the fact that this was the first time both sides—the food makers and the scientist/nutritionists—had agreed to work together. On reflection, it was a significant milestone, and my only regret was that it hadn't taken place years earlier.

One of the experts, Martijn Katan, a world-renowned molecular biologist and professor of nutrition at Vrije Universiteit, Amsterdam, took his turn at the podium. He recited some standard technical data for the attendees, but there were a few significant snippets that I remembered from my notes.

> *Each fat molecule has three fatty acids, and these are often different. . . . A food fat is never 100 percent saturated or unsaturated. . . . A "hydrogenated" fat can be okay for blood lipids if its trans fat content is low. . . . The term "hydrogenated fat" is no longer useful for consumers. . . . Terminology is a real problem. . . . Let's just take palm oil. I've seen it in liquid form in Malaysia but in solid form in Rotterdam, where I am. I wouldn't label palm oil as healthy oil. . . . What you see isn't exactly what you get because there are four different kinds of palm oils on the market.*

When you added all this up, you realized that good fats and bad fats provide the same number of calories. Katan knows this; his colleagues know it; and I know it. The question that remained in my mind was: How do you translate this notion into something simple that the general public can easily understand?

I could see the challenges already.

Katan is a brilliant scientist, of course, yet I couldn't help feeling a little disheartened. There are no absolute answers in food and nutrition, he appeared to be saying, and his colleagues eventually came to the same conclusion. The more we drill down, the more we search for guidance in the technical data, the more we don't know. Yet we tend to ask the experts for some sense of closure on an important problem. The more information we have, the more we crave a definitive answer, the last word, the more elusive this seems to be. *Tell us what to eat, doctor.* But life doesn't work like this. Such is the way of nutrition science; there is no holy grail. Suddenly, I felt the frustration of the American consumer puzzling over the nutrition labels in the supermarket aisle.

But the primary reason everyone was assembled was that they were hopeful and optimistic that there was common ground on which to stand, where solutions could be forged to stem the tidal wave of obesity and its related illnesses. It was absolutely critical to look ahead, not behind. It was also important not to waste time analyzing how we got where we are, but to get a sense of what we had to do.

The food we eat is further complicated as you look beyond the American borders. People eat differently around the world, and the diets in various locales—from India to China to Mexico—suggest that it will be difficult to find a one-size-fits-all solution. Nutrition researcher Barry Popkin is well versed in how other cultures eat, and he leans toward aggressive action. He's been squarely on the side of taxing sin foods, especially in Mexico where sugared beverages are a major cause of obesity and of grave concern among government officials. Sugar consumption is one of his main targets. "It's not just cake and Pepsi," Popkin said. "Their sugar intake is up more than twice as much in the past seven years. They add six to eight teaspoons of sugar to their coffee."

But back to the United States, for now. One of Popkin's slides showed a large increase in intake of added sugars during the 1990s across every age group. Americans consume 377 calories a day from added sugar. The top 20 percent of the population gets 896 calories of added sugar a day.

Sugar sources:

- 1965—mostly from desserts
- 1977—desserts and beverages are about equal
- 2004—sodas dominate, at about 158 calories per person per day

We're also fat not just because of what we drink but because of the *way we eat*, Popkin explains. We have to take responsibility for much of this because in the 1950s, Americans, at least, spent two hours preparing dinner. Today, the average is closer to twenty minutes. "It's not just McDonald's," Popkin reported. We've created fast food at home, thanks to prepared and frozen foods, and microwave ovens.

Bob Langert, the vice president for corporate responsibility at McDonald's, lamented, "I wish we sold more salads than double cheeseburgers." I believe him; it would make his job easier—and they'd likely produce higher margins.

It wasn't long before the defense—the food companies—took the field. They justified their positions, of course, but they also reflected a conciliatory mood. They appeared to embrace the notion that a healthy customer was a long-term one. General Mills said it had converted its portfolio of products so that the level of "healthy" foods accounts for about a third of their sales. Hershey cited the creation of a Center for Health and Nutrition. Coke's portfolio was slowly changing so that they're selling more water and artificially sweetened beverages and fewer sugared drinks. In fact, Coke now has a Beverage Institute for Health and Wellness. General Mills, Danone, and Kellogg's are making commitments toward healthier food, too, publicly and privately (some of which I've already detailed in the chapter on Stealth Health).

General Mills's Susan Crockett, the company's vice president and senior technology officer for health and nutrition, reminded us that her company's theme is "nourishing lives." Green Giant is the biggest vegetable brand in the world, she said, and nothing would make her company happier than to see more people eating more vegetables. Nobody argued with her; I certainly agreed that string beans are probably the last thing we needed to tamper with.

To be sure, the food industry folks cited a number of noble product efforts on the health front, and they included: Capri Sun Roarin' Waters (35 calories); Kool-Aid Singles (30 calories); Country Time On the Go (35 calories); South Beach Diet Snack Bars (100 calories); Sugar-Free Oreos (100 calories per two-cookie serving); Sugar-Free Jell-O and puddings; reduced-sodium Campbell's soups; WIC (for Women, Infants, and Children)-approved low-sugar cereals; and so on.

General Mills was not shy about mentioning its failures, including its Dora and Clifford Crunch healthy cereals. Dora was already pulled from the marketplace, and Clifford Crunch was not selling well. Fruit Crisps, a dried sliced apple, was supposed to be an alternative to the potato chip, but the buy rate among groceries just couldn't support the product. Often a company has to give up because the supermarkets won't stock anything that isn't a high-turnover item.

The scientists and nutritionists sitting in the room came to understand this cold fact, and they accepted it. It has to taste good, and it has to sell. While this may seem obvious, it's far from it. Looking around the room, I couldn't help but think that just getting the scientists to fully appreciate this perspective would have been difficult ten years ago. Seeing the researchers there, nodding their heads in skeptical agreement as the food industry execs explained the pressure they're up against to make money and provide healthy fare, I couldn't help but think that we were moving things forward, one small step at a time.

During the second day, the atmosphere of wariness dissipated and there was more of a sense of camaraderie, as the participants began to understand the different agendas, various subjects in the presentations, fresh points of view, and the business challenges of the food companies. It was heartening to see that everyone understood we were all in this together.

It also was refreshing for me to listen to and learn from Dr. George Bray, the esteemed biomedical researcher and professor of medicine at Louisiana State Medical Center in Baton Rouge. To many insiders, he's known as the founding father of the obesity issue. Bray is a doctor and scientist who has been practicing his craft for fifty-one years, and he still has the energy and curiosity of colleagues who are half his age. When he first began studying obesity, he was a doctor gently sounding a warning bell, but nobody was listening. The American population was about 14 percent overweight at the time. Now 30 percent of us are fat, so he said the problem has doubled since he began his work.

Much of the nutrition research done by Bray and others centers on tabulating just how much food their subjects actually eat. I've always been fascinated by how we all lie to each other—and worse, to ourselves—about our eating habits. This has been well documented, and I mentioned it to Bray during one of the coffee breaks. How can we be certain whether people accurately recall what and how much they eat? How do we know when they're lying—either out of embarrassment or because their motive is to "help" the results? Bray conceded that this is a problem, and why it's extremely difficult to gather reliable data. Perhaps Brian Wansink, the Cornell behavioral nutritionist, who conducts his eating experiments surreptitiously, is one of the few who can report solid results. It was good that he was appointed the czar of the government's new Food Pyramid. Despite the skepticism I have about how much of an effect the pyramid will have on American obesity in the future, I believe Wansink is a guy who fully understands the culture of eating more than most of the others in the field.

It was instructive to hear Cynthia Bulik, a clinician and researcher in the department of psychiatry at the University of North Carolina, Chapel Hill, take the wheel of the Straight-Talk Food Express. She has spent several years studying eating behavior and using the knowledge she's gained to impart advice to her clients about responsible consumption. Bulik contends it's harder to get someone to resist food than it is to get an anorexic to eat. Something is going on that is triggering all the food cues, she said, and a lot of it comes from "industrial strength advertising and marketing, all the time." It's very hard to go through a day not thinking about eating something no matter how strong your wall of resistance is. We're bounced around the marketing juggernaut in ways we don't even notice, and our brains are absorbing and responding to the deluge of messages as if we're a Stepford community of serial eaters. Bulik said, "I call this the 'dopaminic pinball machine.' We've taken 'sometimes' foods and made them 'all-the-time' foods." Someone in the group mentioned that Taco Bell was marketing the "fourth meal," and described it as a horrible idea if there ever was one. As if we need a reminder to eat.

Bray told a few stories that resonated with me. The first one was related to the forum's discussion of portion control. Bray said, "I went into a supermarket just the other day when I was in Washington, D.C. I went up and down the aisles looking for a snack that would be in a 100-calorie pack, and I couldn't find one. The food companies blurt out that they have them. And this is true. But they're still hard to find. They're not ubiquitous by any means." Nobody in the audience doubted this.

Bray said he had recently spoken with a colleague, a pediatrician, and he asked the doctor to name the biggest issues facing children in reference to obesity. First, the physician said, we have to eliminate the ads on Saturday-morning television. They're almost all food ads, and they're for horrible food. Again, nobody disagreed, and the food company emissaries mentioned their voluntary effort to reduce or eliminate the marketing of high-sugared cereals. The pediatrician also told Bray that he would jettison all the vending machines in the schools.

And that brought Bray to the second story I noted. He was asked to work with a local principal to try to reduce obesity among the children in her school. But before doing so, she stipulated that he had to agree not to replace the bottled sodas in her vending machines with bottled water. This somewhat startled me, and I suppose Bray as well. The principal's argument was that the bottled water came exclusively in plastic bottles, which are oil-based products, and they were causing a huge pollution problem. In other words, Bray wondered whether littering and recycling was overshadowing obesity. He hadn't thought about this. The attempt to solve one problem easily can create another. Perhaps she could have just banned all those soda machines.

It was gratifying to hear that someone in the science community suggested that we have given short shrift to the notion that there are some foods that we shouldn't change, even if they're not necessarily "good" for us, especially in large quantities.

Martijn Katan segued easily into this issue. When he held up a humble croissant and described it to the forum, it was abundantly clear that everyone was preoccupied with items like this one as well. Croissants were served at the hotel with breakfast, and you'll excuse me if I refer to this as a delicious example of what's known in the trade as "indulgent" or "comfort" food. The French croissant is a universal symbol of an elegant pastry, revered and respected more abroad than here, requiring a delicate touch to bake it correctly. Katan knew his way around the croissant. It should be crispy on the outside, yet fluffy and light on the inside, and the texture should yield an effect of melting in your mouth. A good croissant has a very short shelf life. Anyone who has tasted an old lousy one knows it's not an easy thing to bake. As Katan described the perfect croissant, he made me instantly hunger for one.

Yet Katan wondered aloud whether we could reengineer the croissant in a healthy way. More important, he asked us whether we should even try. He said this not because he's pessimistic, but because it represents a real challenge. Puff pastries have layered dough, and this is hard to do with a healthy oil substitute. Cookies pose a similar challenge because most baked goods assume a form and a texture that are constituted from butter and lard or high–trans fat hydrogenated oils. If we decided to change them—and there have been some halfhearted attempts; they just don't taste the same—then we would have a lot of work to do.

There is a strong case for leaving indulgent food the way it is, but then we're still relying on the consumer's ability to eat sensibly on a consistent basis. It's hard to do for all but a few of us. That's changing consumer habits, and I had given up on that some time before I decided to write this book. Ice cream is another feel-good food. (I'm thinking of substitutes such as ice milk, and how they put more air in ice cream, or make it low-fat in some way.) Should we tamper with coatings, glazing, and powders? If so, can we make them healthy but still taste rich with the proper texture?

Katan did not think there was much we could do with cocoa butter, and this is an opinion that will likely comfort the chocolate companies. Debra Miller, PhD, Hershey's senior nutrition scientist, had mentioned earlier that when there was talk of making chocolate with vegetable oil instead of coca butter, some 30,000 people wrote or blogged in protest. She said people want their chocolate—perhaps the ultimate comfort food—real, or not at all.

As I pondered this, I wasn't sure I totally agreed. Some food company nutritionist, somewhere in the industry, I hoped, was at least trying. I thought about reconditioning our taste buds. My coauthor, Doug Garr, constantly reminded me throughout this project that after years of drinking coffee with sugar, he finally gave it up and now can't even sip a cup with any kind of sweetener in it. Diet Coke has the right level of sweetness for him and has become his favorite soft drink; he can no longer drink a real Coke without gagging.

Some low-calorie chocolate treats are coming close. I've tasted them. Yes, they're not quite the same as the real thing. But my taste buds have been fooled before, and I'm certain mine—and millions of others'—can be fooled as we do more work to develop better foods. So in my view we shouldn't stop trying to invent a terrific-tasting diet chocolate.

The chocolate issue is obviously one that stirs our passions, and it connected with the presentation of Dr. Richard D. Mattes, associate professor of medicine at Indiana University School of Medicine, who went into some very detailed technical analyses—complete with slides and charts—about the human interaction with foods that contain sweets.

Mattes asked, "Do we have an inherent liking for sweetness? Or is it something that's learned?" In fetal studies, the answer is yes, we have an inherent liking. The same holds in infant studies, so our craving for sweetness is likely rooted in our formative years.

Photos of babies with their sweetened fingers in their mouths—compared to other flavors—showed absolutely gleeful smiles on their faces. I thought, no surprise there. How many of us are hooked at birth, or before birth? Scientists are still struggling to know whether sweetness is a learned behavior or something that's with us from the womb.

I began wondering how this could affect the future of obesity. Today, we can't definitively conclude whether our addiction to sweets is genetic or acquired. But now that we've mapped the human genome, maybe scientists can identify a "sweet" gene that causes certain people to become fat. In 2008, several months after the conference, my speculation was given some credence. Researchers from Toronto found evidence that a tendency toward regular consumption of sweets might be connected to a genetic variation. The study was published in the journal *Physiological Genomics.* Previous work noted that there were possible connections between "glucose sensing" in the brain and its regulation of food intake. Perhaps the pharmaceutical industry might discover a drug that retards our cravings. Today it's a stretch; maybe tomorrow there's a real application and solution for an obese segment of the population who cannot understand why they can't resist a cookie or a cupcake.

Sugar in soft drinks has been controversial for many years now, and it's been countered with the advent of artificial sweeteners. I remember Royal Crown's Diet Rite Cola from my youth, and Tab thundered into the marketplace shortly thereafter. Then there were various health scares about the use of artificial sweeteners, most notably those involving cyclamates and NutraSweet. The beverage companies are very aware that a groundswell of parents do not want their children drinking artificially sweetened beverages. So it wasn't long before one of my colleagues posed the question to a panel: "So what do you feed your children when water isn't an alternative and they need something sweet? Do you give them a sugared drink or an artificially sweetened drink? Which is ultimately safer and healthier?"

Barry Popkin replied, "You've asked a horrendous question." People are confused because government and industry haven't given anyone sufficient direction. There is not enough research data to support a reasonable answer. This is something of a surprise, given how long artificial sweeteners have been approved and marketed.

Another topic that appears to stimulate endless debate in the food community is nutrition labeling, and the advent of "symbology," or a simplified version of packaging identification—either icons or stars—that immediately convey what kinds of food consumers are about to buy. Other countries already have turned to symbol labeling requirements, and many of us wondered whether our own laws needed updating. The UK has designed a system using green, yellow, and red dots to rank fats, sugar, and salt as low, medium, or high. The Swedish government has a program featuring a green keyhole-shaped symbol to identify the healthiest choices within a food category, and the Netherlands has a similar program.

Mexico is considering placing caution claims, such as "increases the risk of obesity, increases the risk of diabetes, increases the risk of adverse health outcomes," on beverages whose consumption is targeted to be minimized.

The notion of caution claims on packaging is provocative, and I understand their purpose. The theory here is that these kinds of warnings had some success in lowering cigarette smoking levels in the United States, so maybe it can induce Mexicans to think twice before reaching for another sugared can of soda or highly sweetened juice beverage. Where I disagree is—at least in my interpretation of the proposal—that they would just as easily be placed on a 6.5-ounce bottle of Coke, or next to a small order of fries on a McDonald's menu board. I could see caution claims on items that nobody would argue are patently over the top, such as on 64-ounce cups of sugared soda and the 2,000-calorie combo meals. That might be effective in cutting back their usage. I just don't see it as an across-the-board initiative. One issue that government regulators and nutrition advocates will face, especially given the lobbying efforts of the industry: If they adopt some sort of reasonable approach on this issue, there will be some spirited debate on which products qualify for such a warning label.

And that brings us to the labeling consistency issue here in the United States. Some companies have voluntarily come up with their own nutrition labeling codes, with some success. Kraft, PepsiCo, and General Mills all use some basic guidelines in their product labels, but consumer advocates say this is not enough, and it certainly isn't a uniform system. The companies sheepishly concede to the critics here. When a reference was made to "evaporated cane juice" on one of Kraft's packages, everyone laughed. Did anyone know what that was? And if you did, was it good for you or bad for you? Labeling certainly has run amok.

Most agreed that it would only be beneficial or work at all if it's done in addition to normal nutrition labeling already in effect. It's not a substitute but rather a supplement. There was some concern—especially at the science and nutrition end of the room—that too many positive symbols would cause many consumers to simply think, "If it's healthy I can eat more." This reminded me of the Law of Unintended Consequences that often permeates decision making in the food business.

Kellogg's, which had nearly $11 billion in revenues in 2006, noted that it was in the process of introducing Nutrition-at-a-Glance labels on the top right corner of cereal boxes. Already in place in Europe and Australia, the new labels will take information printed on the side panel of the boxes from the Nutrition Facts panel, which is mandated by the federal government, and include its key highlights on the box's front panel. The new labels will show consumers the number of calories and grams of total fat, sodium, and sugar in a single serving. Guideline Daily Amounts (GDAs), based on a 2,000-calorie daily diet, will display the percent of daily requirements delivered.

While highlighting side panel information on the package front is laudable, the mandated nutrition panels themselves can be misleading. For instance, less-sweetened, more adult cereals use one cup as a serving size. In the case of Kellogg's Corn Flakes, that translates to 100 calories and 2 grams of sugar per serving. But when one compares that to the more child-oriented Frosted Flakes, a strange thing occurs. The serving size, presumably because kids consume less than adults, drops to three-quarters of a cup, delivering 110 calories and 11 grams of sugar. While the sugar is much higher, the calories compare favorably to the less-sweetened Corn Flakes.

If, however, these products were more accurately compared using the same serving size, the discrepancies would become more apparent. For a serving size of one cup, the Frosted Flakes really contain 147 calories and 15 grams of sugar. This represents a 47 percent higher caloric content and a sevenfold increase in the amount of sugar. If we're revamping labels, this would be a good candidate for reexamination.

One retailer, Hannaford Brothers, a grocery chain in the Northeast, has developed a "guiding star" system, in which products are rated with zero, one, two, or three stars. If you're eating three stars you're eating healthier foods, and if you're buying no-star packages, you're in high-calorie, high-salt territory. Hannaford, to its credit, even rates its own private-label brand. Healthy foods have seen increased sales since the system was implemented.

Mark Doiron, a senior vice president for Hannaford, claimed that no single individual in the company's high command walked into a meeting with a mission to save the world from obesity. He said the idea came from several discussions about simply trying to identify healthier products in their aisles and help consumers make informed decisions. Doiron said the program has been met with positive reaction and is gaining traction. In an interview he said, "The parents are using this when they're shopping with their children. They go down the cereal aisle, and the kids are picking out the cereal and the parents say, 'You can pick out anything provided it has a star.' So they go on this little 'star search' and find their favorite item. The other thing—one of our associates overheard a conversation in the aisle—there was this woman that was quite obese shopping with her very young daughter. She picked up a cereal item—it was a nonstar item—put it in the basket, and the child said, 'Mommy, you should get one with a star because it would make you better.'" Doiron expects this kind of behavior to continue, a new definition of peer pressure, if you will.

At Hannaford, they've done more than track the anecdotal evidence. Initial results indicate that people are shifting their buying habits toward the better products, and despite any shortcomings, the labeling system appears to be effective. "We have five thousand new items a year," Doiron said. "It's going to start shifting the dynamic. So, when we started this, twenty-two percent of our portfolio was starred. It's now twenty-four percent. But we didn't do that on purpose. We're letting consumers drive that shift, and they are."

A 2 percent positive shift in this kind of volume is, in fact, significant and noteworthy. But I suspected, however, that the system was imperfect, and Barry Popkin privately confirmed my suspicions. I know Barry, and he's hardwired toward big solutions and giant steps. During a break in the conference he mentioned how Hannaford went only partway. "They're only labeling one-seventh of the products in their stores," he complained. "Every vegetable—a hundred percent of the items that could be called a vegetable—is a three-star item." Popkin wondered, how is a potato anything like a brussels sprout in terms of nutrition and ingredients? From an outsider's perspective, the basic deficiency with Hannaford's system is that a no-star package can be misleading. Was it rated and failed the star test? Or was it simply not considered at all? The consumer doesn't know (and Hannaford's marketing literature does not elaborate).

This also got me to thinking: Is it better to have a single, consistent, nutrition labeling program that every packaged food seller is compelled to follow? Or would it be preferable for every company to be pressured to comply by adopting its own, like Hannaford's? Again, my answer to this question relates to my inherent distaste for too much (and the wrong kind) of government intervention. I'd like to see other companies follow Hannaford, and perhaps improve on what they've begun.

Just as I was contemplating this issue, Brian Walker of Cadbury Schweppes brought up a good point as well, and Martijn Katan agreed: If one single company abuses symbol labeling and it becomes a small scandal because of biased or inaccurate ratings, it could damage the credibility for the entire industry no matter how responsible the major companies are. It could turn out to be a disastrous case of no good deed going unpunished.

Indeed, there are government rumblings about this. Saber rattling can be heard on the federal level. A month before our obesity forum, the FDA held a series of hearings in Washington over two days to address the need for a universal system in the United States. Food companies, international nutrition experts, and government officials all testified about the confusion in the supermarket aisles and the need to develop a program from which everyone can immediately discern the value of a given item without having to slog through multisyllabic jargon that few of us truly understand. It's worth noting the comment sent to the FDA by Dr. Mark Etzel of the University of Wisconsin-Madison:

> *Please require the use of simple labels on the front of processed foods that indicate by color the level of fat, sugar, salt, and calories per government-defined serving size. Please require food manufacturers to use the government-defined serving size instead of making up their own serving size. For example, all beverages have a 240 ml [milliliter] government-defined serving size, but soda manufactures frequently label an entire 500 to 600 ml bottle as one serving. Younger people such as students eat diets low in fruits, vegetables, and dairy, and high in salt, sugars, and fat. Many students do not know what they should*

*eat and should not eat. Simple labels on the front of the package, given using a common definition of serving size, will help educate the consumer and help provide a step forward in solving the national obesity epidemic.*

Would this be a be-all and end-all? Of course not. But I'm hoping that Etzel's comment about the beverages will be taken seriously, especially considering that Coca-Cola has taken the initiative to put both the serving size and the total calorie content on their bottle. On one hand, this is good for consumers. They're giving us more information. On the other, government regulations can create additional confusion and chaos. One forum attendee inspected a 20-ounce bottle of Coke that contained 100 calories per serving. The serving size was 8 ounces (1 cup). The total calories in the bottle were listed at 240. Perplexed, this attendee said, "When you do the math, it comes to 250 calories, not 240, doesn't it?" This was not faulty computing; the FDA apparently allows companies to "round down." Coke said that consumers have asked for both serving and bottle notices, and they're simply following the FDA requirements. In my opinion, identifying total calories for any "single serve" container is a good idea because it reflects the way the product is usually consumed.

I think this issue will gather more steam within the general public, and I expect that if the industry cannot agree on a standard, the FDA will eventually impose one. The food and beverage industry has been warned.

In two days of intensive meetings, it was impossible to cover every issue regarding the obesity crisis, but the major topics did get a substantial airing. Was there a consensus on what we should do to end the scourge? Was there a course of action recommended that every attendee found palatable? No.

By the end of the conference, there was a sense among most of the people I spoke with that we could put an end to the adversarial relationship between the food and beverage industry and the science and nutrition side. In fact, I believe there was a strong feeling that we all needed to work together to find the right solutions to our seemingly intractable eating problems. This was a dialogue—not of talking heads yelling at each other and rattling off bullet points—but with actual substance, one that brought the two sides together and allowed them to lay out their cases.

Did it solve everything? No, in fact in that capacity I would argue that it left many people with more questions than answers. Was it worthwhile? Absolutely, because at least people had started to talk, think, and interact. The food industry needs the endorsement and support of serious scientific researchers and nutritionists if it is going to restore public faith in the industry and its products. Likewise, the researchers and nutritionists need the involvement of the food industry if they are going to see a widespread reduction of obesity. It may not have looked like much, but it was a start.

This is not a situation that will be solved through one meeting of the minds—no matter how smart and willing those minds may be. It took us more than fifty years to get into this situation; there's no magic bullet solution that will get us back to where we were overnight. No government mandate, line of miracle weight-loss drugs, or superfood is going to be able to do the job alone. As such, the need for the two sides coming together is clear; it is only through efforts like these that we'll be able to make actual progress. The more that each side acknowledges the other, the more we'll be able to encourage and promote health in all food products, not just a select few.

The obesity crisis can be solved in a way that benefits us all, but the food companies have to be the ones to take the first steps. Some already have, others are still coming on board, but with each passing day the imperative becomes more urgent, the realities more unavoidable. Going forward it should be their mandate to work with America, not against it, to help their customers live longer and better. Because if we survive, they survive.

# epilogue: full circle

*Reunion Weekend, May 3–4, 2008,*
*Minneapolis, Minnesota*

It's always strange going back from whence you came. On the one hand, you look forward to seeing the people you've carried a special bond with throughout your life. On the other, you don't really know how you will feel when you enter through the portals of a place you were once an integral part of. A place you spilled your guts to help make successful. A place where you forged such indelible memories. Yet so foreign and distant now.

This was the weekend when General Mills's "alumni" came back home and reminisced about where they've been, what they're doing with their lives, how many children they have. Very much like the typical high school or college reunion. Humorously named "The Mills Afterlife Foundation," almost a hundred former friends and associates gathered and shared drinks, stories and hors d'oeuvres at the local Marriott hotel. If you left in 1993, you were the Class of '93. Each name badge reflected your "graduation" year.

It happens that one of the graduates was married to a senior executive at General Mills and coordinated the first-ever invitation by General Mills to former employees to come back and tour their new headquarters. Several of General Mills's top executives turned out for the tour and reception, including chairman Steve Sanger, chief executive officer Ken Powell, and chief operating officer Ian Friendly.

Much had changed since I last set foot inside the Mills. The company had acquired its hometown rival Pillsbury in 2000. Never in my wildest imagination had I envisioned that Betty Crocker would dance in the supermarket aisles with the Doughboy, but then again, there was a lot about the industry that was pretty different from when I first got into it. In the intervening years, General Mills had acquired a host of other brands—everything from breakfast cereals to vegetables to Mexican foods to barbecue. The company's landscape looked little like it had when I was there.

As if the mergers and acquisitions of the company weren't enough, there was actual evidence of all this change right in front of us. Recently General Mills had expanded their worldwide headquarters and we were given a tour. The new HQ, while architecturally exciting, still maintains General Mills's small-town flavor and modest Scandinavian influence. The original building and campus were designed in 1958 and reflected the traditional rectangular feel of corporate buildings post World War II. This new complex clearly was designed for the twenty-first century. The Champions Center, a 140,000-square-foot, three-story "town center," serves as the new hub of the company. All kinds of food vendors, coffee bars, and even a dry-cleaning service are there. The Total Fitness exercise center is replete with scores of exercise machines, and employees are allowed to use the facility any time of the day. Conference rooms are equipped with state-of-the-art features such as wireless "Room Wizard" technology.

Perhaps the most interesting visual impression was the new Betty Crocker kitchens. Here was the heartbeat of where new product recipes were developed. Floor-to-ceiling windows graced the two-story structure, which consisted of nineteen fully-equipped kitchens. I was reminded of the cake mix recipes I had enjoyed sampling in my younger days with the company. And we all chuckled as our tour guides relayed how the old, formal (some say stodgy) executive suite was converted into a food-service kitchen.

In many respects the building itself reflects the sea change that has gone on since I broke into the industry thirty years ago. There were a handful of things that were just as I remembered: the unique massive sculptures that graced the well-kept lawns; the gray Canada geese with their distinctive black beaks that still roam the grounds; and the fresh-water ponds that transform into solid ice under the frigid Minnesota winter. But the real treat for most of us was when we were permitted to revisit our old office areas. Here was the epicenter for how the company would market its products: where the Cheerios box was crafted, Bisquick side panel recipes were determined, and Yoplait packages were designed. This is where a few of us had decided what America would eat.

Looking at those old office areas, it was obvious that more than just the building had changed. Of course, all those iconic brands are still around with their logos largely untouched and their taste largely the same. It was everything behind those brands, behind the boxes that was different. It was a foreign world from the one I had been a part of all those years ago. Back then there were a lot of things that we didn't think about—not because they weren't important, but because we simply weren't trained to. This was not an industry of evil people; no one ever set out to addict people to food or make them overweight. But it happened and the food industry cannot afford to ignore that history.

Seeing this space and walking the halls that day simply reinforced my beliefs that ultimately the food industry can and must be the agent of change on the issue of health and food. It's come down to the food sellers. They are how we got into this mess, and they'll be a part of how we get out. And when they heed this call, they will be happy they did because it will benefit everyone—consumer and seller.

Ultimately, these are people who want to do the right thing, but it's taken far too long for them to realize just what that means. It may seem hard to trust the very people who played such a broad role in bringing us to this point. But the fact is that food is a business, big business, and the government has proven inept at helping to run this business. This is not about to change any time soon.

While it may appear that government is the right institution to force the industry's hand, nothing could be further from the truth. The blunt arm of legislation will only make the transition that much harder, regardless of how well meaning it might be. Our government officials—local, state, and federal—are searching their hearts and souls for the means to protect us from ourselves when it comes to nutrition issues. None truly wants to pass a law that is ill conceived or ineffective. Our legislators see that we're fat, and they see that obesity is costing society billions of dollars, not to mention the heartbreak of families caring for loved ones with food-related illnesses, so they want to do something, and many of our regulations regarding safety are sensible.

The kind of government intrusion that most nutritionists and scientists advocate will not solve our problems. The small steps suggested by concerned nutritionists, governing bodies, and health officials will always be woefully inadequate. These Band-Aids will not stop the hemorrhaging. We need to get the industry involved in a major way—hopefully voluntarily—if we're going to stem the tide of our deteriorating collective health.

Weaving down the halls of General Mills, I couldn't help but think that this just might be possible. If more companies began to adapt the aggressive strategies of a place like General Mills, the industry just might be able to adapt, make money, and promote health all at the same time. This is not to say that General Mills is perfect, but if a company as storied and entrenched as they are can lead the charge on this, who's to say that any of the other big concerns can't develop their own models to build health into their bottom line. Doing so will take time; it won't happen next week. It will also take a level of innovation and creative management that to date seems to have evaded these companies, particularly the restaurant chains. And yet if they're committed, actually 100 percent behind changing their food products, it will happen.

As we strolled through the building, I commented to Steve Sanger that General Mills appeared to be doing some good things to make their products healthier and to incent their managers to follow such a course. His response to my observations was unrehearsed and immediate: "It's just good business."

There it was. Its simplicity captured the essence of the journey we have taken throughout this book. It's just good business to see the trends, understand what the consumer is looking for, and then take the lead in doing what's best to serve those customers. It's exactly the attitude I believe the industry needs to follow to create that necessary win-win so that companies can make their profits, the consumer can expect healthier products, and the country can regain its health.

I didn't start out to single out General Mills one way or another. The maker of those healthy whole-grain Cheerios still has some work to do to improve the health profile of many of its products. But they've made a commitment. A commitment to do the right thing, and make money doing it.

Everything had come full circle. What started out for me as a desire to be a great consumer products marketer with a top company has turned out to be rewarding look at how much good can accrue from America's food marketers. General Mills offers hope that the right thing can be done. And others should, and must, take their lead.

Sometimes it's good to come back home.

# acknowledgments

First, I would like to thank my editor, Matt Harper, for his many suggestions and tenacious review of the material, which resulted in a substantially improved manuscript. With his guidance, each draft brought the story into much better focus.

A special thanks to two publishing pros. To my agent, Joëlle Delbourgo, for recognizing the need for another voice to be heard on America's worsening obesity crisis. Her thorough understanding of the publishing industry and what it takes to get things done have been a tremendous asset to the project. And to Sandy Goroff-Mailly, an exceptional publicist whose creativity, passion, and tenacity contributed to ensuring that my message would be heard.

I have had the privilege of meeting and engaging with so many who have served in the food industry that it would be impossible to thank them all. I do wish to express gratitude to those who have directly contributed to my thinking and the writing of this manuscript, including Jack Greenberg, former chairman and CEO of McDonald's; Rick Lenny, former CEO of The Hershey Company; Chris Lowe, president of Coca-Cola FoodService; Chris Policinski, CEO of Land O' Lakes; Bob Goodale, former president of the Harris Teeter grocery chain; Tom Ryan, chief concept officer extraordinaire for McDonald's and Smashburger; Hala Moddelmog, former president of Church's Chicken and the current CEO of the Susan B. Komen Foundation; Irwin Kruger, longtime McDonald's franchisee in New York City; John Kimber, a former executive with Burger King and Hardees; Glenn Armstrong, an early role model for healthier eating and formerly with Quaker Oats and Wrigley's; Steve Allen, a vice president for Nestlé; and Steve Carley, the CEO for El Pollo Loco ("Crazy Chicken") restaurant chain.

# acknowledgments

Several in the nutrition field were generous in providing their views regarding how America got to the point where overweight and obesity reign, and what could be done. I would specifically like to thank Kathleen Zelman, director of nutrition for WebMD Health and the WebMD Weight Loss Clinic; Marion Nestle, professor of Nutrition, Food Studies, and Public Health at New York University and author of *Food Politics* and *What to Eat*; and Brian Wansink, author of *Mindless Eating* and presidentially appointed executive director of the U.S. Department of Agriculture's Center for Nutrition Policy and Promotion.

Particular thanks are extended to Barry Popkin of the University of North Carolina–Chapel Hill, where he directs UNC-CH's Interdisciplinary Center for Obesity. I have had the privilege of working with Dr. Popkin in directing the annual Global Obesity Business Forum, which brings together the food industry and the scientific community to advance solutions to the obesity crisis.

Not to be forgotten are those who have served as sounding boards for ideas and kept me on track: I would like to thank Rusty Myers, James Benedict, Britt Carter, Judy Safern, Gerry Sindell, Patrick Meyer, and Frank Kuhar. The friendship and caring of these "nutritious" people were powerful motivators to complete the book.

And thank you, Rachel Warner Bussel. You have elevated the cupcake to the ultimate food icon that it deserves to be.

I would like to thank those close to me from whom I have always received unconditional support. To my wife, Mary, a bedrock of encouragement, for stretching my thinking beyond my comfort zones so that all possibilities were considered. I thank her for her love, creativity, resourcefulness, resilience, and endless optimism.

To my children, Erin and David, for their perpetual cheerleading, urging their father on in this important project. I thank my parents for their values and instilling the vision, focus, and drive to see an undertaking like this through. To my brother, Thomas, for nurturing this sometimes untethered balloon back to reality and viewing situations more concretely. And to all the friends, family, relatives, and mentors who have always been there for me.

And finally, I would like to thank my writer, Doug Garr, without whom this book would not be readable. His gifts of observation and colloquial writing have been invaluable to making this project come alive.

# index

# about the authors

**hank cardello** is chief executive officer of 27°North (www.27degNorth.com), a consulting firm that helps businesses take the lead on solving social issues. For more than three decades he was an executive at some of the world's largest food and beverage companies, including Coca-Cola and General Mills. Today he chairs the annual Global Obesity Business Forum, sponsored by the University of North Carolina at Chapel Hill. Cardello lives in Chapel Hill, North Carolina.

**doug garr** is the author of *IBM Redux: Lou Gerstner and the Business Turnaround of the Decade*. His work has appeared in *BusinessWeek*, *Fortune's Technology Review*, *GQ*, *Popular Science*, *Worth*, *New York*, and *MIT's Technology Review*. Garr lives in New York.